Images of Modern America

EAST BRANCH & LINCOLN RAILROAD

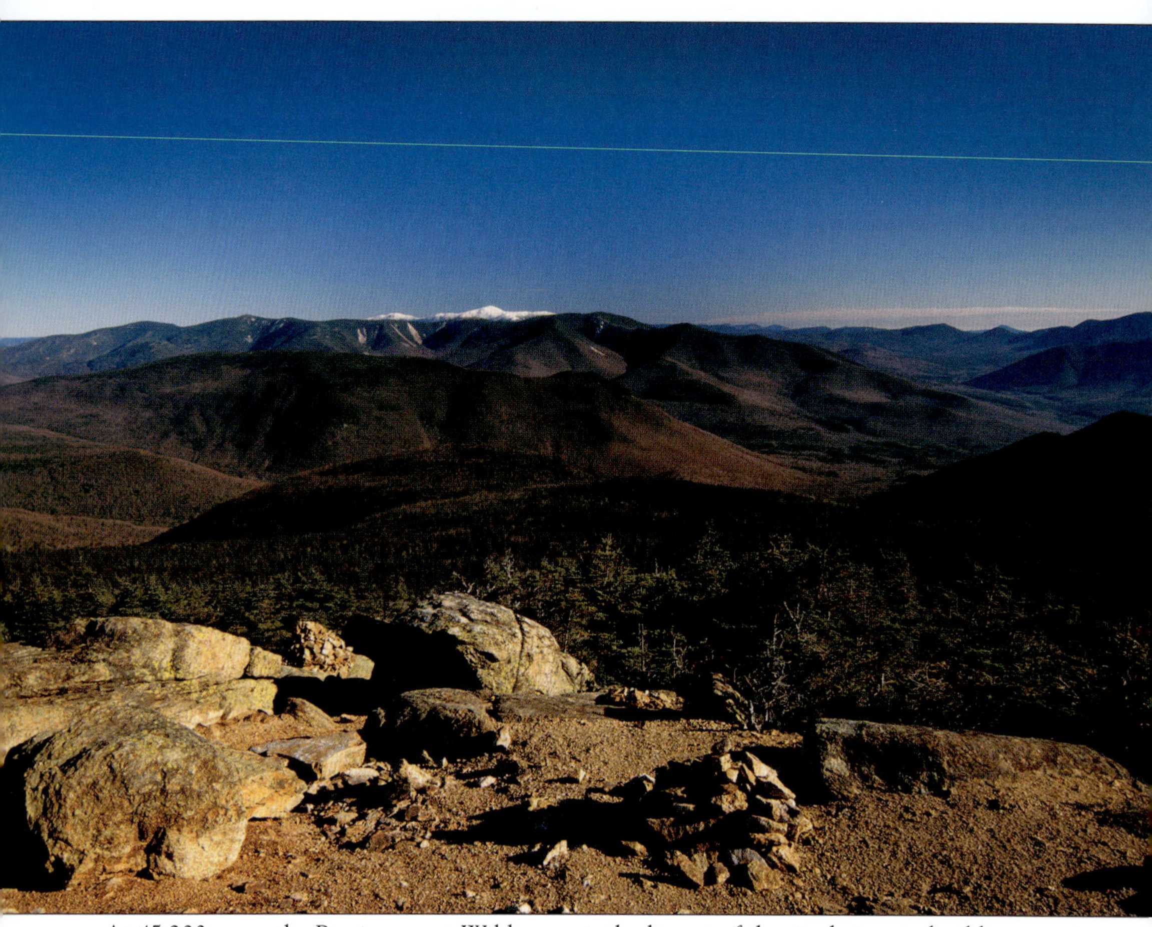

At 45,000 acres, the Pemigewasset Wilderness is the largest of the six designated wildernesses in the White Mountain National Forest. This wilderness is known throughout New England and beyond, but not for its wilderness designation. It is known for what took place here from 1893 to 1948. Once known as Henry's Woods, these valleys hold the story of James Everell Henry and his mighty East Branch & Lincoln Logging Railroad. (Author's collection.)

Front Cover: The East Branch & Lincoln Railroad's Porter 50-ton saddle tank engine locomotive, on display at the entrance to Loon Mountain ski area, is pictured in 2011. (Author's collection.)

Upper Back Cover: The Burnt Brook (North Fork of the East Branch of the Pemigewasset River) drainage in April 1912 shows the devastation caused by forest fire. (Courtesy of the National Archives & Records Administration.)

Lower Back Cover (from left to right): James E. Henry and his family pose for a photograph in the early 1900s (courtesy of the Upper Pemigewasset Historical Society), trestle No. 16 along the East Branch & Lincoln Railroad (author's collection), woodsmen posing for the camera at one of the logging camps along the East Branch & Lincoln Railroad (courtesy of the Upper Pemigewasset Historical Society).

Images of Modern America

EAST BRANCH & LINCOLN RAILROAD

Erin Paul Donovan

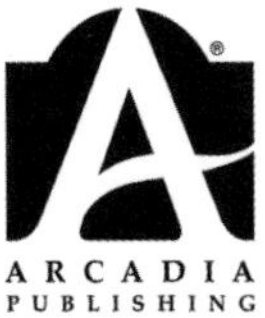

ISBN 978-1-4671-2862-9

Published by Arcadia Publishing
Charleston, South Carolina

Printed in the United States of America

Library of Congress Control Number: 2017956430

For all general information, please contact Arcadia Publishing:
Telephone 843-853-2070
Fax 843-853-0044
E-mail sales@arcadiapublishing.com
For customer service and orders:
Toll-Free 1-888-313-2665

Visit us on the Internet at www.arcadiapublishing.com

Dedicated to the memory of James Everell Henry, who unknowingly created the greatest trail system in the White Mountain National Forest—the Pemigewasset Wilderness trail system.

Contents

ACKNOWLEDGMENTS

This book project has been a long time in the making, and it would not have been possible without the assistance of a number of organizations, local historians, and various other individuals.

A special thank-you is given to Carol Riley, president of the Upper Pemigewasset Historical Society in Lincoln, New Hampshire. Carol gave me access to the historical society's large black-and-white photography collection of the East Branch & Lincoln Railroad, which includes the expansive Bill Gove collection. Without them, this book would not have been possible. I also need to thank the volunteers of the Upper Pemigewasset Historical Society who answered my questions and provided beneficial information for this book. In particular, David Thompson.

I also would like to thank Becky Fullerton, archivist for the Appalachian Mountain Club; Eben Lehman, director of library and archives for Forest History Society; Gina McNeely of Gina McNeely Picture Research, and the archivists at the National Archives and Records Administration. All went out of their way to help locate a number of the incredible black-and-white photographs used in this book. I would also like to thank Linda Dammann, development assistant for the Society for the Protection of New Hampshire Forests, for providing historical information pertaining to the town of Lincoln.

I would also like to thank Steve Smith, owner of Mountain Wanderer Map & Book Store in Lincoln, and Mike Dickerman, owner of Bondcliff Books in Littleton, New Hampshire. Their knowledge of the White Mountains is incredible, and their willingness to share it helped me out greatly while working on this book. And lastly, I want to thank my editor, Liz Gurley, for pointing me in the right direction during this entire project.

INTRODUCTION

In 1764, Gov. Benning Wentworth granted 24,000 acres of land to James Avery of Connecticut and others. Lincoln was named after Henry Fiennes Pelham-Clinton, second duke of Newcastle, ninth earl of Lincoln. The town was settled in 1782, and farming was the main source of income throughout the 1800s. The rocky terrain created tough growing conditions for farming. However, the virgin forest and abundance of rivers to supply water to sawmills made the area perfect for logging operations.

In the late 19th and early 20th centuries, railroad logging was a way of life in the New Hampshire White Mountains. Thus, the story of James Everell Henry and his East Branch & Lincoln Railroad is forever engrained in New Hampshire history. Henry's clear cutting logging practices made him one of the most controversial figures in White Mountains history, but he is also among the most interesting. His business practices earned him the label of "Lumber King of the Granite State," and his logging practices earned him the less desirable label of "Woods Butcher." Nonetheless, his employees were loyal and considered themselves to be well treated, and were even offered health insurance for 50¢ a month.

Born on April 21, 1831, in Lyman, New Hampshire, James E. Henry was no stranger to railroad logging when he moved his army of woodsmen to Lincoln. In the years around 1880, he had built the village of Zealand, which included a large sawmill, charcoal kilns, store, and company houses for the workers, and operated his Zealand Valley logging railroad.

In 1892, the small mountainous town of Lincoln was put on the map when Henry moved his logging railroad operation from Zealand to Lincoln. He bought the area known today as Lincoln village and the entire East Branch of the Pemigewasset River watershed, known as Lincoln Woods during the East Branch & Lincoln Railroad days.

Henry wasted no time in Lincoln, building tenement houses, a sawmill, a company store, a school, a hospital, and later, a pulp mill and paper mill. Lincoln was a true company town. The Henrys owned the town, mill, school, company store, hospital, boardinghouse, and hotel. Members of the family held various town jobs, such as selectmen and postmaster. By 1894, the East Branch & Lincoln Railroad was hauling virgin spruce out of Lincoln Woods down to the mill in Lincoln village.

Henry was not the first to seek out the virgin spruce in the East Branch watershed, however. During the mid-1800s, there were a few small sawmills operating on the Pemigewasset River. And the Fiske and Norcross Company, incorporated as the Merrimack River Lumber Company in April 1850, was cutting timber on land it owned in the Lincoln and Woodstock area, and did log drives on the Pemigewasset River. The drives began in the Lincoln/Woodstock area, and the logs were floated down the Pemigewasset River to the Merrimack River, eventually ending up in Lowell, Massachusetts, where the company had a sawmill.

By 1883, the Boston, Concord, and Montreal's Pemigewasset Valley Railroad had reached North Woodstock, New Hampshire. The Pemigewasset Valley Railroad connected Plymouth to North

Woodstock. The Concord & Montreal Railroad took over the railroad in 1889, and in 1895, the line was leased to the Boston & Maine Railroad. During this period, travelers were becoming interested in the White Mountains, and the Pemigewasset Valley Railroad allowed tourists to visit the hotels, lakes, and mountains in the area.

When Henry arrived in Lincoln, his intention was to do log drives on the Pemigewasset River down to Massachusetts, where he planned to build a sawmill, and he did do at least one log drive, but he ran into problems and abandoned the idea. Realizing that the railroad would be the best option to transport lumber, in 1893–1894, he negotiated a deal with the Concord & Montreal Railroad to connect the short length of railroad that he had already built in Lincoln village to the Pemigewasset Valley Railroad in North Woodstock. The East Branch & Lincoln Railroad was now connected to the outside world, and it was the beginning of a logging railroad empire that would last for 54 years. By January 1948, the last log train had rolled out of Lincoln Woods for good.

The East Branch & Lincoln Railroad traveled deep into the region known today as the Pemigewasset Wilderness, a designated wilderness area consisting of 45,000 acres. Including spur lines and rail sidings, the railroad was estimated to be 50 to 60 miles long. It was the largest logging railroad in New England and survived longer than any other logging railroad in the New Hampshire White Mountains. During its 50-plus years of existence, one billion feet of logs were hauled over this railroad.

James E. Henry retired a wealthy man in 1908 and died in 1912. His sons continued to operate the family business after his retirement until selling the railroad, land, and the town to the Parker-Young Company in 1917. Parker-Young sold all company assets again in 1946 to the Marcalus Manufacturing Company. The East Branch & Lincoln Railroad came to its demise by January 1948 under the ownership of Marcalus Manufacturing. Marcalus reorganized as the Franconia Paper Corporation in 1950 and continued to operate the Lincoln mill. In the early 1950s, with the use of trucks, it hauled pulpwood out of Lincoln Woods from its Black Mountain Camp operation to the mill. In June 1960, the last log ran through the sawmill, and because of pollution problems, the paper mill shut down in June 1970. The paper mill attempted to operate under different ownerships until 1980, when all mill operations came to an end because the mill failed to meet Environmental Protection Agency pollution standards. The final day for the Lincoln mill operation was June 11, 1980. In 2009, the remaining mill buildings were torn down.

The logging empire James E. Henry built employed thousands of workers over its 70-plus years in existence. Henry's logging tactics influenced the passing of the Weeks Act in 1911, which authorized the federal government to purchase private land in the eastern United States and maintain it as national forests.

With the use of black-and-white and color photographs, this book explores the history of the East Branch & Lincoln Railroad, while showing the abandoned railroad as it looks today. Beginning in the village of Lincoln, then documenting the early years of the railroad, this work is laid out in chronological order following the path of the railroad and the woodsmen as they moved throughout the East Branch country to harvest spruce.

One

Lower East Branch

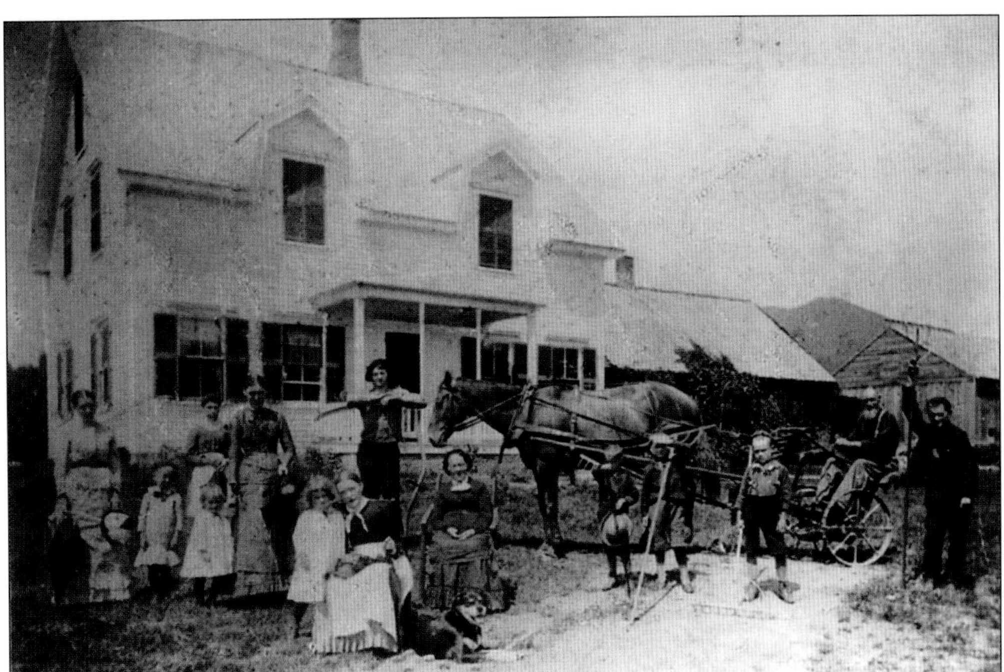

The town of Lincoln was settled in 1782. By the 1850s, the Merrimack River Lumber Company (Fiske and Norcross Company) was logging land that it owned in Lincoln and Woodstock. The Dearborn farm, seen here, was one of four farms in Lincoln village (known then as Pollard's) in 1892 when James Everell Henry arrived. (Courtesy of the Upper Pemigewasset Historical Society.)

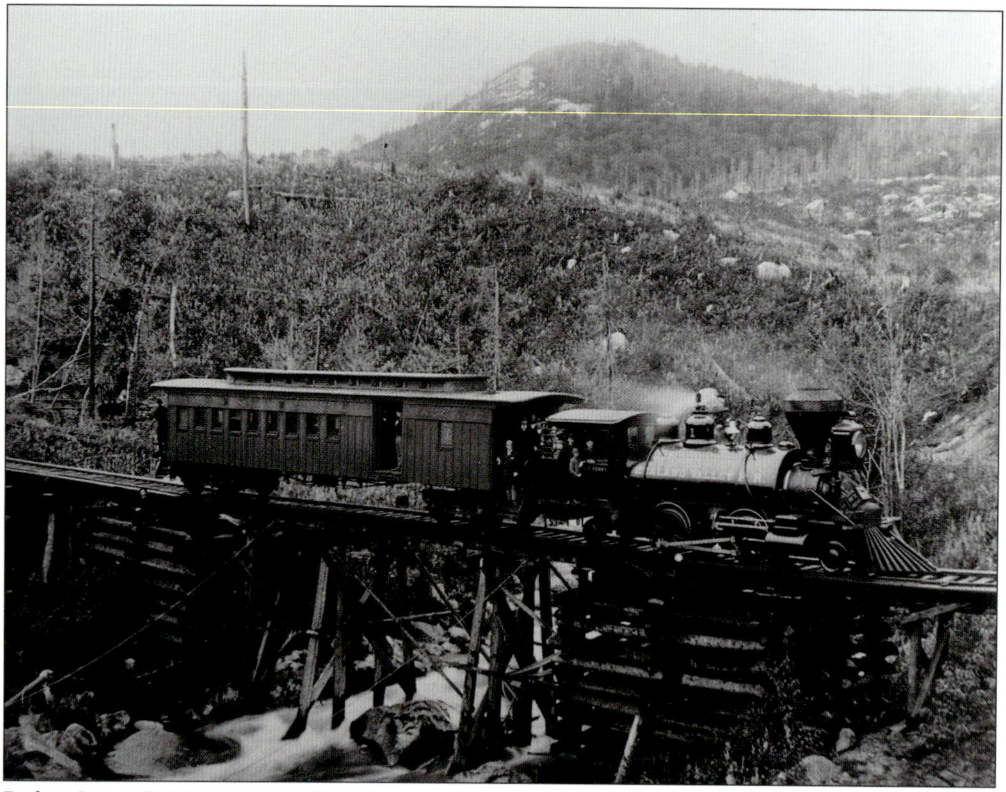

Before James E. Henry arrived in Lincoln, he had already been involved in sawmill operations and in railroad logging. In the late 1800s, Henry harvested timber from the Zealand Valley of the White Mountains. Pictured here on a trestle along the Zealand Valley Railroad is the first locomotive Henry purchased for the Zealand Valley Railroad, the 25-ton Baldwin locomotive No. 1, the *J.E Henry*. (Courtesy of the Upper Pemigewasset Historical Society.)

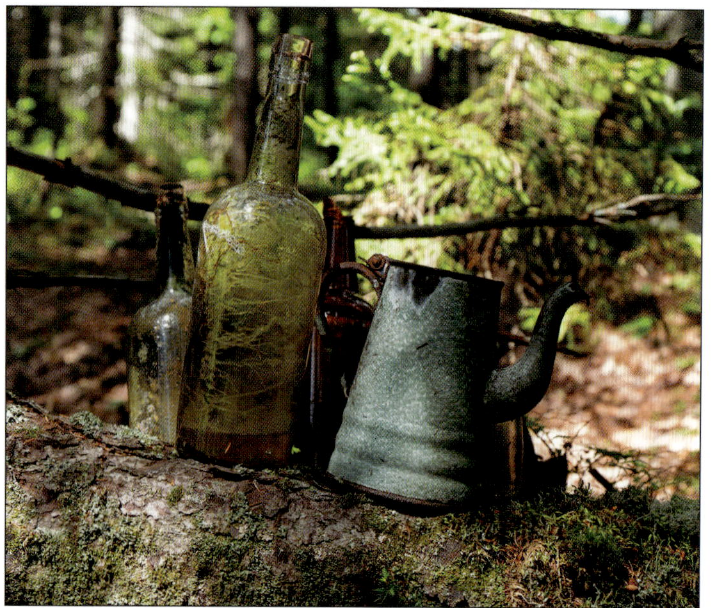

The total number of logging camps and their locations along Henry's Zealand Valley Railroad is a mystery. The camps were made out of logs, and between mother nature reclaiming the Zealand Valley area and devastating forest fires, very little remains of them. Here, hikers have placed artifacts on display at one of the possible old logging camps along the railroad. (Author's collection.)

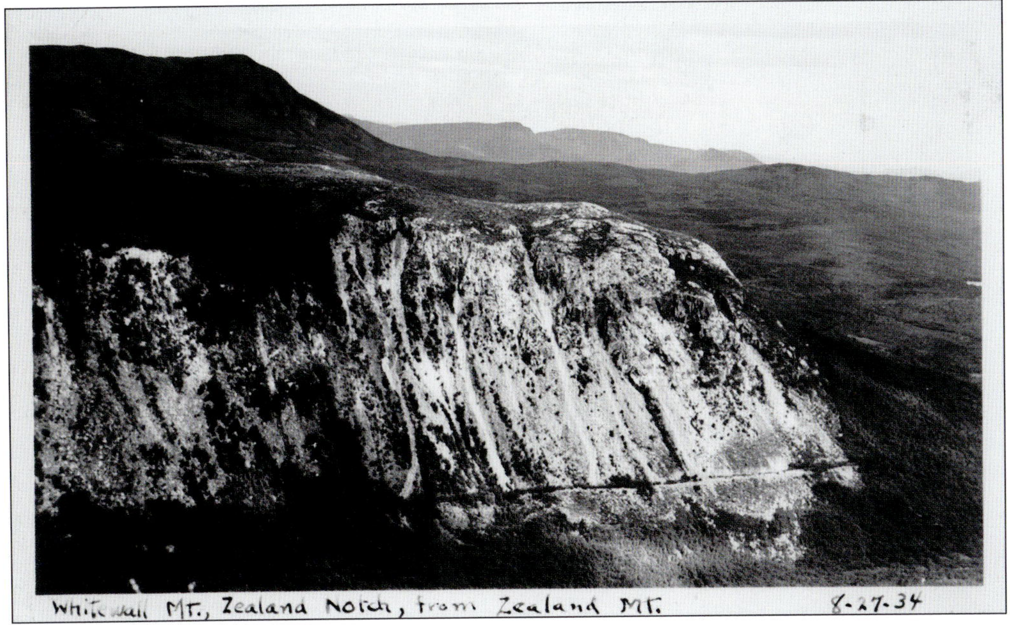

One of the grand accomplishments of James E. Henry's 11-mile-long Zealand Valley Railroad was building through Zealand Notch. The 1934 photograph above from Zeacliff shows the old railroad bed that Henry cut into the side of Whitewall Mountain in Zealand Notch. Today, the Ethan Pond Trail, a section of the Appalachian Trail (below), utilizes this section of the railroad. (Above, courtesy of the Appalachian Mountain Club Library & Archives; below, author's collection.)

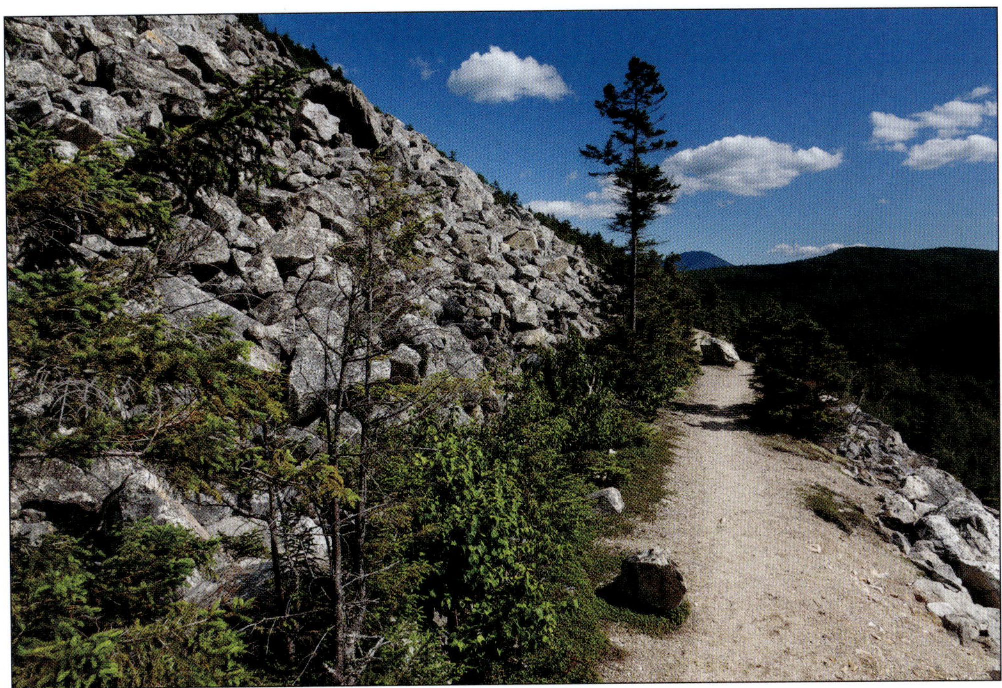

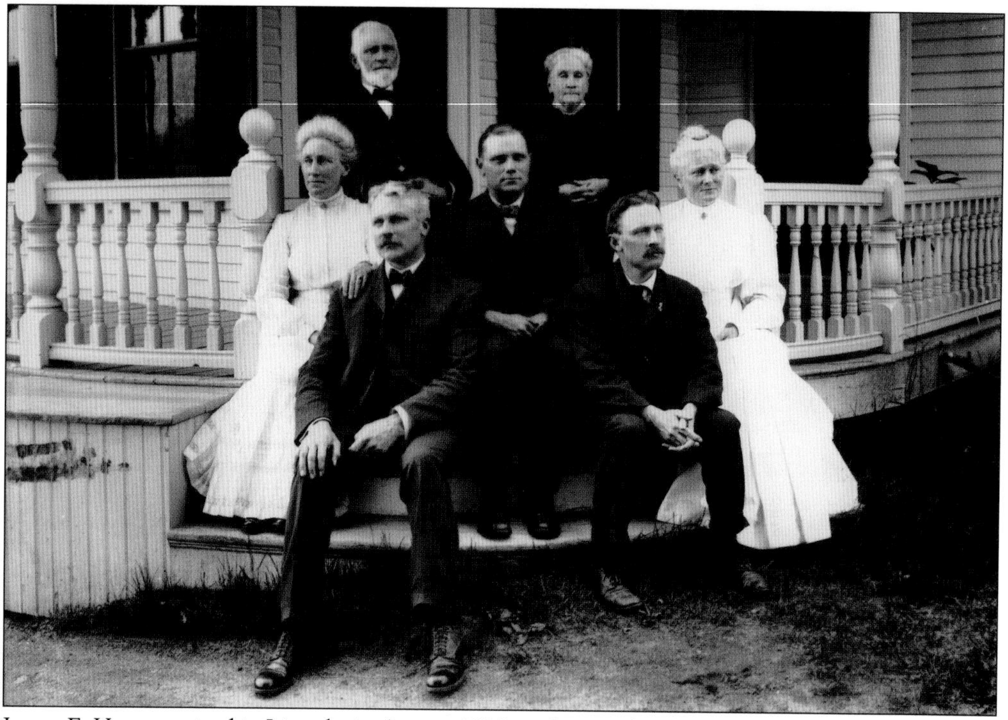

James E. Henry arrived in Lincoln in August 1892, and immediately started building his mill town and his East Branch & Lincoln Railroad. Henry's three sons were involved in the business, which operated as J.E. Henry and Sons. Sitting on the steps are, from left to right, (first row) Harriet, John, George, Charles, and Ida Henry; (second row) James E. and Eliza Henry. (Courtesy of the Upper Pemigewasset Historical Society.)

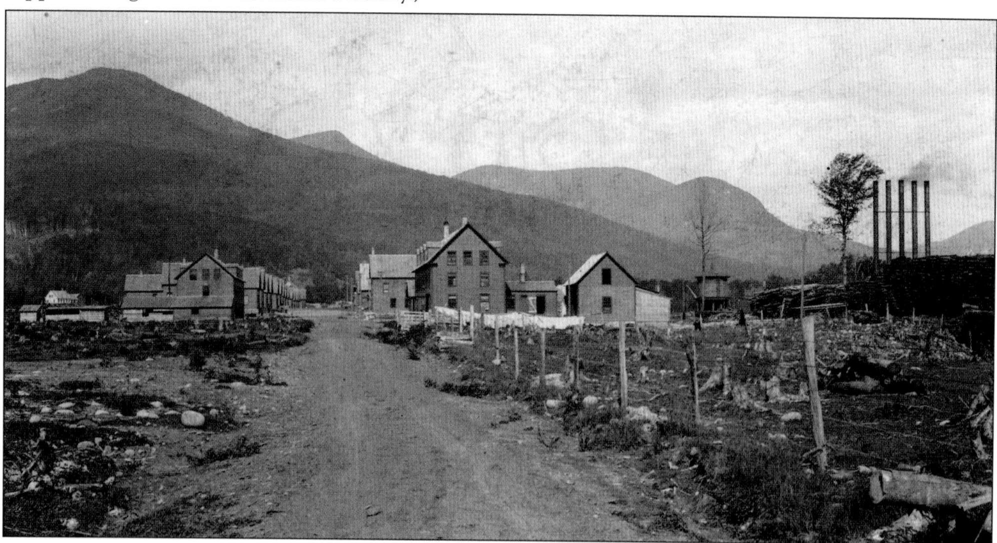

Lincoln was a small wilderness town until J.E. Henry and Sons transformed it into a thriving mill town. The company not only owned the town, it built it and owned thousands of acres in the East Branch of the Pemigewasset River watershed, known as Lincoln Woods. This early 1890s photograph looking east along Main Street shows Henry's first sawmill, identified by the five smokestacks at right. (Courtesy of the Upper Pemigewasset Historical Society.)

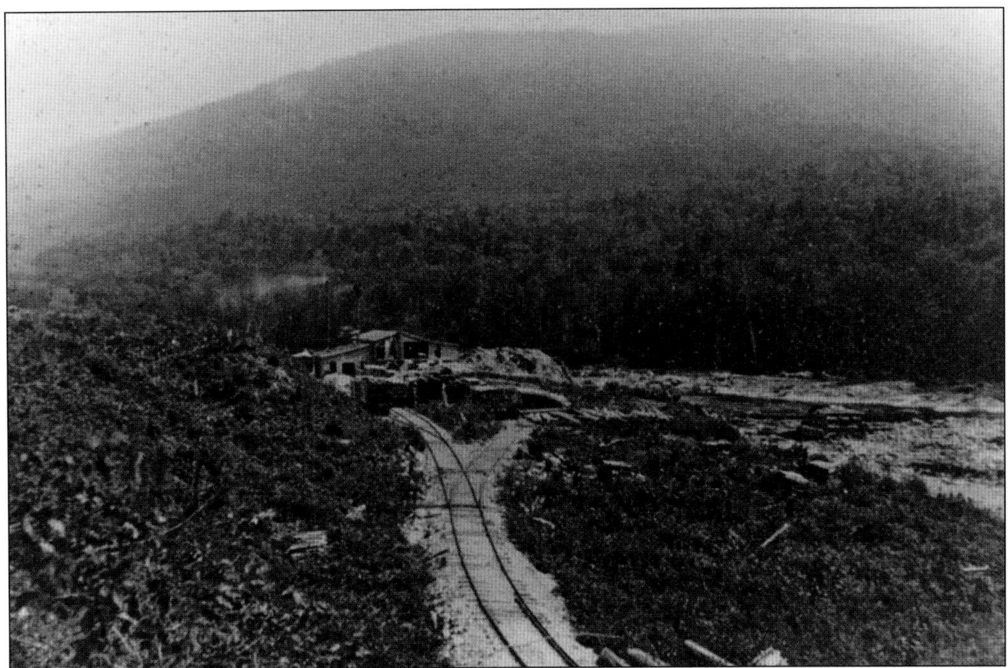

This early sawmill on the East Branch of the Pemigewasset River is believed to be the G.E. Dupee sawmill that James E. Henry leased to saw lumber for the original houses and sawmill he built when he first came to Lincoln in 1892. Dupee purchased the mill from C.M. Stuart, who purchased it from W.R Park. The Dodge Clothespin Factory was later built in this area. (Courtesy of the Upper Pemigewasset Historical Society.)

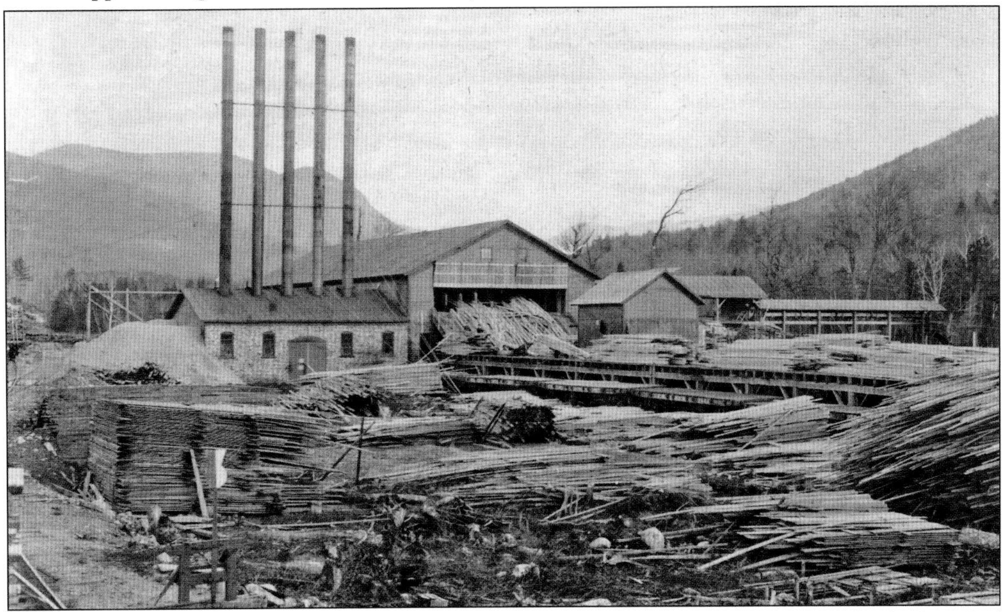

Built in 1893–1894, J.E. Henry and Sons' first sawmill was one of the largest in New England. Identified by its five smokestacks, it operated from 1894 until it was destroyed by fire on Christmas Eve 1898. Henry rebuilt the sawmill in 1899, and mill operations continued. Piles of cut lumber can be seen in this undated photograph of the first mill. (Courtesy of the Upper Pemigewasset Historical Society.)

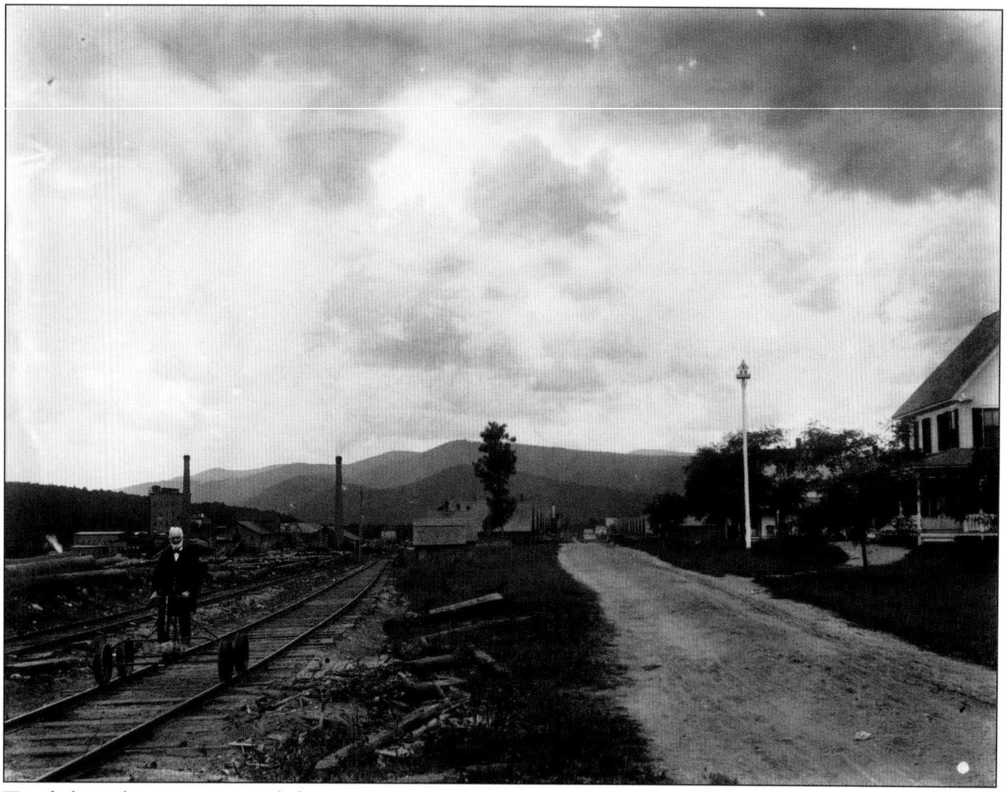

Track bicycles were one of the means of transportation for getting around the East Branch & Lincoln Railroad. In this 1902 photograph of Lincoln village, James E. Henry rides a track bicycle east along the tracks. The paper mill, the pulp mill, and the second sawmill are behind him, and Main Street is on the right. (Courtesy of the Upper Pemigewasset Historical Society.)

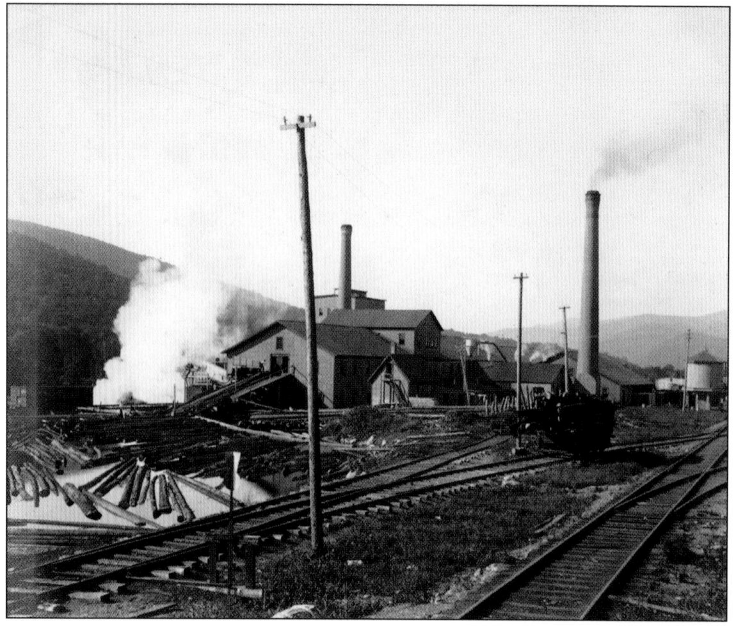

Built in 1899 and operating by 1900, J.E. Henry and Sons' second sawmill was a double mill. This west-facing view of Henry's second sawmill shows the mill log pond full of logs. The top of the pulp mill, built in 1898, can be seen behind the sawmill. Henry also built a paper mill in 1901–1902 that operated under the name Henry Paper Company. (Courtesy of the Upper Pemigewasset Historical Society.)

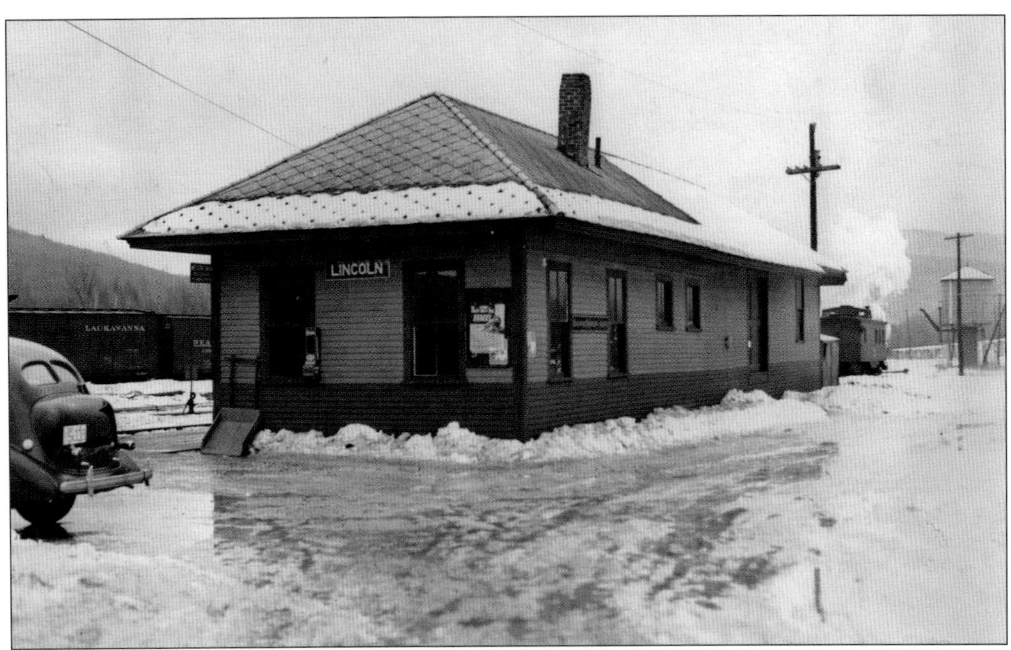

In the early days, James E. Henry wanted to do log river drives down the Pemigewasset and Merrimack Rivers to Massachusetts, where he planned to build another sawmill, but he ran into problems and had to abandon the idea. Realizing that the railroad would be the best way to transport lumber, Henry connected the short length of line that he had already built in Lincoln to the Concord & Montreal Railroad (Boston & Maine Railroad) in North Woodstock. The Concord & Montreal Railroad built a depot at the end of the Lincoln yard. The depot can be seen to the right of the water tank in the upper portion of the 1940s photograph below. (Both, courtesy of the Upper Pemigewasset Historical Society.)

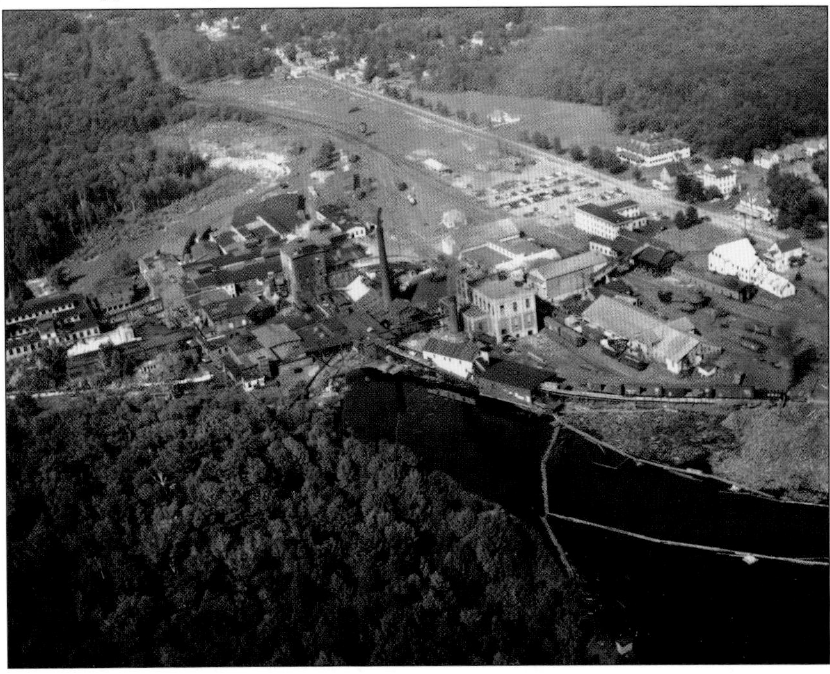

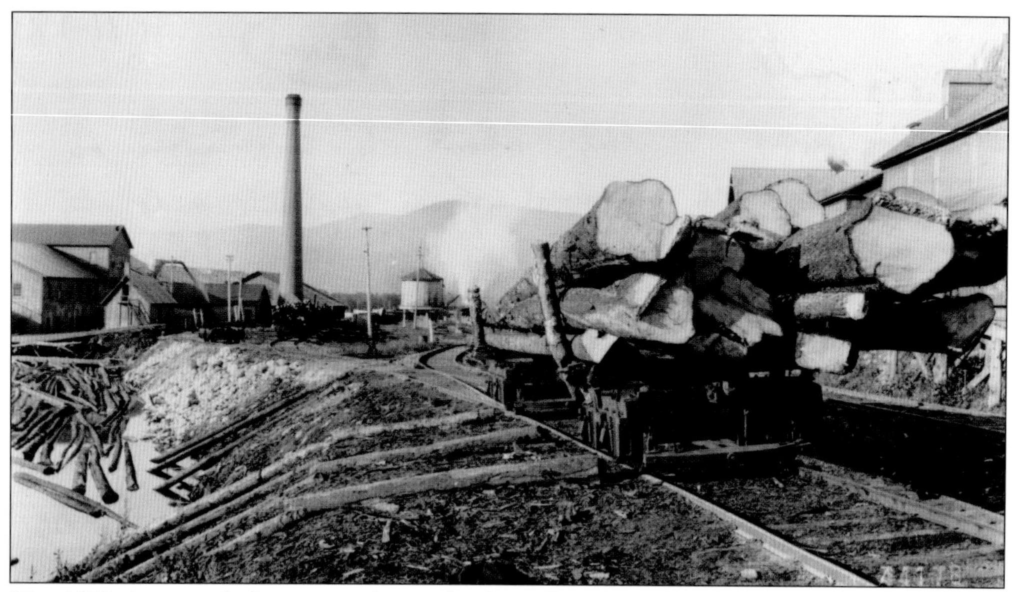

This 1903 photograph shows an early wooden frame log car ready to have its load of logs dumped into the log pond next to the sawmill. To dump the logs, the two wooden stakes on the pond side of the log car were removed by a worker on the opposite side of the car using a seven-foot wrench. (US Forest Service photograph, courtesy of the Upper Pemigewasset Historical Society.)

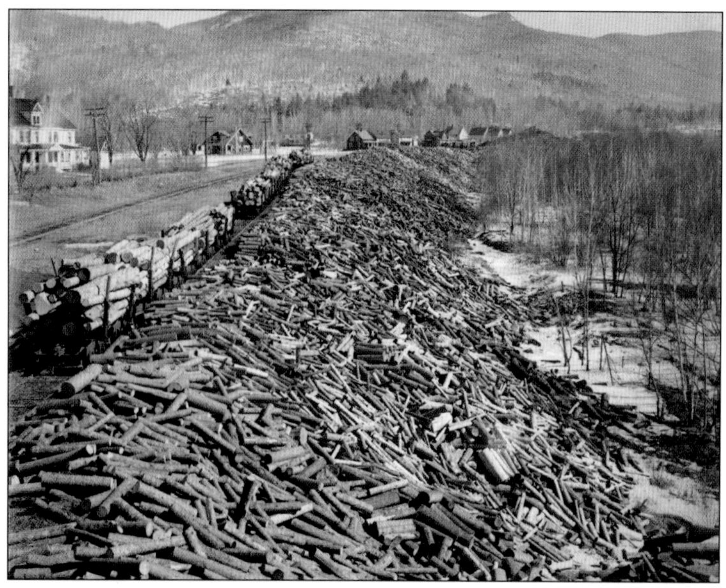

This undated photograph shows loaded log cars and piles of pulpwood as far as the eye can see. When James E. Henry came to Lincoln, he brought with him the wooden frame log cars (and other railroad equipment) that he used on the Zealand Valley Railroad. Around 1910, the log cars were updated with steel frames and stakes. (Courtesy of the Upper Pemigewasset Historical Society.)

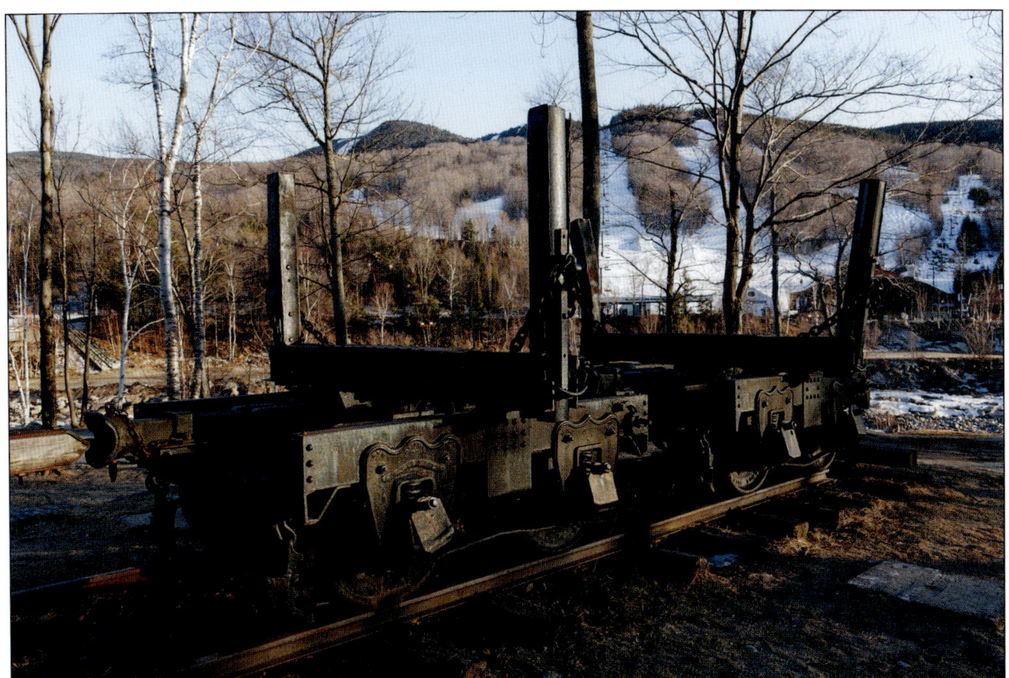

Along the Kancamagus Scenic Byway, a few miles above Lincoln village in the picnic area next to the entrance to Loon Mountain ski area, a couple of steel framed log cars are on display. One of the log cars (below) has a load of logs on it. The East Branch & Lincoln Railroad's Porter 50-ton saddle tank engine locomotive is attached to the loaded log car. Even though climbing on this display is not allowed, it interests both the young and old and allows for a close-up view of the equipment used on the railroad. (Both, author's collection.)

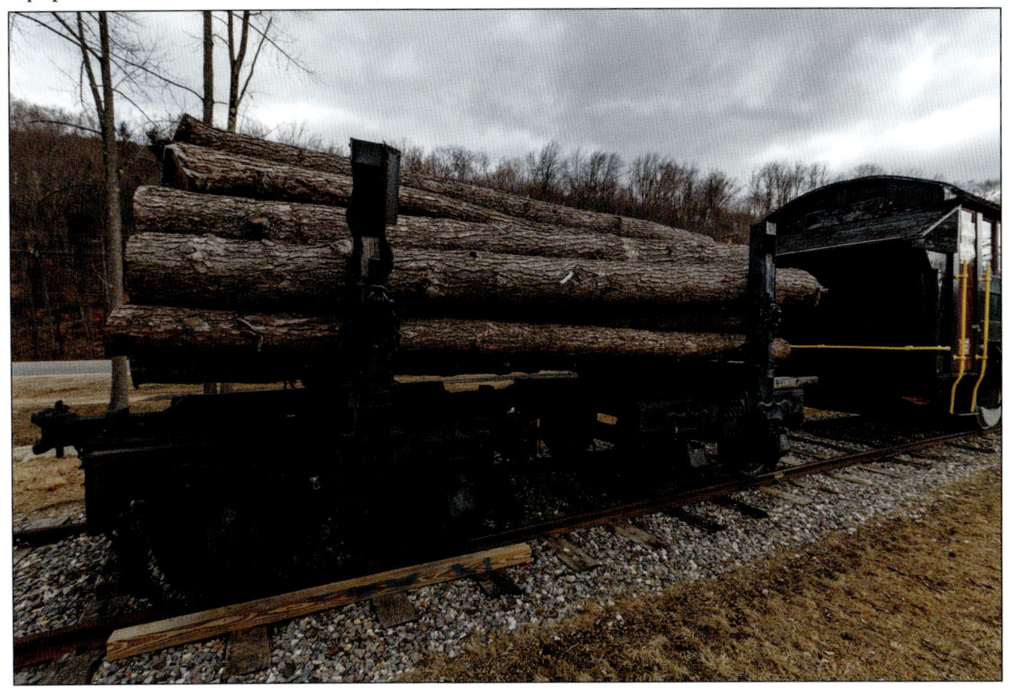

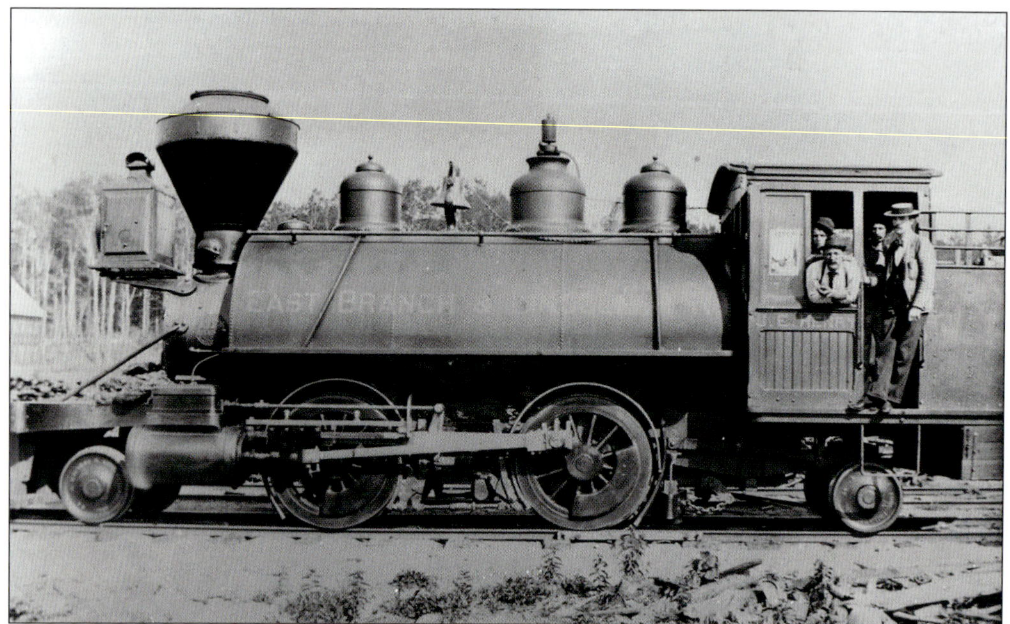

James E. Henry also brought with him from the Zealand Valley Railroad the Baldwin locomotive No. 1, the *J.E Henry*, and the Baldwin locomotive No. 2, the *Tintah*. In this c. 1895 photograph, four unidentified men pose in the cab of the *J.E. Henry*. Note the attire of the two men in front. (Courtesy of the Upper Pemigewasset Historical Society.)

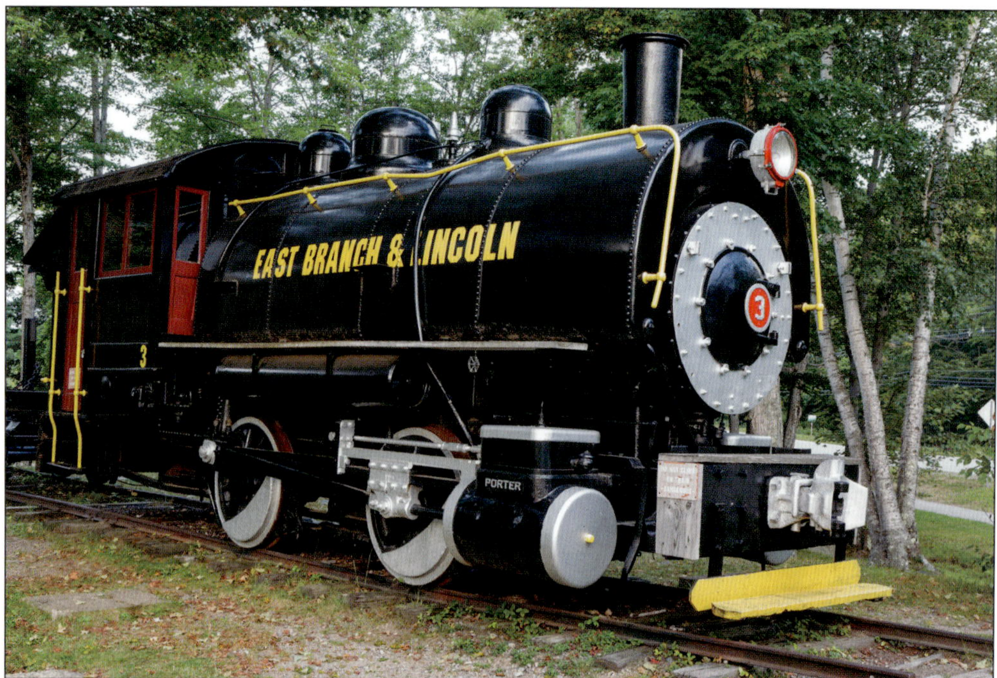

Built in 1917, the Porter No. 3 50-ton saddle tank engine locomotive was purchased from the US Army in 1945. It was used mainly in the Lincoln railroad yard during the Parker-Young years. Today, it is on display at the entrance of Loon Mountain along the Kancamagus Scenic Byway in Lincoln. (Author's collection.)

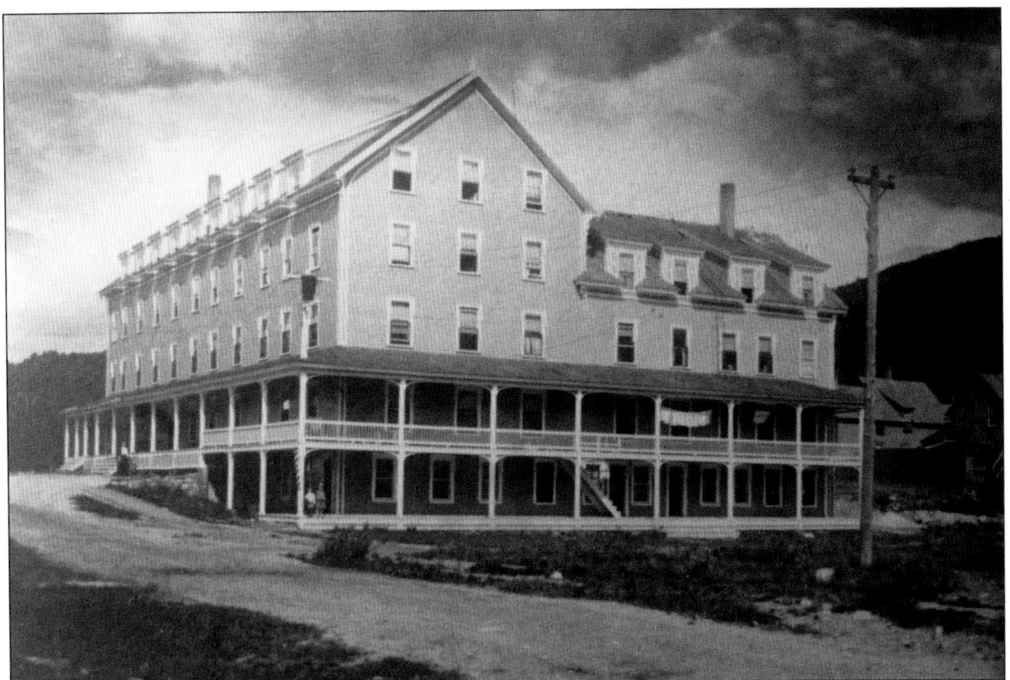

In 1902, James E. Henry built the Lincoln Hotel (Lincoln House). It lasted for over 70 years until it was destroyed by fire in 1975. This undated photograph shows the hotel in its early days. Lincoln's firehouse on Church Street now occupies the hotel site. (Courtesy of the Upper Pemigewasset Historical Society.)

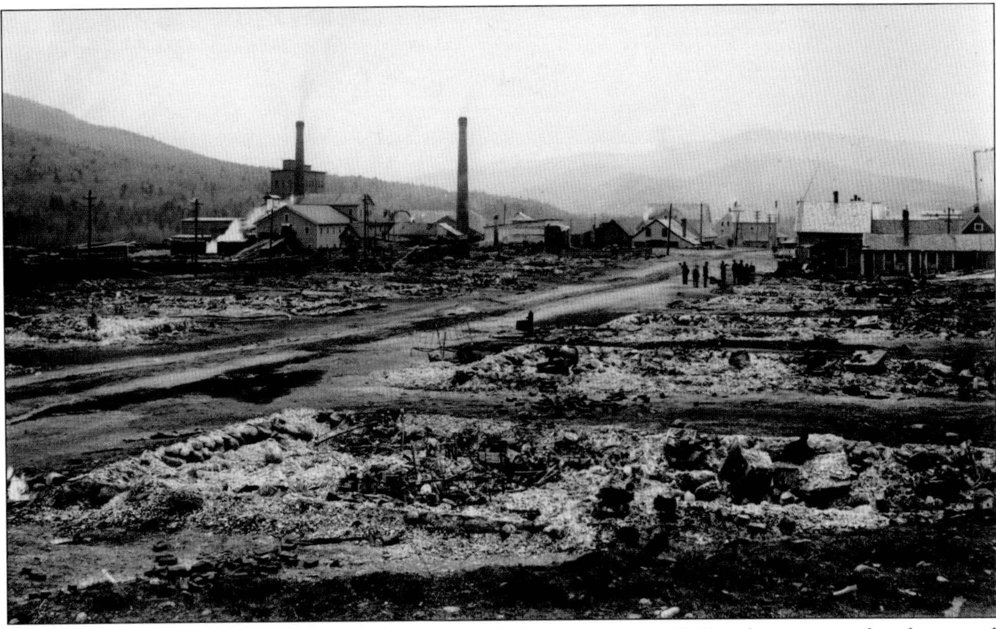

The paper mill was heavily damaged by fire in 1906. On May 13, 1907, a devastating fire destroyed a number of dwellings along Main Street in Lincoln village. This photograph looking into the village shows the damage from the 1907 fire. A number of buildings on both sides of Main Street were destroyed. (Courtesy of the Upper Pemigewasset Historical Society.)

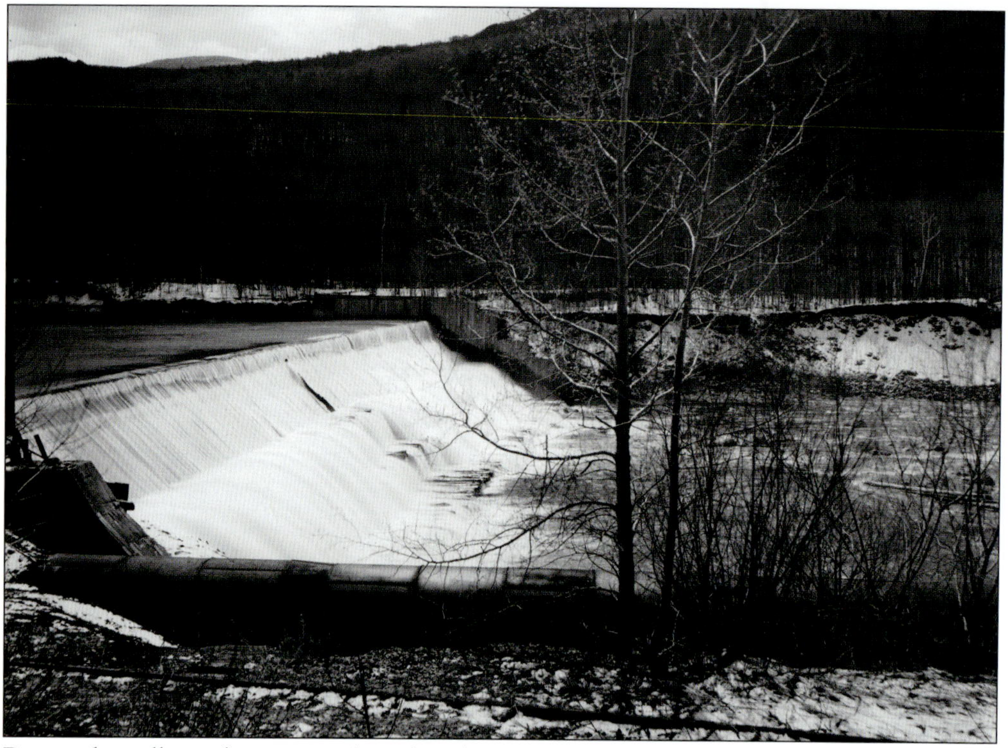

During the mill era, there were at least four dams on the East Branch of the Pemigewasset River. The Crib Dam controlled water flow into the mill pond, Gravity Dam provided manufacturing water to the mill, and the Nos. 1 and 2 Dams generated electricity for the mill and town. All were damaged at one point or another from flooding. In 1904–1905, the two dams that were used to generate electricity were built above Lincoln village. The No. 1 Dam pictured above in an undated photograph was just downstream from today's Loon Mt. Bridge. It would eventually supply both power and manufacturing water to the mill. The cribbing for this dam and the old powerhouse can still be seen along the paved walking path between Pollard Brook and the entrance to Loon Mountain. (Above, courtesy of the Upper Pemigewasset Historical Society; below, author's collection.)

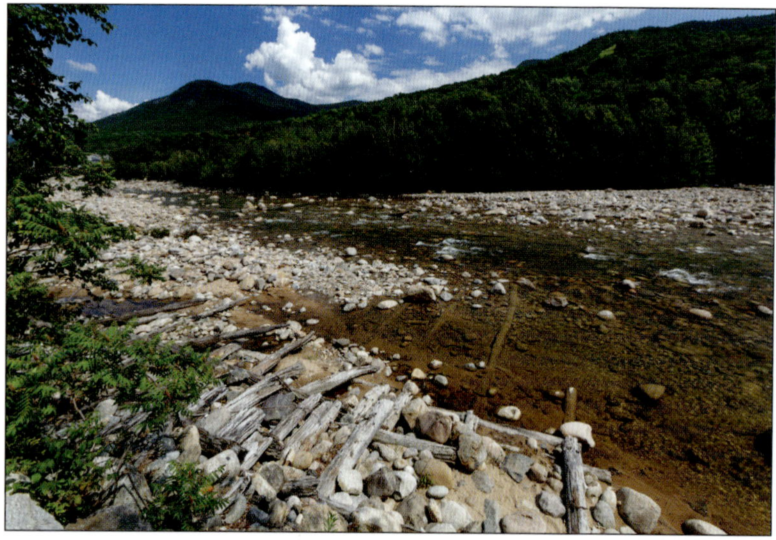

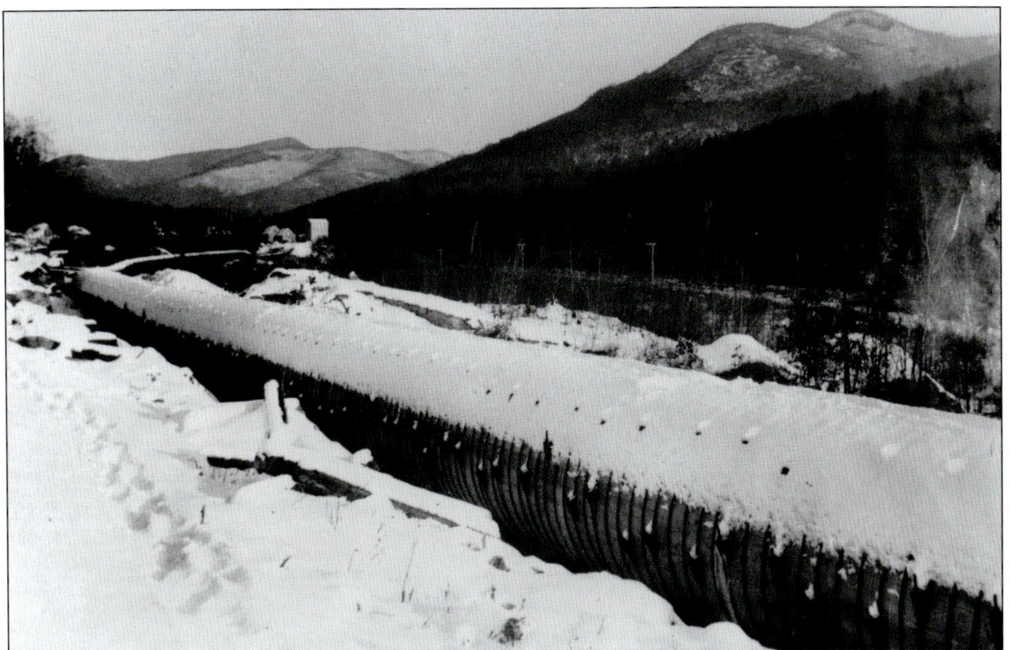

In order to generate electric power for the mill, water at the Nos. 1 and 2 Dams was diverted through large diameter wooden and steel penstock to turbines at the mill. This c. 1907 photograph of the No. 1 Dam penstock shows a section of the wooden penstock and the round steel hoops that held it together. (Courtesy of the Upper Pemigewasset Historical Society.)

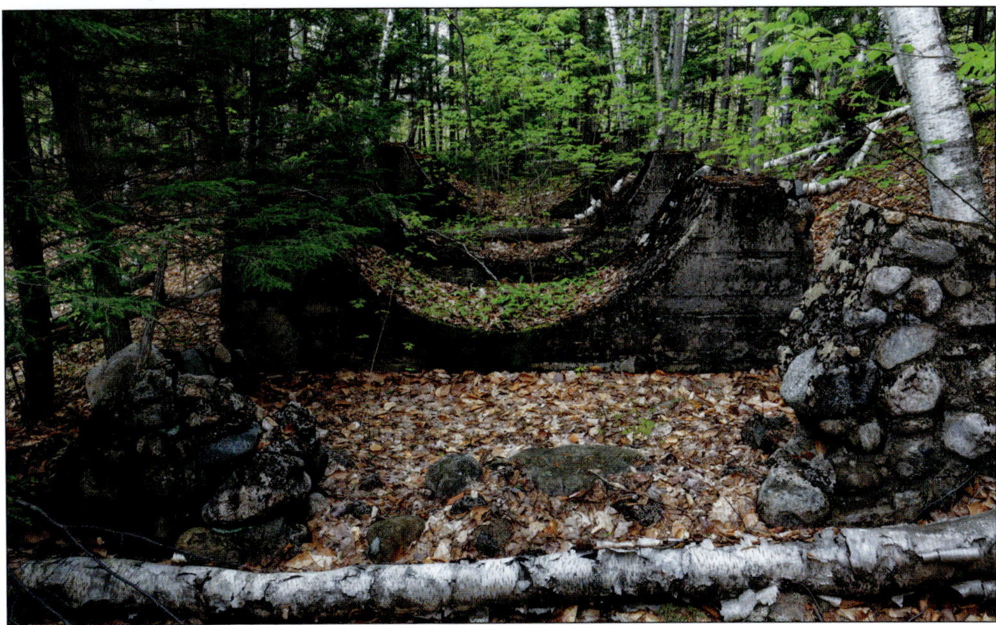

The No. 2 Dam was built upstream from today's Loon Mt. Bridge, just above where Clear Brook drains into the East Branch of the Pemigewasset River. These concrete cradles held the penstock that ran between the dam and the powerhouse, which was downstream from the dam. During the 1927 flood, the west bank of the dam washed away and a new river channel was created, leaving the dam completely dry. (Author's collection.)

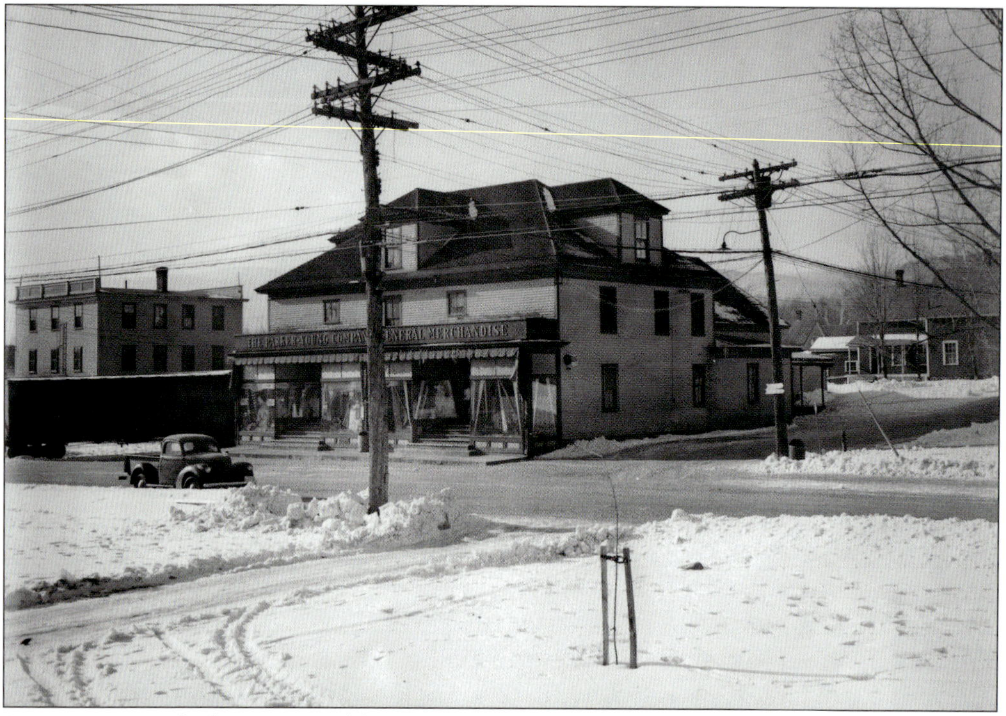

James E. Henry died in 1912, and his sons continued to operate the family business until 1917, when they sold the mill complex, the East Branch & Lincoln Railroad, and all of Lincoln Woods to the Parker-Young Company for $3 million. The sale included the company store that the Henrys built in the early 1900s. Today, Lahout's Country Clothing and Ski Shop (below) occupies the old Parker Young company store. The above undated photograph shows the storefront when it was under the ownership of Parker-Young. The outside of the store has not changed much over the years. (Above, courtesy of the Upper Pemigewasset Historical Society; below, author's collection.)

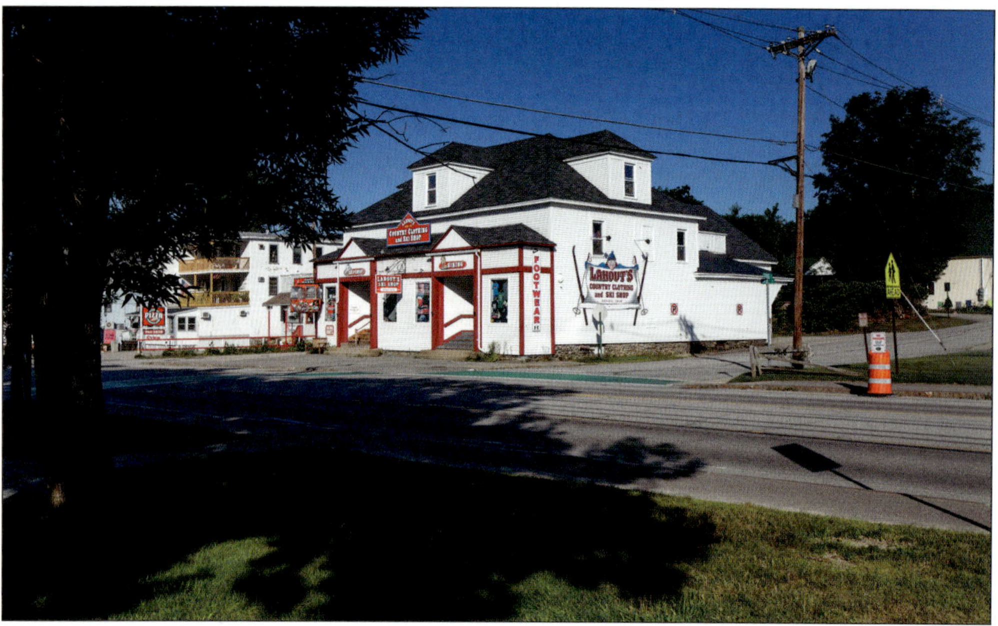

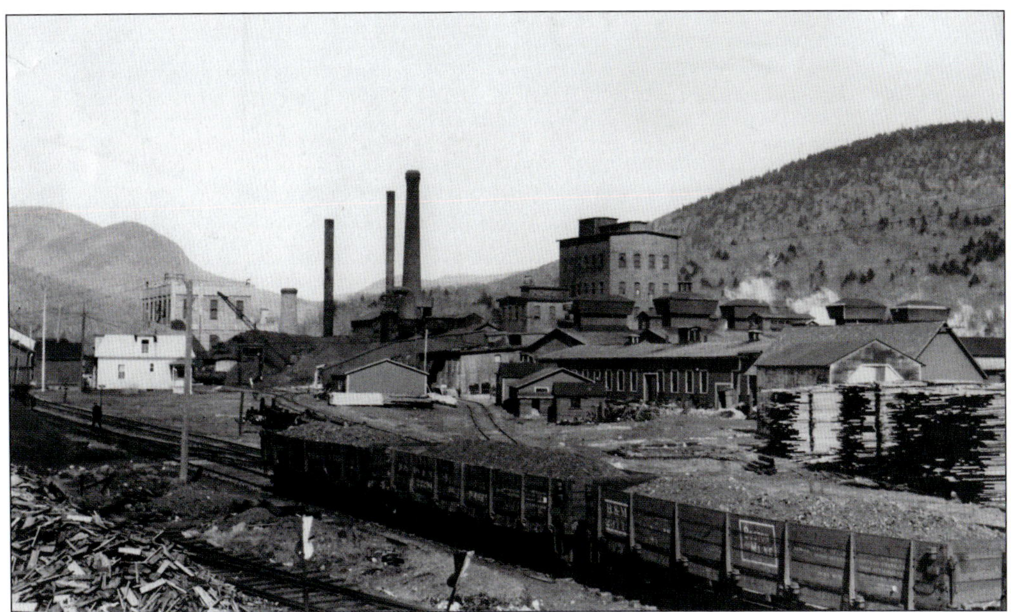

The Parker-Young Company ran the mill and the East Branch & Lincoln Railroad until 1946, when it sold both to the Marcalus Manufacturing Company. Marcalus reorganized in 1950 as the Franconia Paper Corporation. In June 1960, the last log ran through the sawmill, and the paper mill shut down in June 1970. From 1970 to 1980, the mill changed hands a number of times and attempts were made to operate it, but they all failed; the Lincoln mill's final day of operation was June 11, 1980. In 2009, the remaining mill buildings were torn down. The above 1920s photograph shows the mill complex when it was under the control of Parker-Young. Today, restaurants, stores, and the RiverWalk Resort at Loon Mountain (below) occupy the mill complex site. (Above, courtesy of the Upper Pemigewasset Historical Society; below, author's collection.)

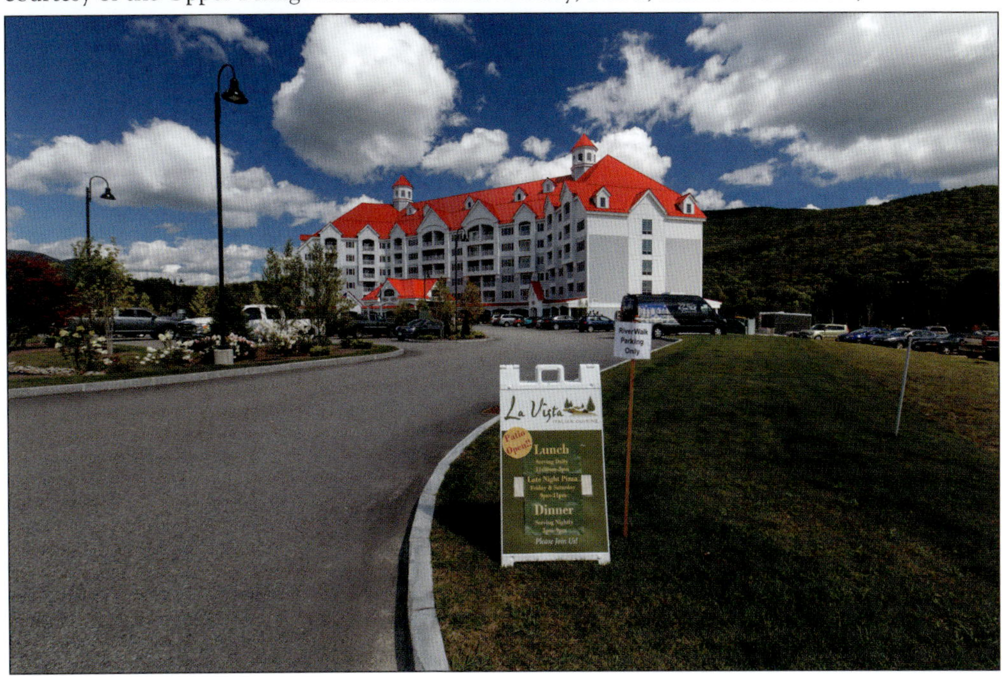

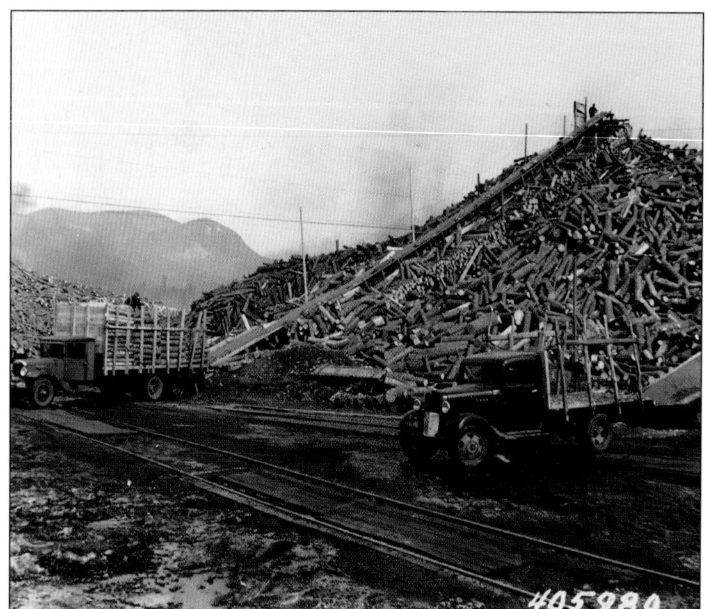

Both the Parker-Young Company and the Marcalus Manufacturing Company used trucks to haul logs out of Lincoln Woods. This 1941 photograph shows a worker hand-unloading pulpwood from a truck onto the conveyor belt that carries the pulpwood to the top of the log pile at the mill in Lincoln village. (Courtesy of the Forest History Society.)

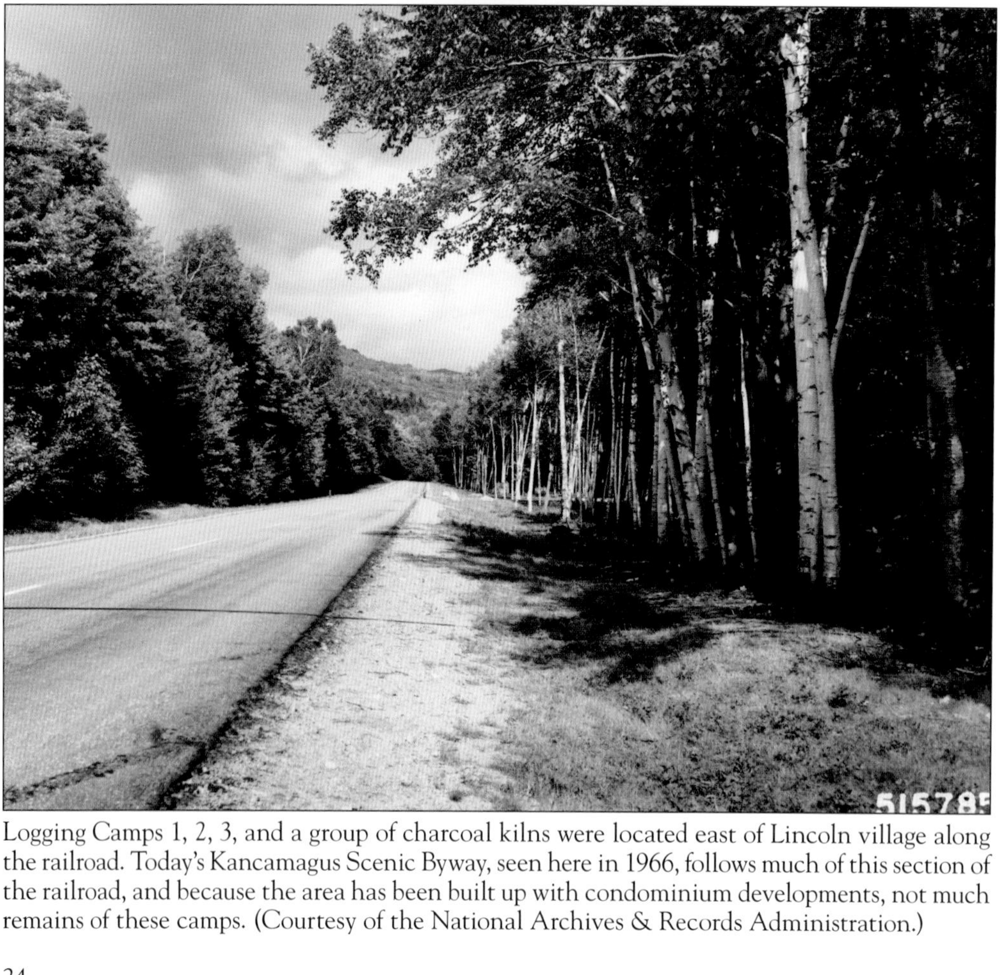

Logging Camps 1, 2, 3, and a group of charcoal kilns were located east of Lincoln village along the railroad. Today's Kancamagus Scenic Byway, seen here in 1966, follows much of this section of the railroad, and because the area has been built up with condominium developments, not much remains of these camps. (Courtesy of the National Archives & Records Administration.)

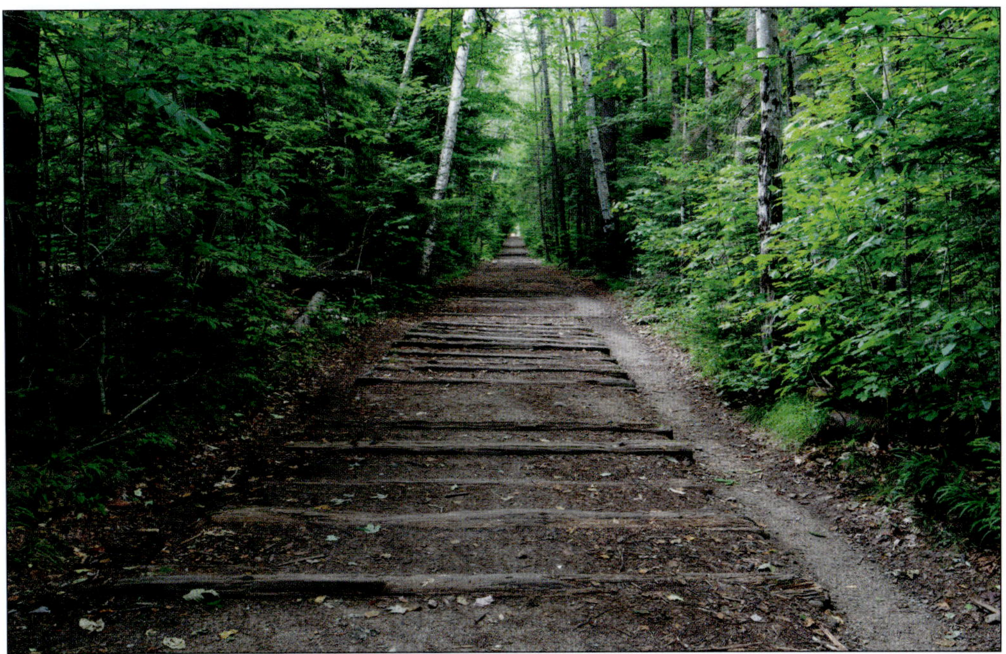

Beyond Camp 3, the East Branch & Lincoln Railroad follows, for the most part, today's Kancamagus Scenic Byway until it crosses the East Branch of the Pemigewasset River, just before the Lincoln Woods Trail trailhead. This crossing was the general area of Camp 4 and was where the railroad split into two branches. The Hancock Branch crossed the river and continued to follow the Kancamagus Scenic Byway, and the East Branch traveled up alongside the East Branch of the Pemigewasset River. Today's Lincoln Woods Trail (above) follows the old railroad grade; the beautiful suspension bridge below is at the start of the trail. (Both, author's collection.)

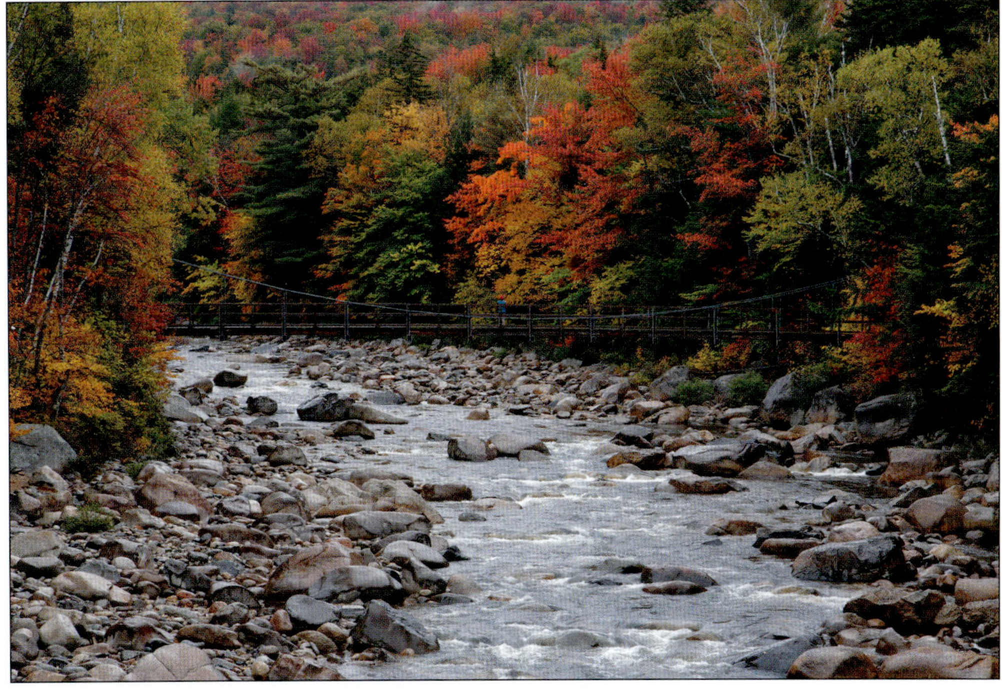

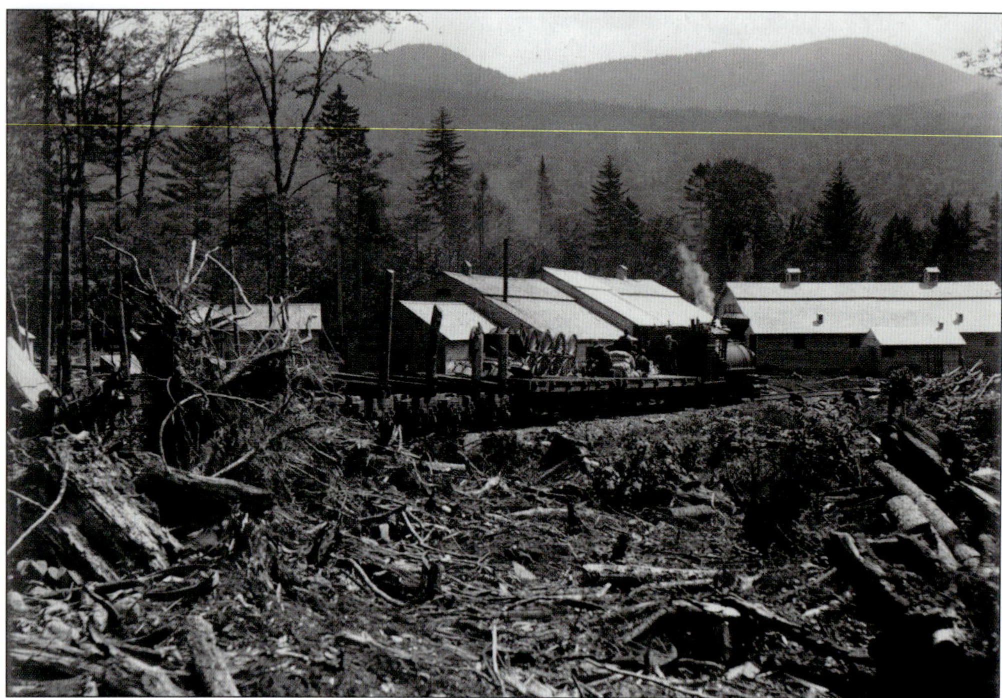

Over the lifespan of the East Branch & Lincoln Railroad, there were at least 41 logging camps along the railroad. Though some were named, such as the Loon Mountain Camp, most were given a number designation. Camps with a letter after the number were mountain camps located off the railroad. The mountain camps, which housed choppers, were much smaller dwellings than the rail-side camps. Four or five logging camps could be operating at one time, some camps were opened more than once over the years, and for some unknown reason, camp numbers were duplicated. In the above c. 1901 photograph, the log train is at Camp 8. The bed frame below is one of the few artifacts that remain at the Camp 8 site today. (Above, courtesy of the Upper Pemigewasset Historical Society; below, author's collection.)

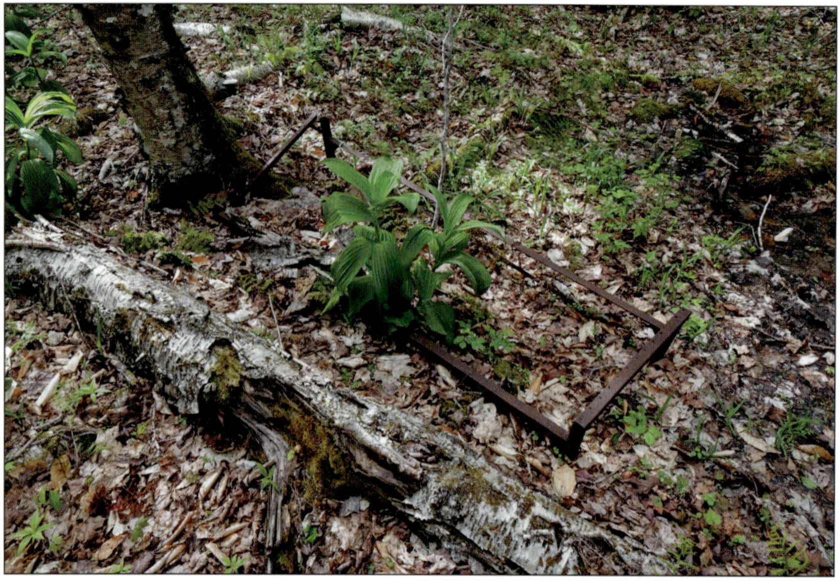

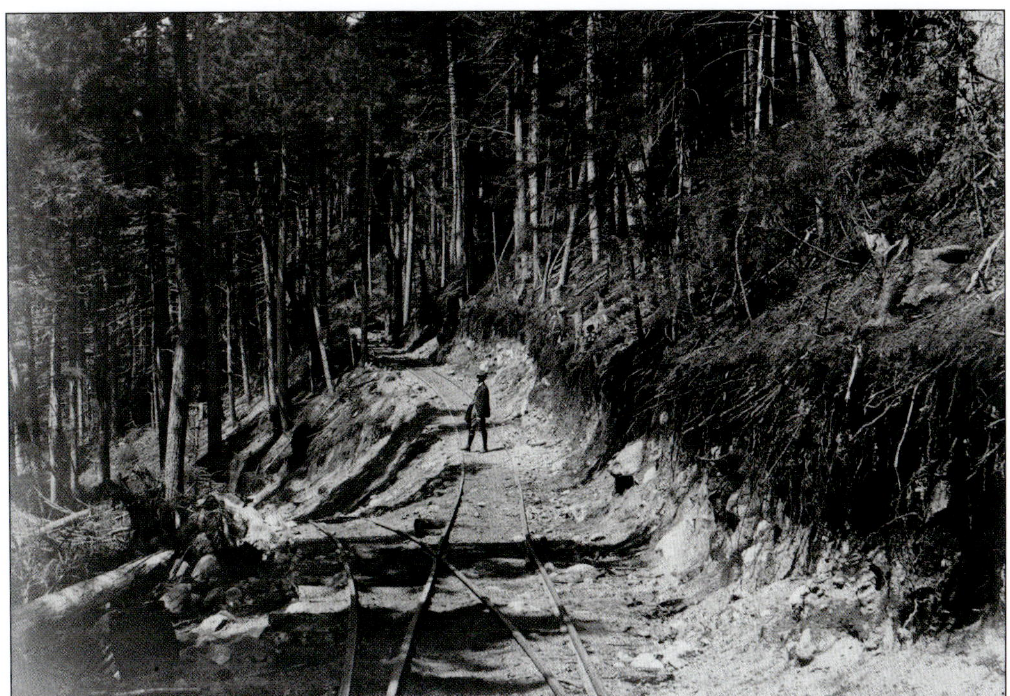

The East Branch & Lincoln Railroad was a standard-gauge railroad, but in 1901, J.E. Henry and Sons used a narrow-gauge line at Camp 8 to harvest timber from the slopes of Whaleback Mountain (Mt. Osseo). This short line traveled into the Osseo Brook drainage and consisted of a series of switchbacks. Horses pulled the empty log cars up the narrow-gauge line. Once loaded with logs, the brakemen released the brakes on the log cars and gravity brought them down the line to the landing at Camp 8. The brakemen rode the logs cars, and operated the hand brakes while coming down the line. This line lasted only for a few years and was discontinued after a brakeman was killed when a loaded log car got out control. Today's Osseo Trail (below) follows parts of it. (Above, courtesy of the Upper Pemigewasset Historical Society; below, author's collection.)

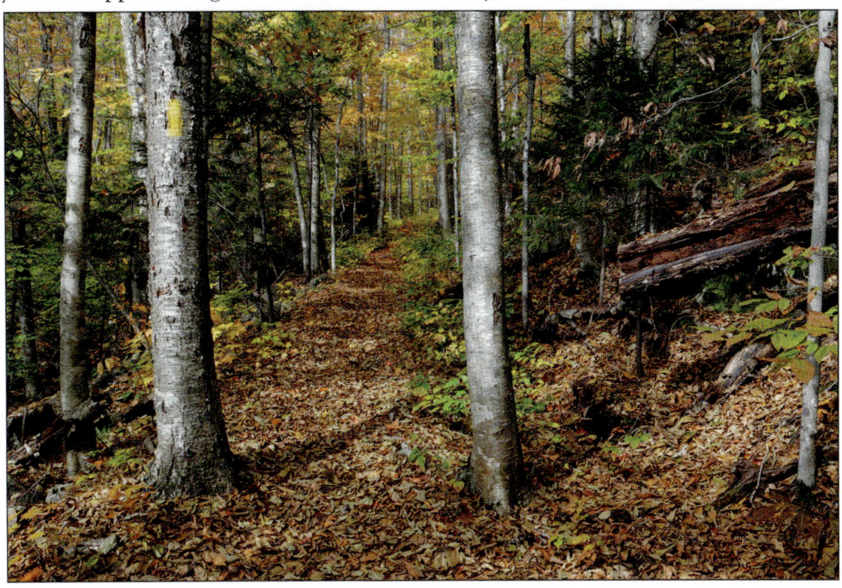

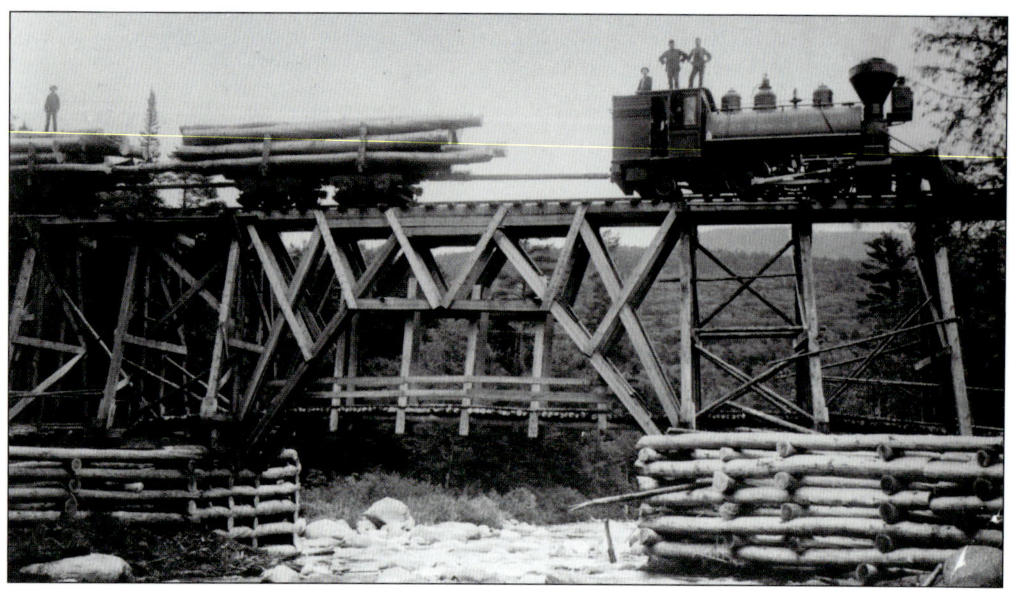

In the 1903 photograph above, the Baldwin No. 3 and crew pose for the camera on one of the grandest trestles along the East Branch & Lincoln Railroad, the original trestle No. 7. Built in 1902, trestle No. 7 crossed Franconia Brook just above where it drains into the East Branch of the Pemigewasset River. It serviced the Franconia and Lincoln Brook Branches and was abandoned in 1911. The trestle was unique in that the bottom deck was used for horses coming in and out of the woods. A few trestle pieces remain at the site today (below). (Above, courtesy of the Upper Pemigewasset Historical Society; below, author's collection.)

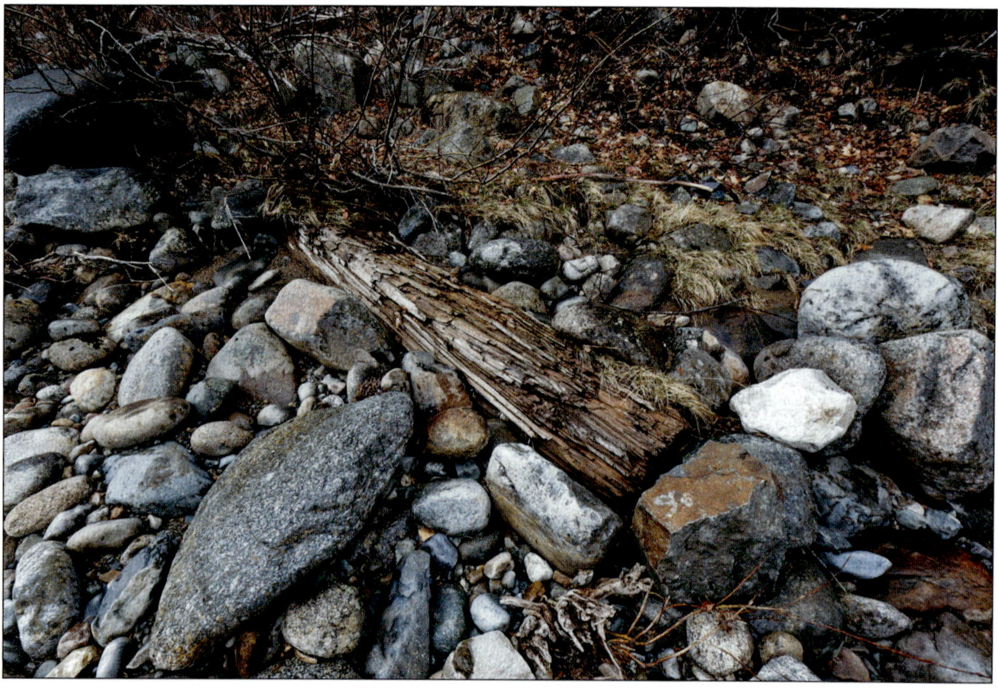

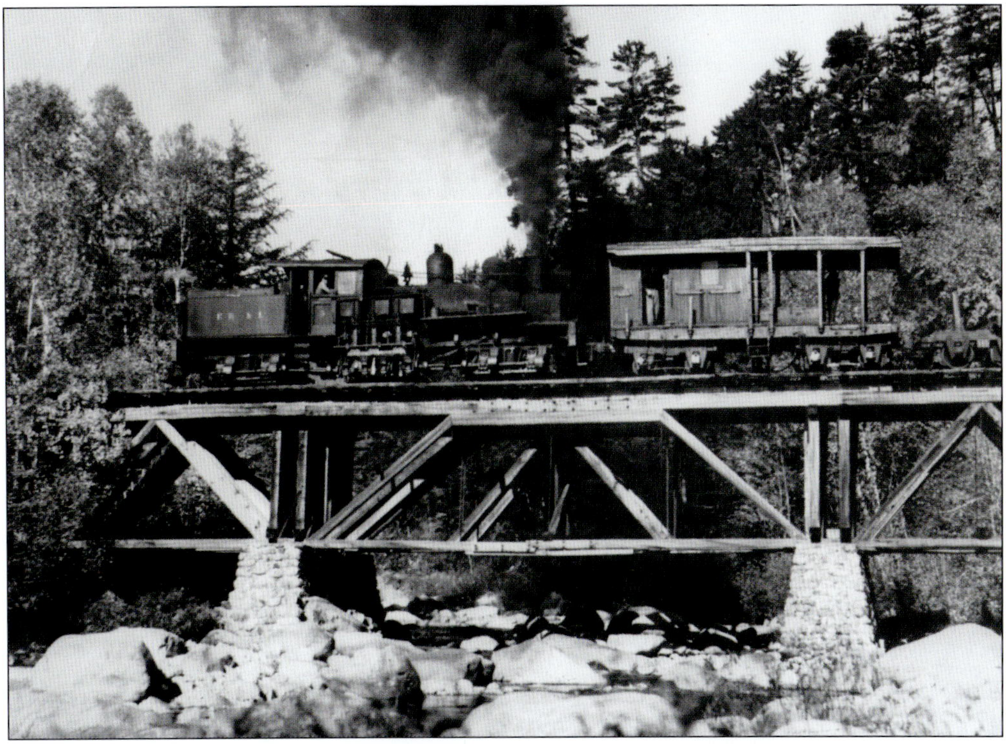

Two trestles were built at this crossing of Franconia Brook. Each serviced different areas of today's Pemigewasset Wilderness. The first trestle, the original trestle No. 7, serviced the Franconia and Lincoln Brook Branches. The second trestle, pictured above in the 1940s with the Shay No. 5 stopped on it, was just below No. 7, and serviced the area surrounding the East and North Fork Branches of the Pemigewasset River. Today, the abutments (below) from the second trestle No. 7 support the footbridge that crosses Franconia Brook. (Above, courtesy of the Upper Pemigewasset Historical Society; below, author's collection.)

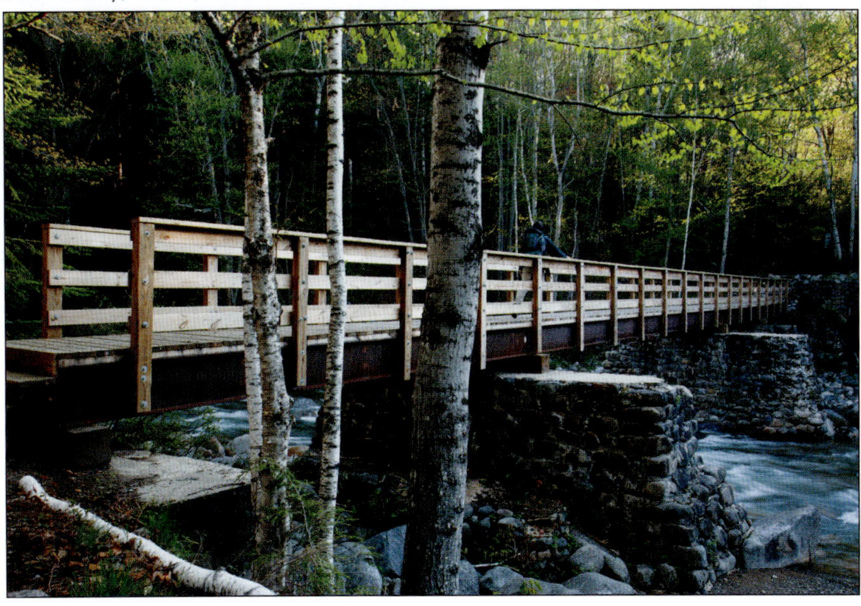

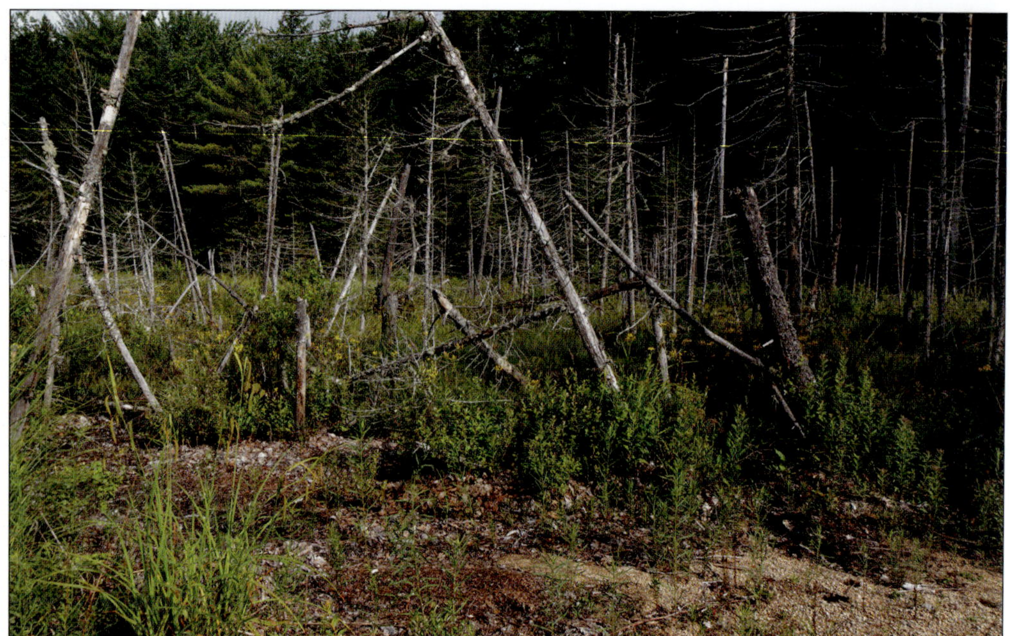

A unique feature of the East Branch & Lincoln Railroad was the ice pond at Camp 7. The large blocks of ice that were cut from this pond were used in iceboxes, predecessors of refrigerators. The blocks of ice were stored at the Camp 7 icehouse and at the company store. The once dammed pond looks more like a swamp today. (Author's collection.)

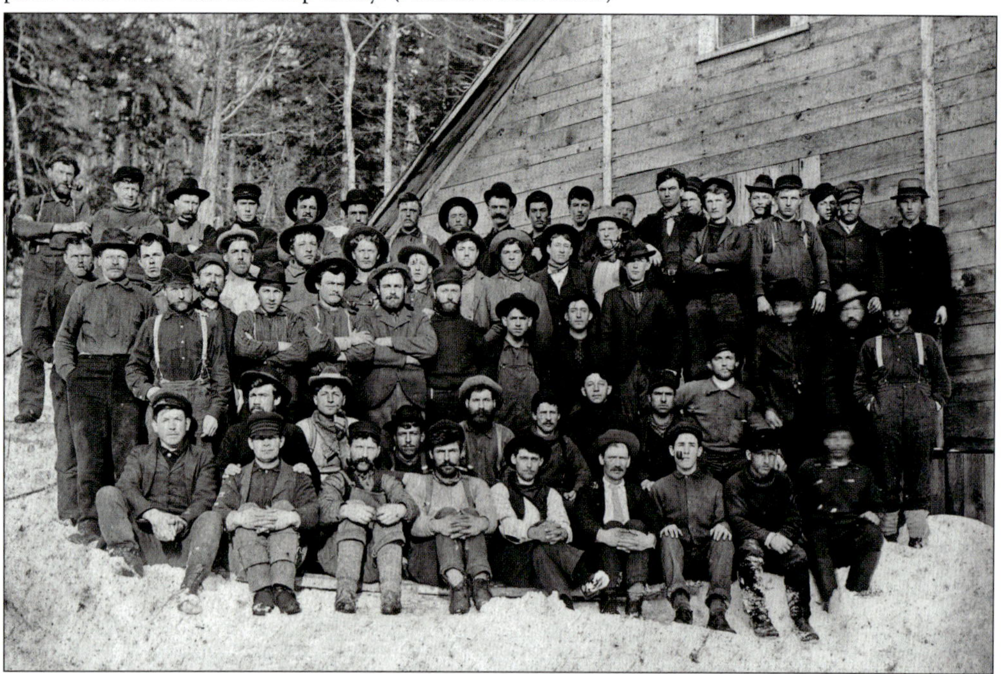

The men working in Lincoln Woods were mostly French Canadian, but there were numerous nationalities represented, including Irish, Polish, and Russians. This undated photograph shows 60 men posing at one of the logging camps along the East Branch & Lincoln Railroad. (Courtesy of the Upper Pemigewasset Historical Society.)

Two

Hancock Branch

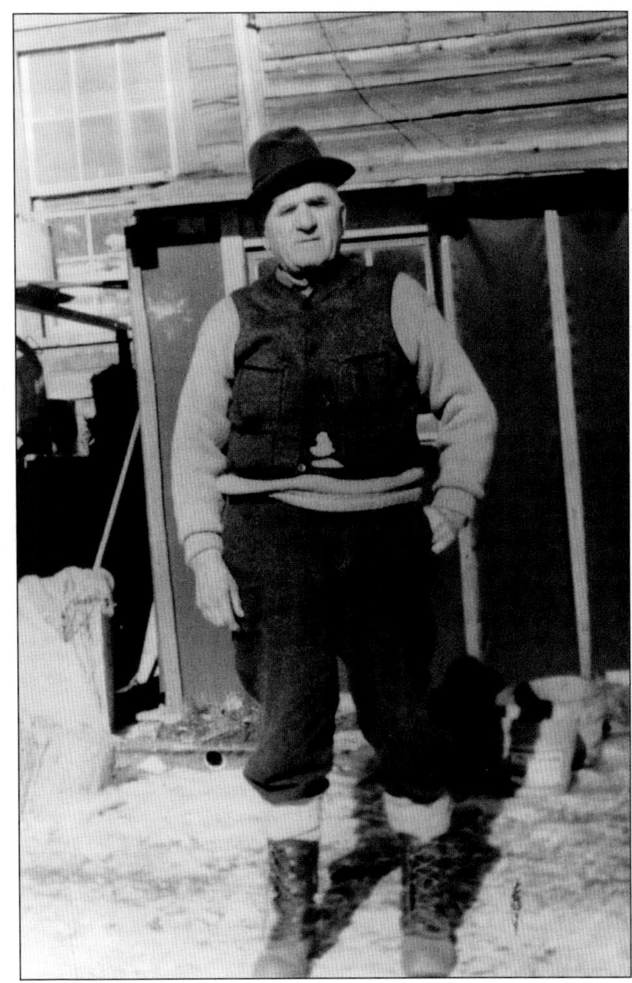

A loyal workforce came with James E. Henry from the Zealand Valley Railroad. The most notable was the James Boyle family, which is still known throughout the Lincoln area today. In his early years, Billy "the Bear" Boyle, seen here, was a teamster along the Hancock Branch; he eventually worked his way up the ladder to walking boss of the entire railroad. (Courtesy of the Upper Pemigewasset Historical Society.)

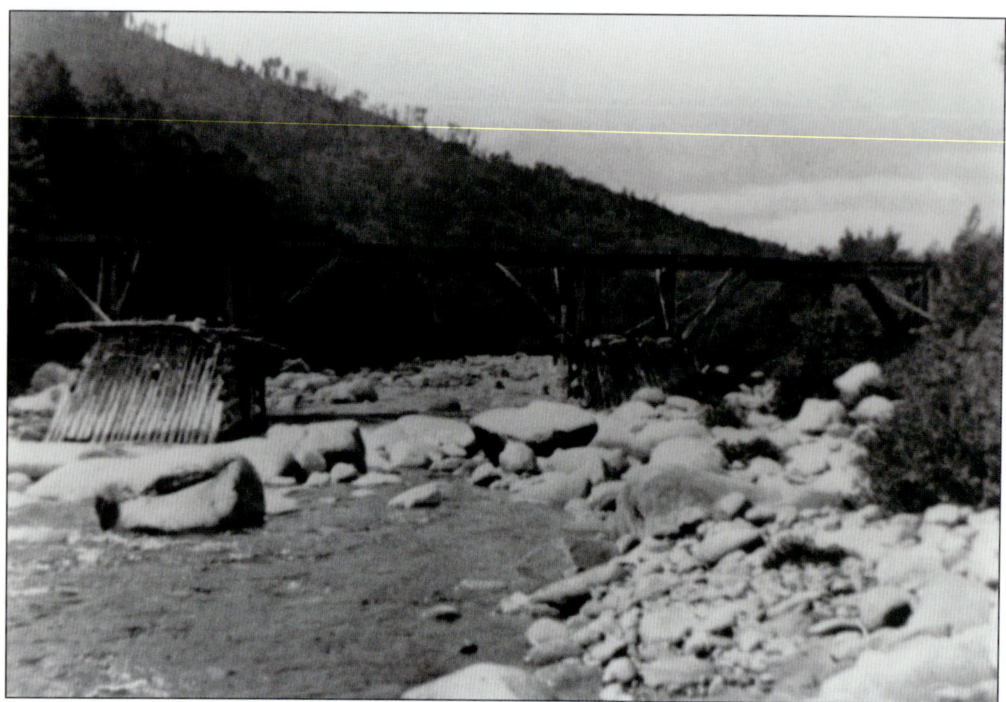

Trestles along the East Branch & Lincoln Railroad took on the name of the nearest logging camp. Trestle No. 4 was near Camp 4, trestle No. 16 was near Camp 16, etc. The trestle at Camp 4, pictured above around 1924, marked the start of the Hancock Branch rail line. The current bridge just west of today's Lincoln Woods Trail trailhead (below) along the Kancamagus Scenic Byway crosses the East Branch of the Pemigewasset River in the same location as the trestle. This scenic byway is one of the top fall foliage drives in New England. (Above, courtesy of the Upper Pemigewasset Historical Society; below, author's collection.)

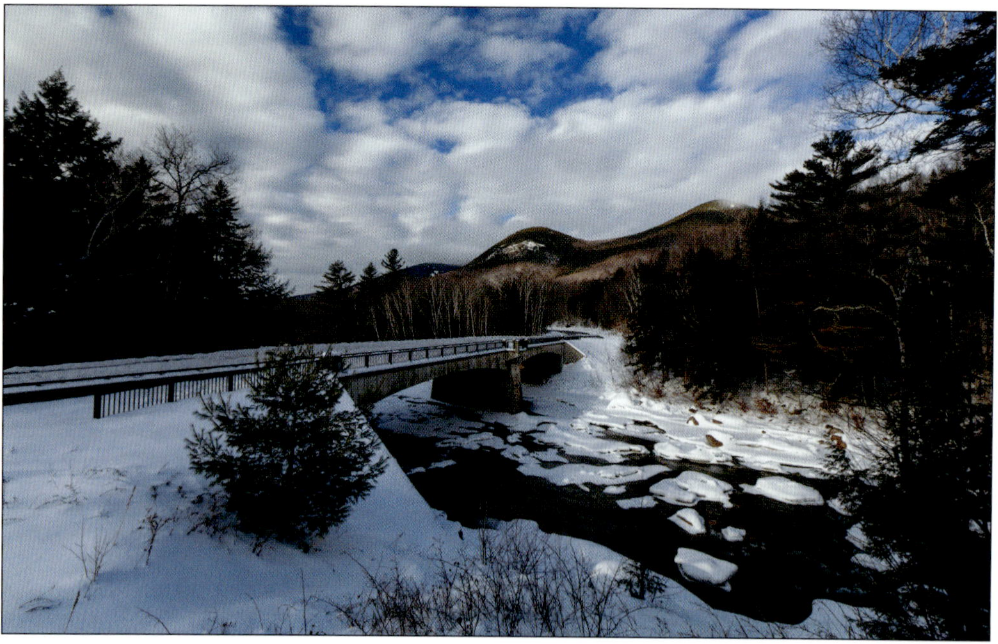

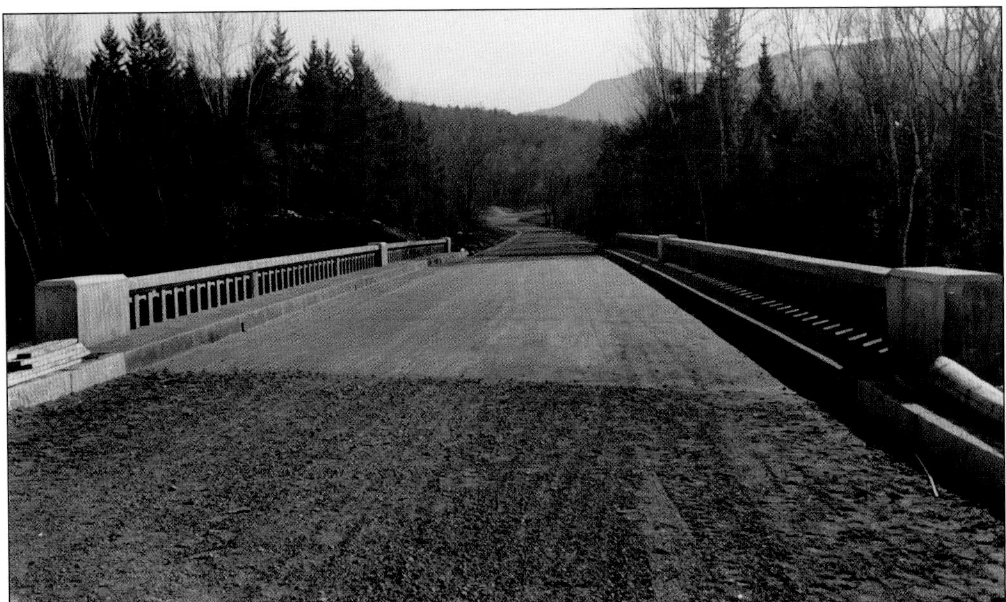

After crossing the East Branch of the Pemigewasset River at Camp 4, the railroad grade followed the route of today's Kancamagus Scenic Byway for about three-quarters of a mile before drifting down to the side of the Hancock Branch Brook. This 1939 photograph of the bridge pictured on the previous page shows it the year after it was built. (Courtesy of the Forest History Society.)

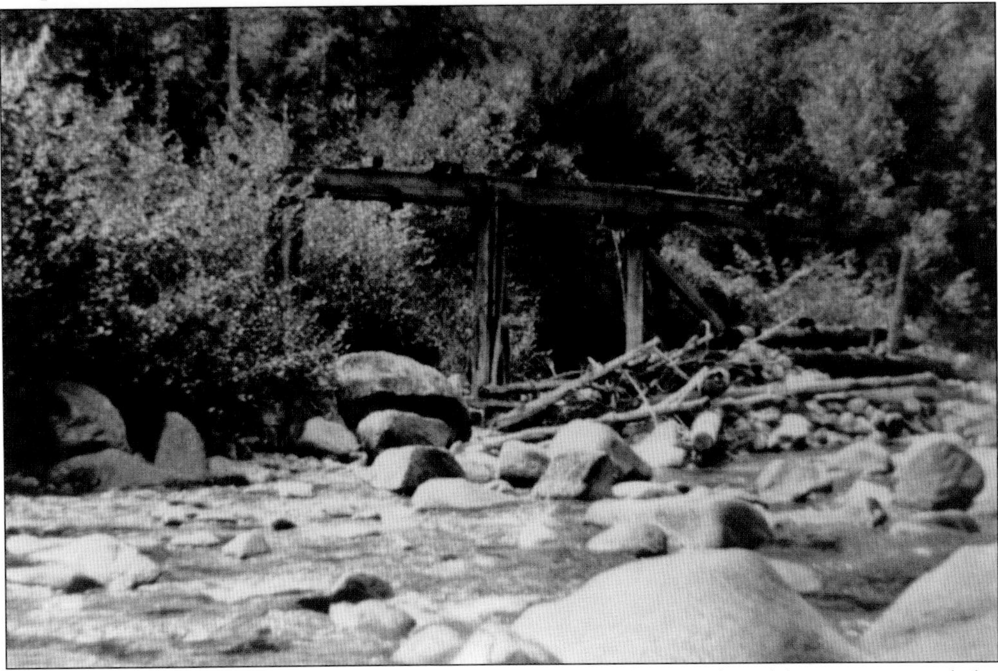

At least 12 bridges and trestles were built on the Hancock Branch rail line: six crossed the Hancock Branch Brook; five were on the mainline; and one was on the Camp 13 spur line near Camp 4. This c. 1924 photograph shows the ruined trestle at the first crossing of the Hancock Branch Brook. All the trestles on this branch were destroyed by the 1920s. (Courtesy of the Upper Pemigewasset Historical Society.)

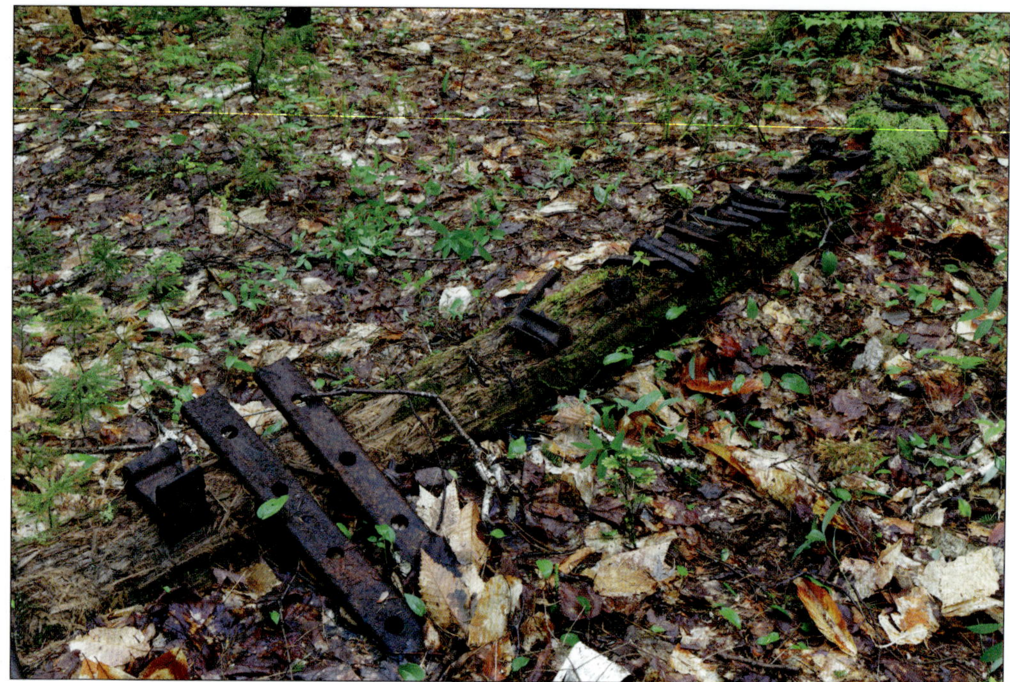

Old railroad spikes and various other artifacts have been placed on display along the Hancock Branch rail line. The removal of historic artifacts from federal lands without a permit is a violation of federal law, and the destruction of artifacts and historic sites is also a crime. Artifacts should be left in place in an undisturbed state. (Author's collection.)

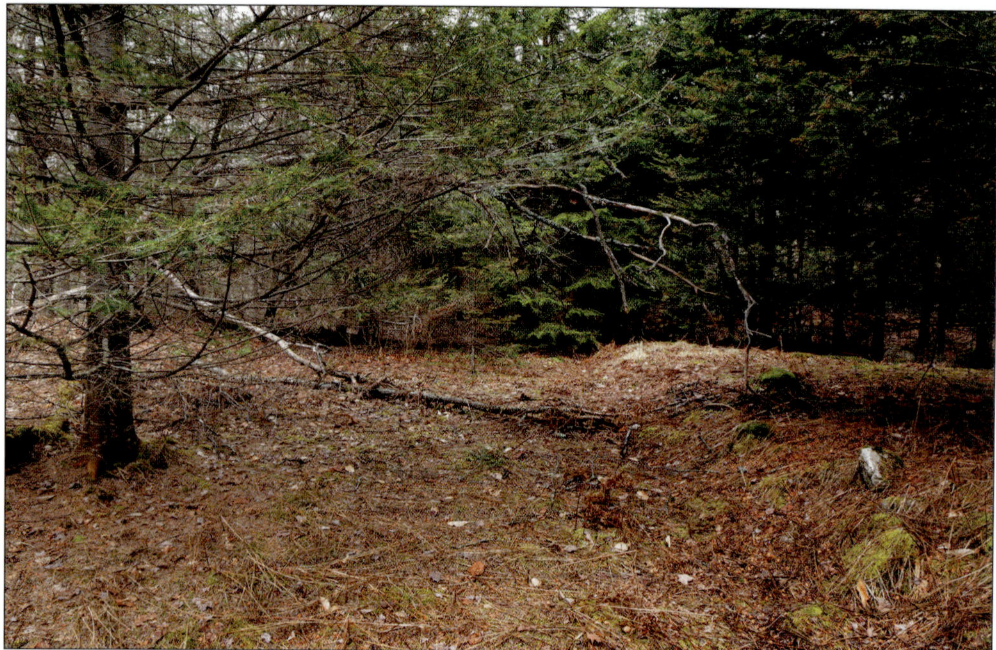

Camps 5 and 6 were rail-side camps located on the south side of the Hancock Branch Brook. The footprint of the old railroad bed is still visible in this area, and for the most part is easy to follow. Other sections of the Hancock Branch rail line are not so easy to follow. (Author's collection.)

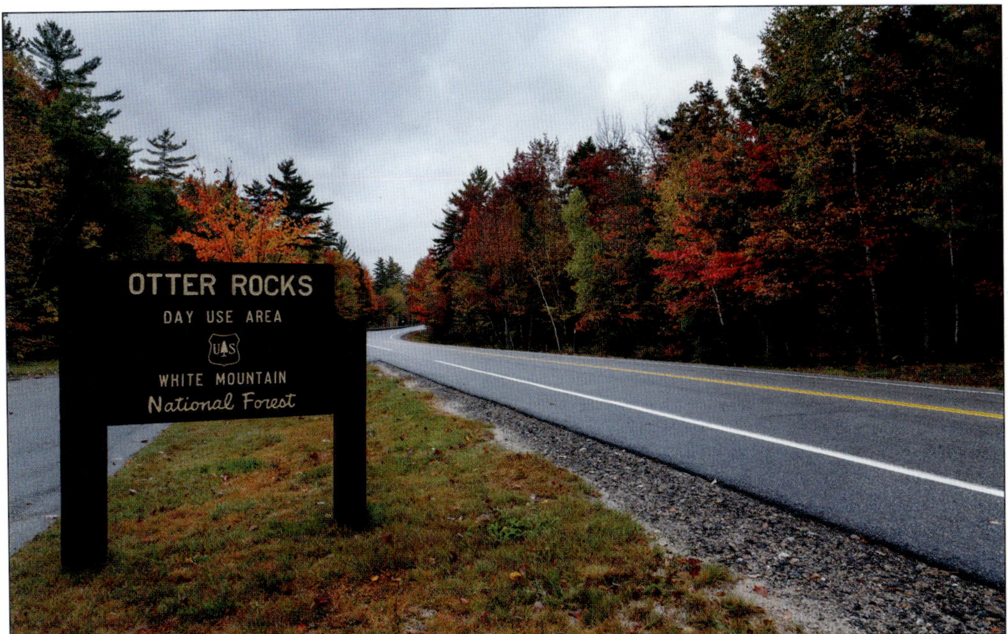

Including spur lines and sidings, the Hancock Branch rail line was about eight miles long. The Kancamagus Scenic Byway follows roughly three and a half to four miles of the old railroad bed. With the exception of about a quarter of a mile near Camp 7, from Otter Rocks, the Kancamagus Scenic Byway follows the old railroad bed up to the hairpin turn just below the Hancock viewing area. (Author's collection.)

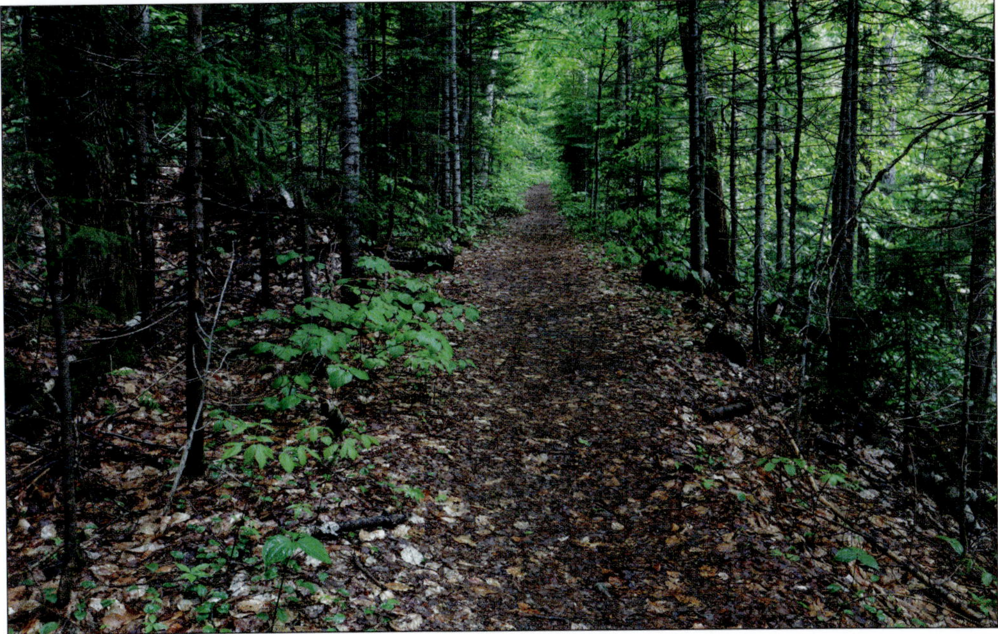

At the last crossing of the Hancock Branch Brook, a spur line referred to as "the Siding" traveled about three-quarters of a mile into the Pine Brook valley, ending at Camp 14. Today's East Pond Trail follows the old railroad bed of the spur line, which ended in the area where the trail crosses Pine Brook. (Author's collection.)

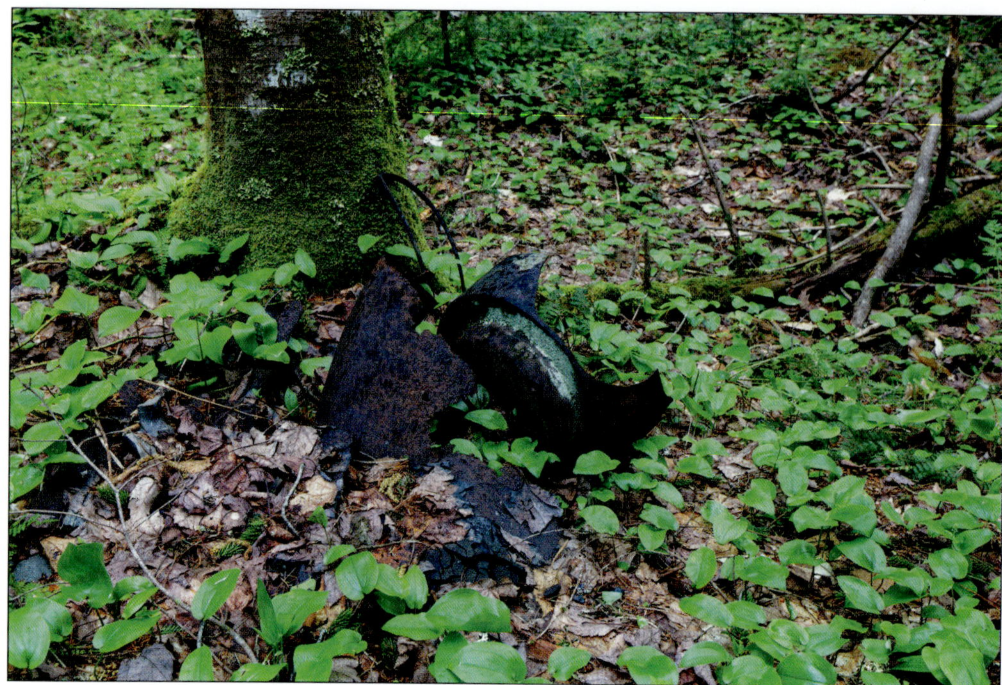

Above the Siding, Camp 7 was the only camp on the South Fork of the Hancock Branch Brook. The East Branch & Lincoln Railroad crossed the brook below and above the camp and one more time higher up where the railroad rejoins with the route of today's Kancamagus Scenic Byway. Like most of the camps along the Hancock Branch rail line, there are almost no visible artifacts at this site, but there are just enough to be able to determine where the camp was. In 2011, Tropical Storm Irene flooded this area, and the railroad track (below) that was at the camp, in the brook, was buried, and is no longer visible. (Both, author's collection.)

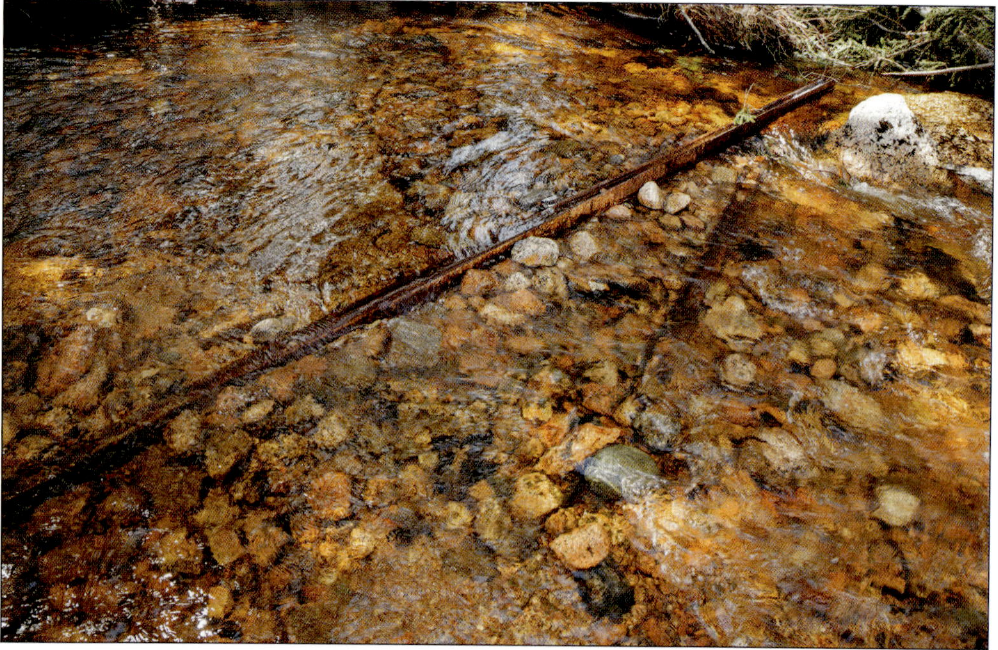

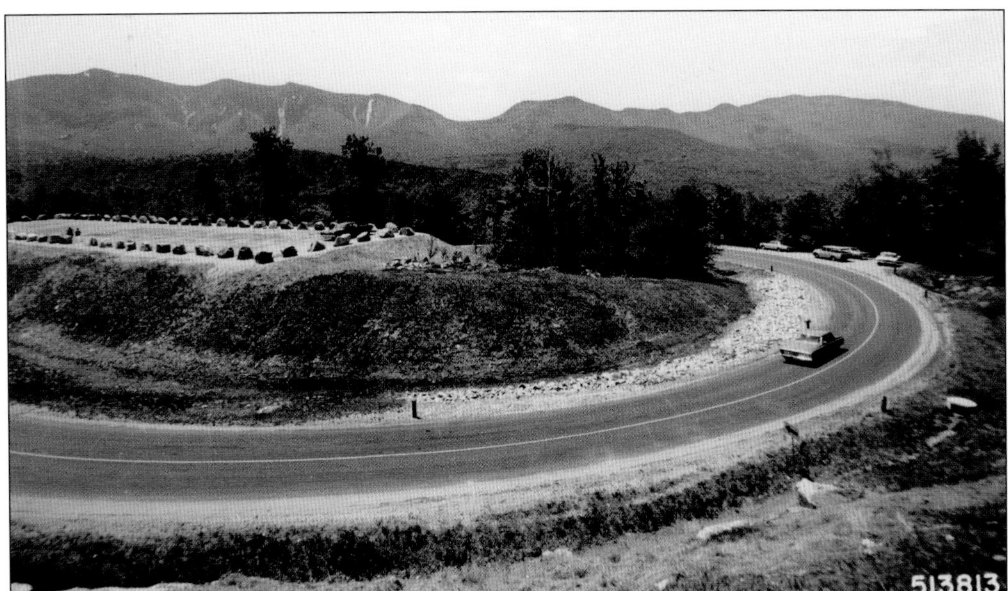

Above Camp 7, the Hancock Branch rail line rejoins the path of today's Kancamagus Scenic Byway and follows it to the hairpin corner at the Hancock Overlook. In this 1965 photograph of the Hancock Overlook, the railroad, when it existed, traveled behind the parking lot and continued straight, where the cars are parked on the road, onto the path of the Hancock Notch Trail. (Courtesy of the National Archives & Records Administration.)

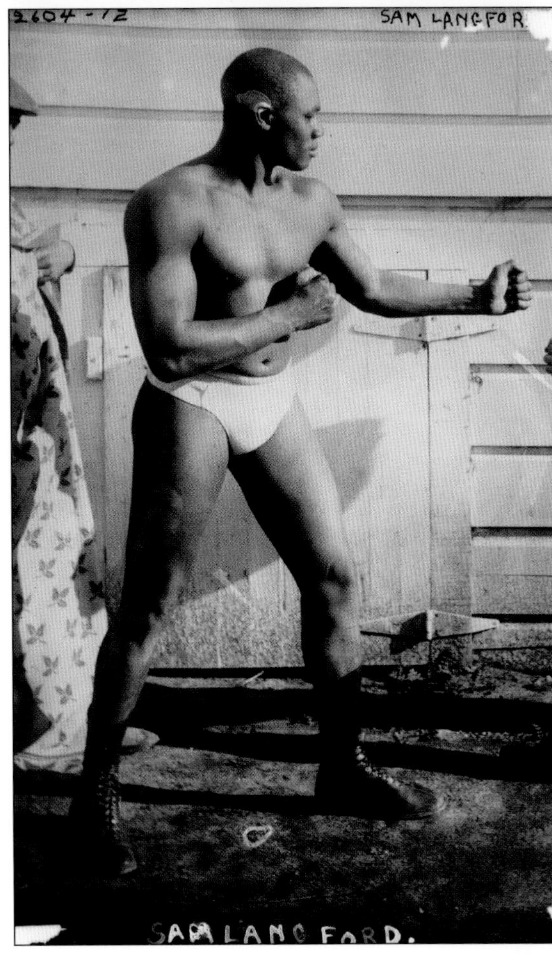

During the early years of his boxing career, Sam Langford (March 4, 1883–January 12, 1956), known as the Boston Tar Baby, Boston Terror, and Boston Bonecrusher, spent time working (training) at the logging camps on the Hancock Branch rail line. He never won a world boxing championship, but he is considered one of the greatest fighters of all time. (Courtesy of the Library of Congress, LC-B2- 2604-12.)

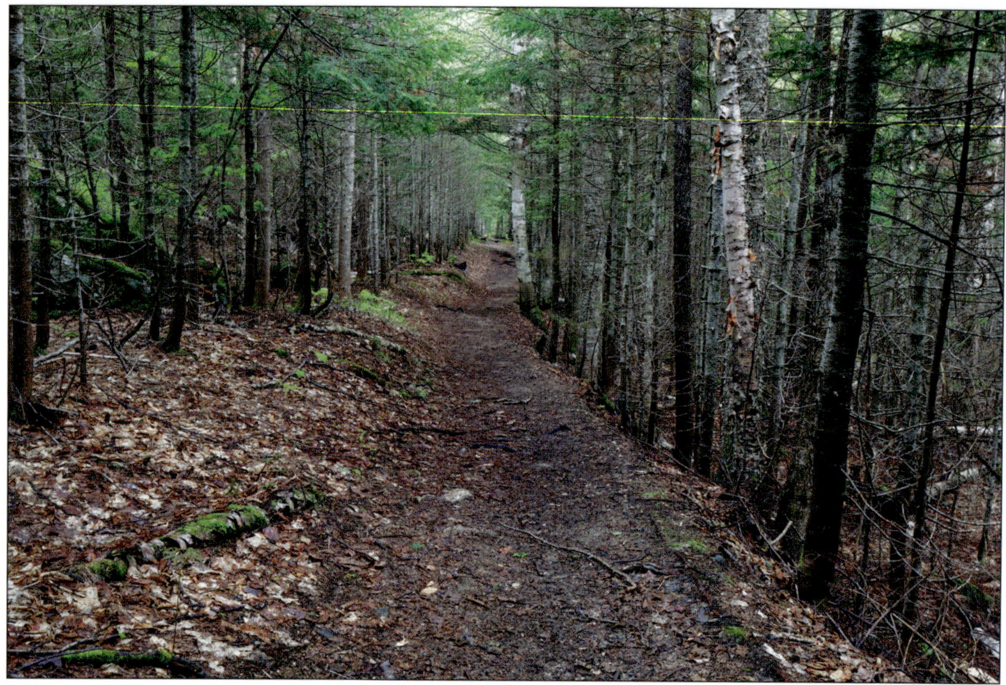

The Hancock Notch Trail follows the old railroad bed for one and a half miles before the railroad leaves the path of the trail and crosses the North Fork of the Hancock Branch Brook, near Camp 9. It ended shortly after crossing the brook. Today, there is little evidence of the railroad along the Hancock Notch Trail. (Author's collection.)

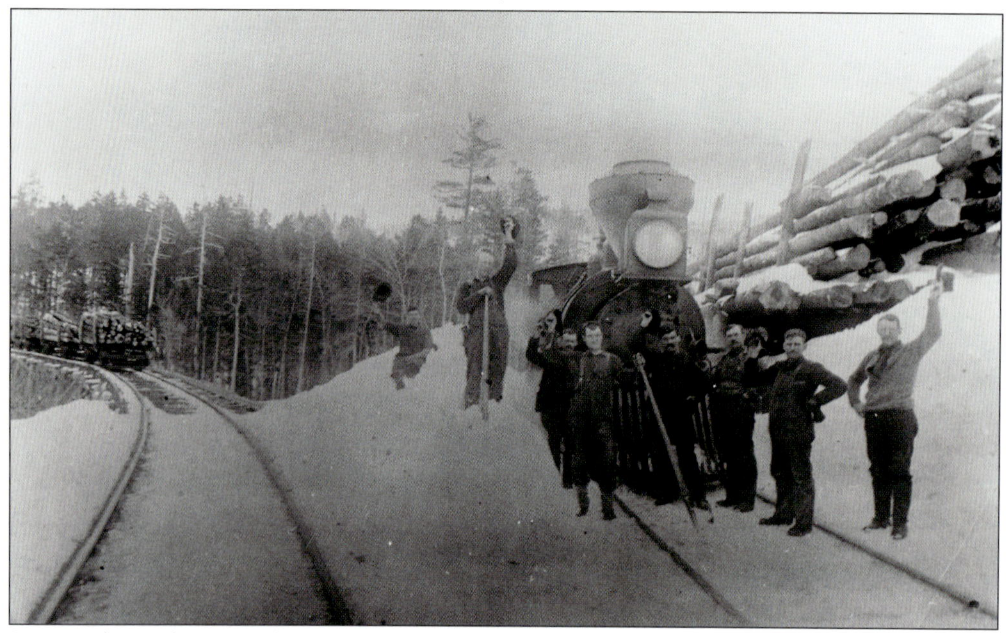

Seen in this early 1900s photograph is the Baldwin No. 2 and unidentified crew and woodsmen at a log landing near Camp 8. The log cars would be positioned underneath the piles of logs so the woodsmen could role the logs onto the cars, a dangerous job. The trestle at left crossed an unnamed brook. (Courtesy of the Upper Pemigewasset Historical Society.)

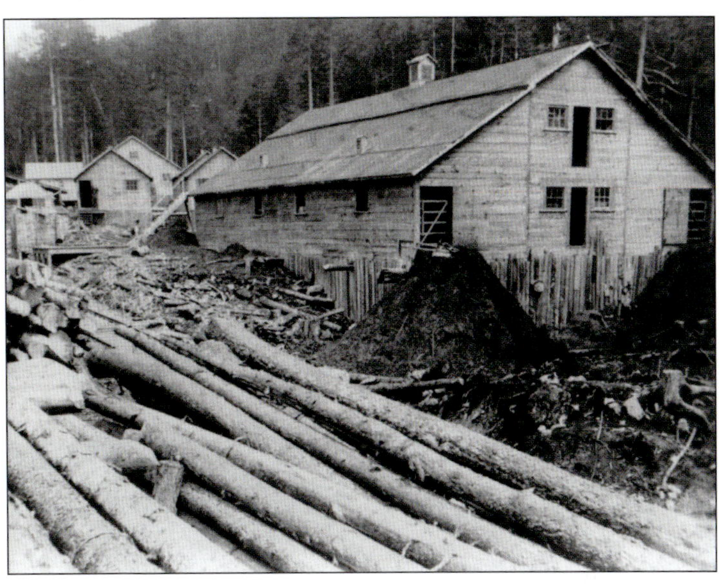

An interesting feature of the East Branch & Lincoln Railroad were the portable camp buildings. These buildings were constructed in sections so they could be moved around on the railroad. When it was time to move them to a new location, they were dismantled and loaded on to railroad flatcars. Seen here is a portable horse barn. (Courtesy of the Upper Pemigewasset Historical Society.)

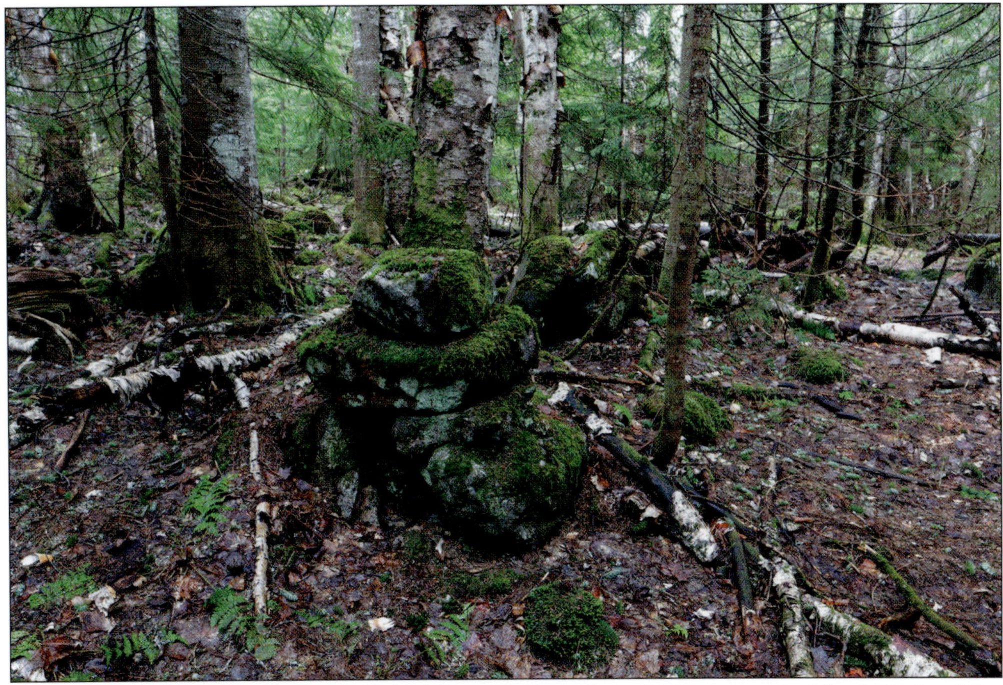

Camp 9 was located at the end of the Hancock Branch rail line, near the North Fork of the Hancock Branch Brook. Because this branch operated in the early years of the East Branch & Lincoln Railroad, little remains of the camp. These piles of rocks at the old Camp 9 site were likely part of the foundation for the portable camps. (Author's collection.)

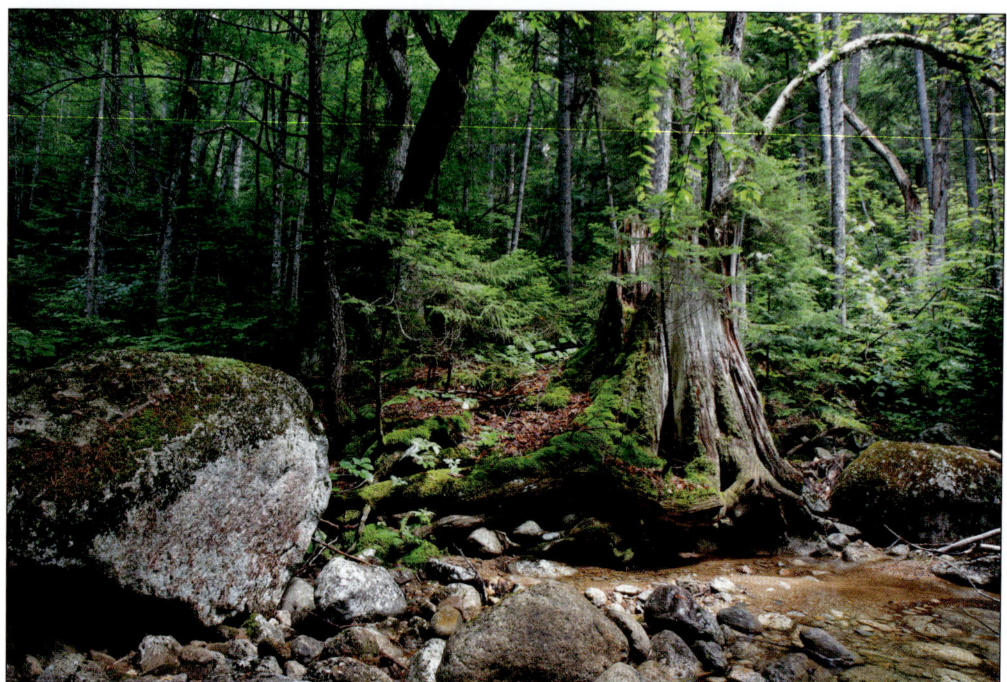

For the first 10 years of the East Branch & Lincoln Railroad, J.E. Henry and Sons focused on the Hancock valley. Henry's log trains and woodsmen worked the Hancock Branch rail line nonstop, cutting and hauling as many spruce logs as they possibly could down to the mill in Lincoln village, and it was just the beginning. The railroad soon made its way into the Franconia Brook valley to repeat the process. Today, the Hancock valley is again the wilderness it was before the woodsmen invaded the area. The forest has recovered, and the brooks are free of logging slash. (Both, author's collection.)

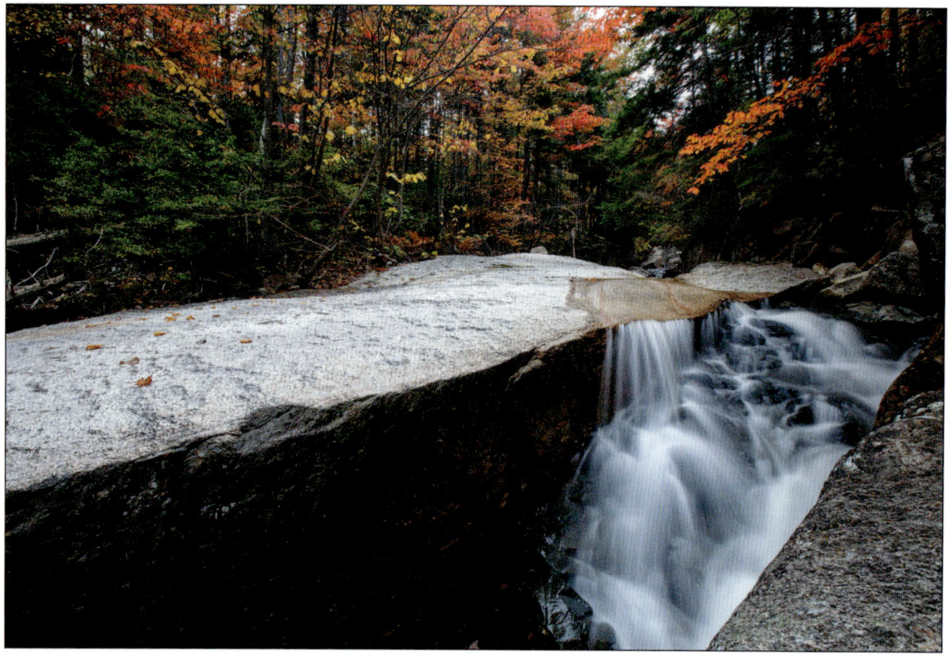

Three

Franconia Brook Branch

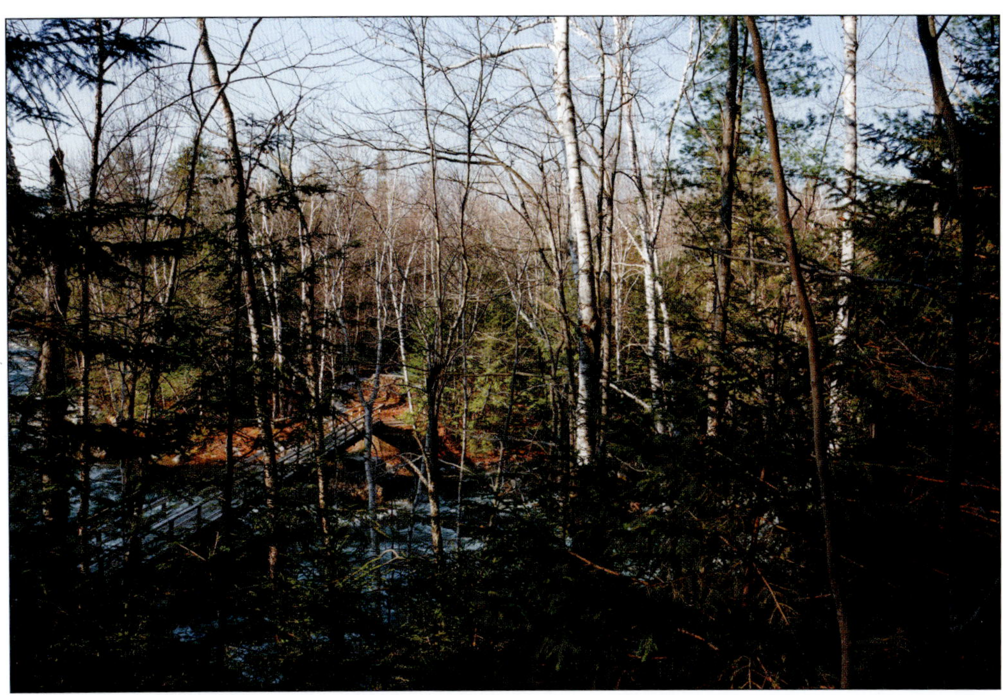

The Franconia Brook Branch of the East Branch & Lincoln Railroad began at trestle No. 7 (see page 28). This view from the east side of the brook is where the trestle joined back into the railroad bed. Including spur lines and sidings, this branch was roughly seven to eight miles long. Today's Franconia Brook Trail follows 5.2 miles of the old railroad. (Author's collection.)

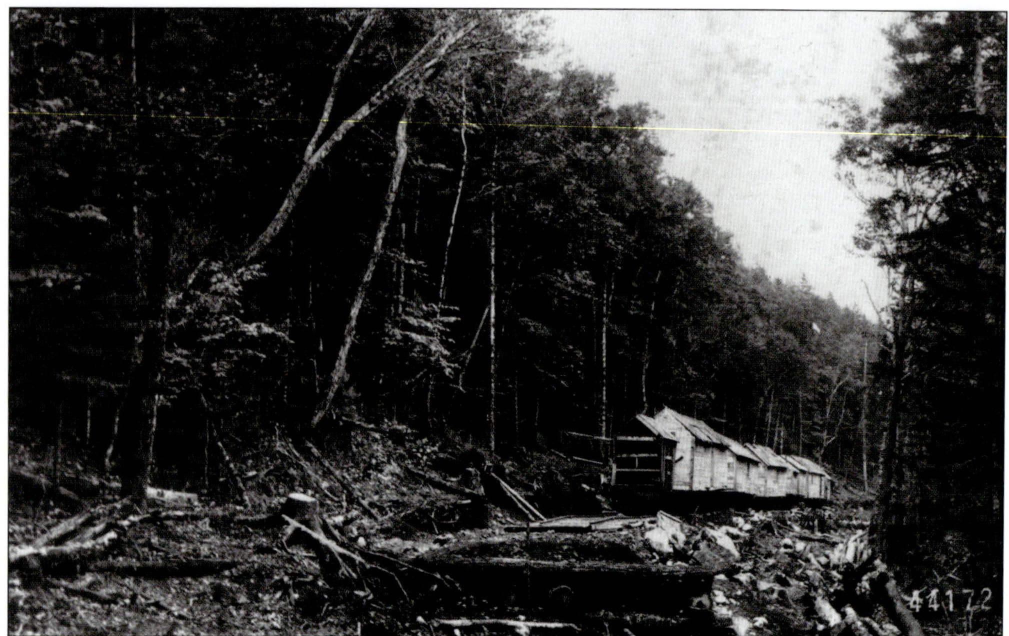

This 1903 photograph shows the J.E. Henry and Sons construction train between Camps 9 and 10 on the Franconia Brook Branch. The new railroad bed being built has hit a point where a trestle is needed. These rolling camps slept 70 workers (24 per car), and had one horse car that held 10 horses, a cook shanty, and a tool room. (US Forest Service photograph, courtesy of the Upper Pemigewasset Historical Society.

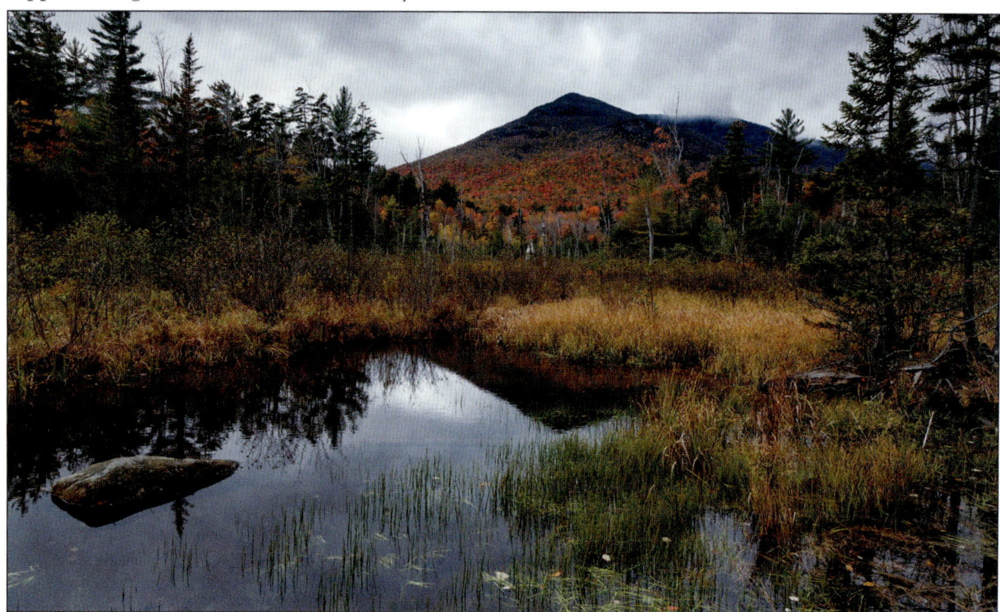

When the Franconia Brook Branch was in operation, this wetlands area was just a small brook, not the wetlands it is today. Beaver activity has flooded the area since the logging era. A spur line beginning at Camp 9 traveled through this wetlands in a northwest direction, crossed Franconia Brook at today's Lincoln Brook Trail crossing, and ended at a landing/work area just beyond the brook. (Author's collection.)

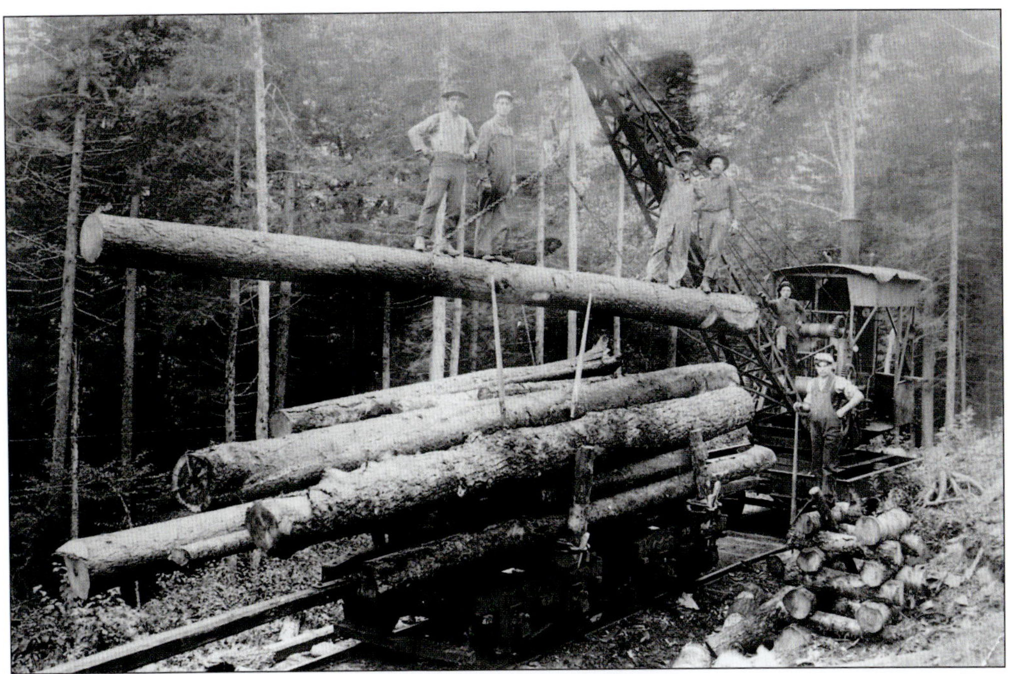

Steam-powered cranes were vital to the East Branch & Lincoln Railroad logging operation. Landings were built so the woodsmen could roll the logs onto the railroad log cars by hand, but when landings could not be constructed, cranes were used. The cranes were also used to dismantle the landings when they were no longer needed. In the above c. 1907 photograph, the steam-powered crane know as the "Dipper Duck" is dismantling a log landing. Below, located at the end of the Camp 9 spur line, is possibly the hoisting system of an old steam-powered log loader. This artifact will be around for many years, and could end up being the last visible artifact along the railroad. (Above, courtesy of the Upper Pemigewasset Historical Society; below, author's collection.)

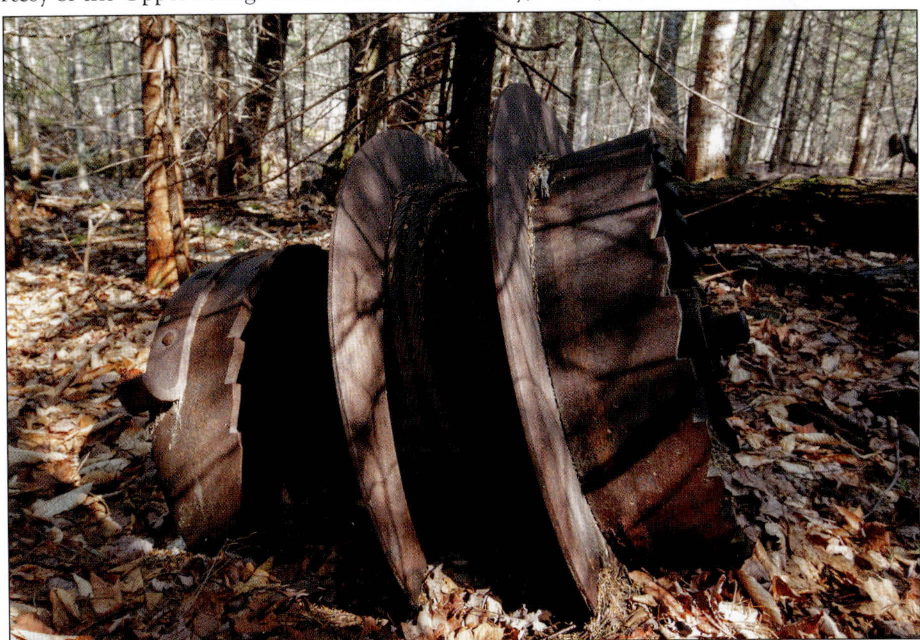

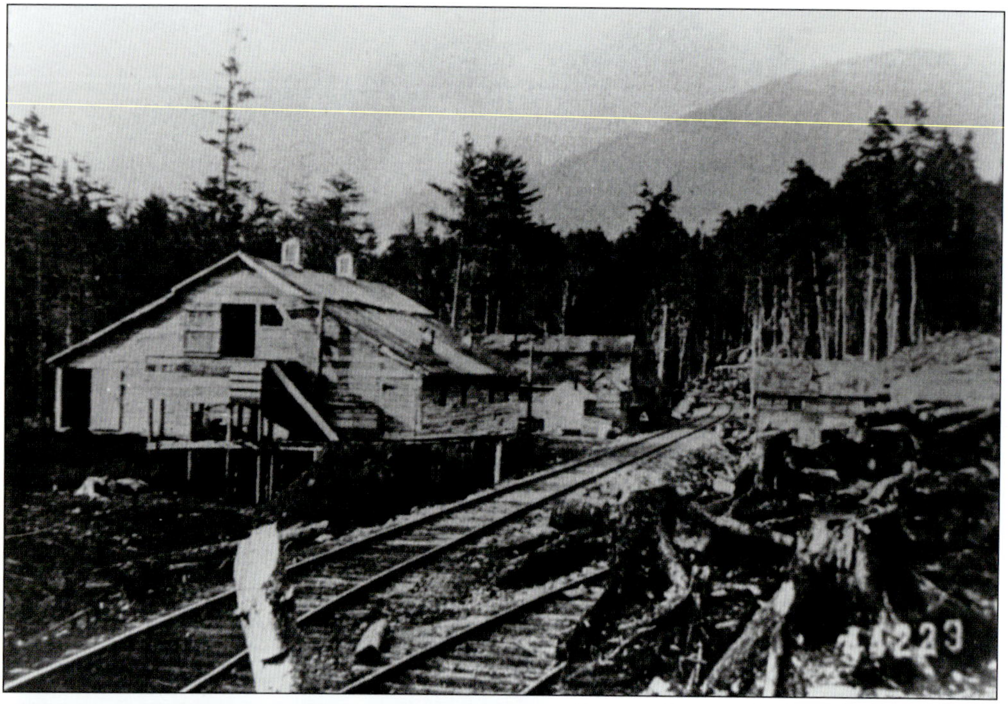

Pictured here in 1903 is the horse barn and other dwellings at Camp 10. The siding on the right reconnected to the mainline a short distance beyond the camp. Most of the rail-side camps were set up close to the tracks, which allowed for easy unloading of camp supplies. (US Forest Service photograph, courtesy of the Upper Pemigewasset Historical Society.)

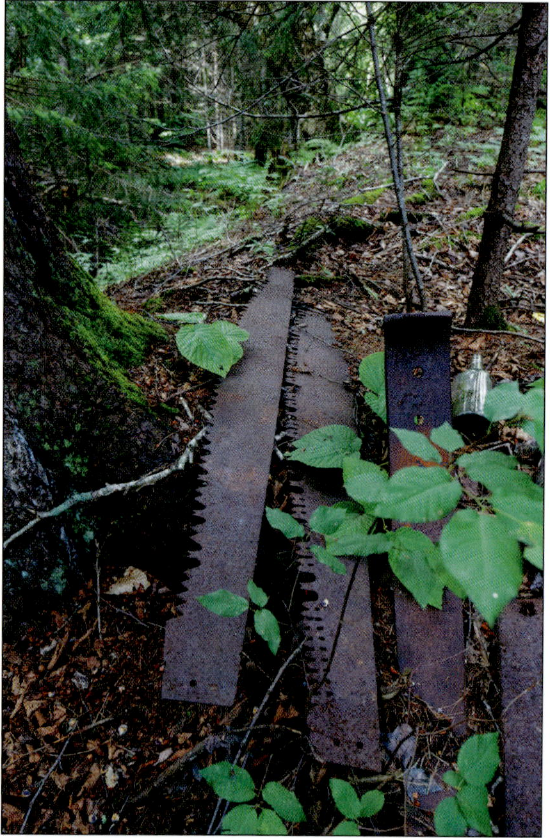

These two-person crosscut saws, now protected artifacts, illustrate two different tooth patterns used for sawing different types of wood. The saw on the left has a champion tooth pattern used for sawing hardwoods and frozen wood. The saw on the right has a perforated lance tooth pattern used for sawing softwoods. (Author's collection.)

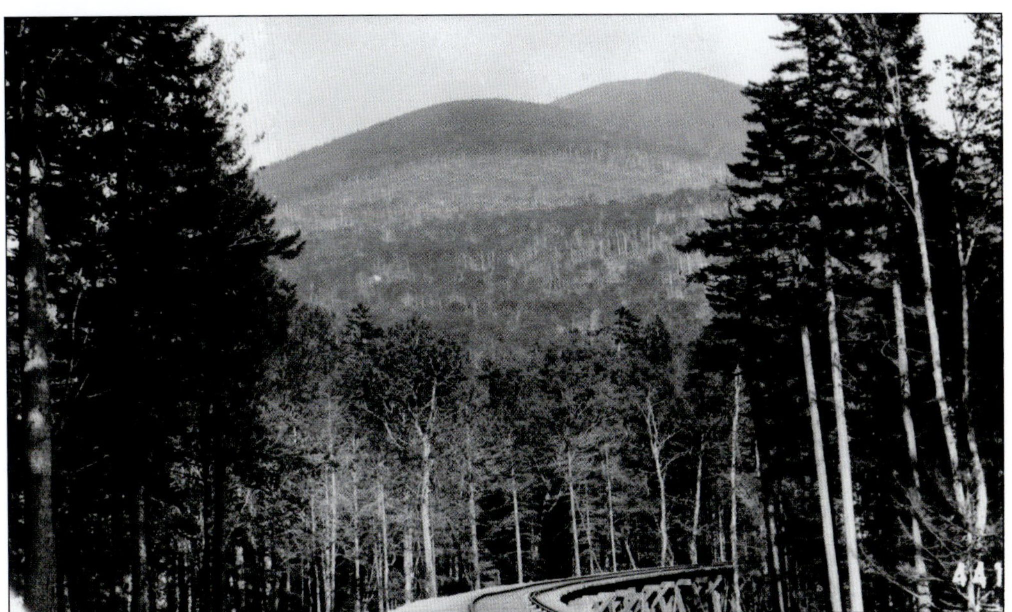

Just above Camp 10, the Lincoln Brook Branch began. It crossed Franconia Brook and then traveled around the southern end of Owls Head Mountain into the Lincoln Brook valley, eventually ending a short distance beyond Liberty Brook at Camp 12. The above 1903 photograph looks east across the roughly 265-foot-long trestle that crossed Franconia Brook. The portion of the brook the trestle crossed is separated by an island. The cutover slopes of a shoulder of West Bond can be seen in the background. A few artifacts (below) and the footer holes for the trestle can still be seen today. (Above, US Forest Service photograph, courtesy of the Upper Pemigewasset Historical Society; below, author's collection.)

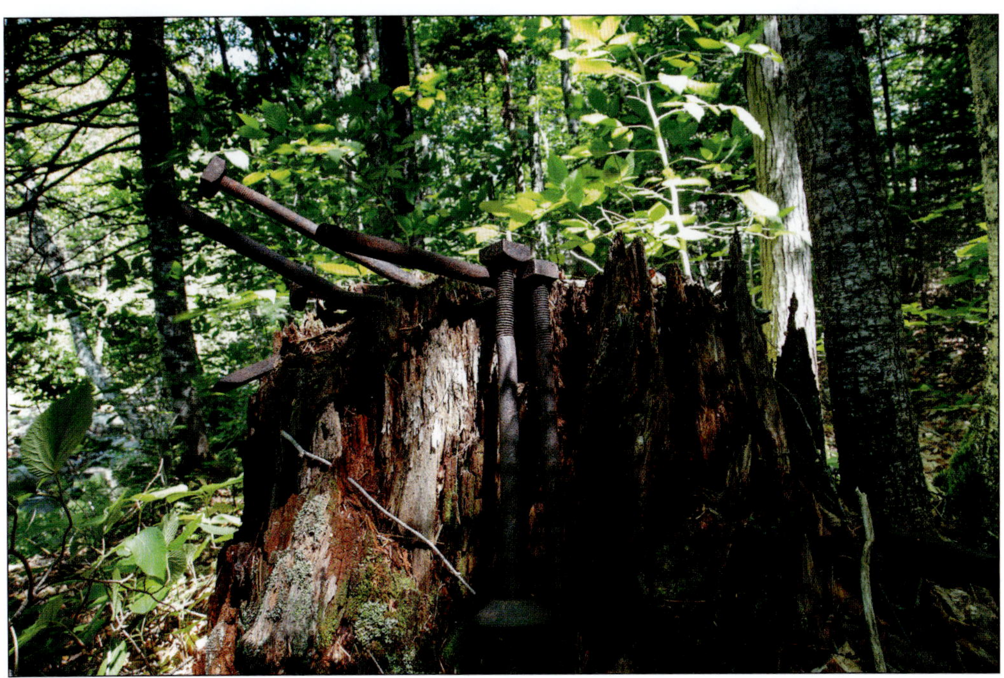

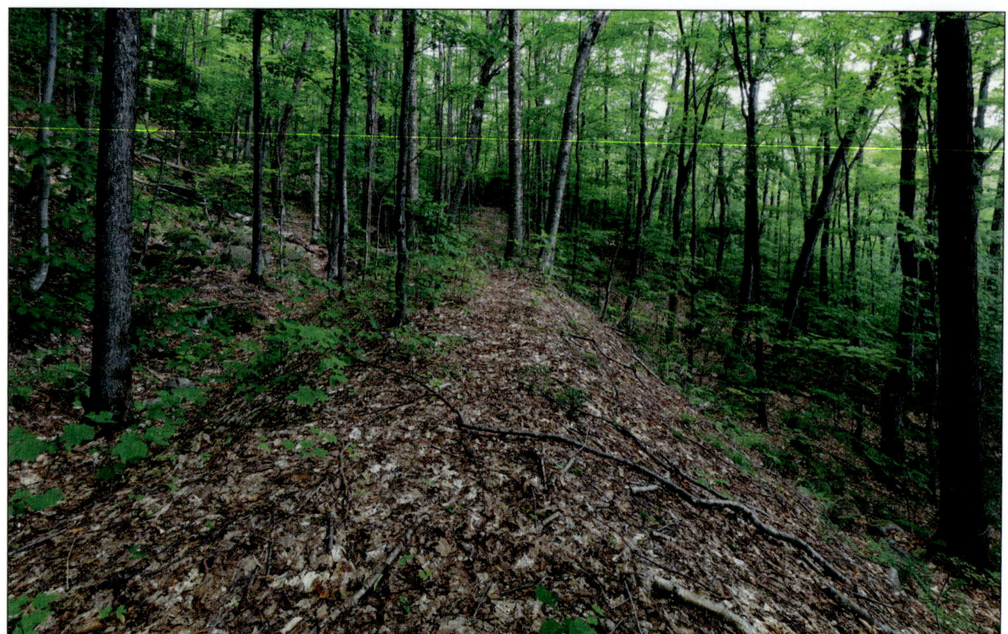

Including spur lines and sidings, the Lincoln Brook Branch was about three and a half miles long, and today's Lincoln Brook Trail follows about half a mile of the old railroad bed. Five out of the seven water crossings along this branch required a bridge or trestle. The other two crossings were small and probably only required buried timber culverts. The railroad bed is still identifiable. (Author's collection.)

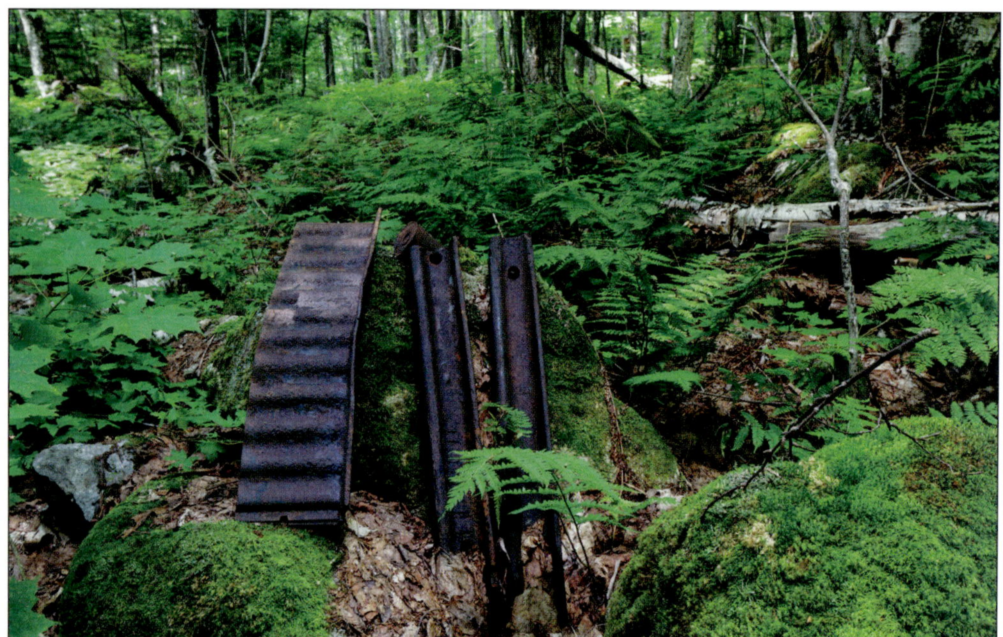

There were two rail-side logging camps along the Lincoln Brook Branch: Camps 11 and 12. Camp 11, the first camp on the branch, was just east of the Lincoln Brook trestle. These pieces of railroad track and other artifacts mark the camp location. A mountain camp was also located in the Liberty Brook drainage; however, it was not one of J.E. Henry and Sons' camps. (Author's collection.)

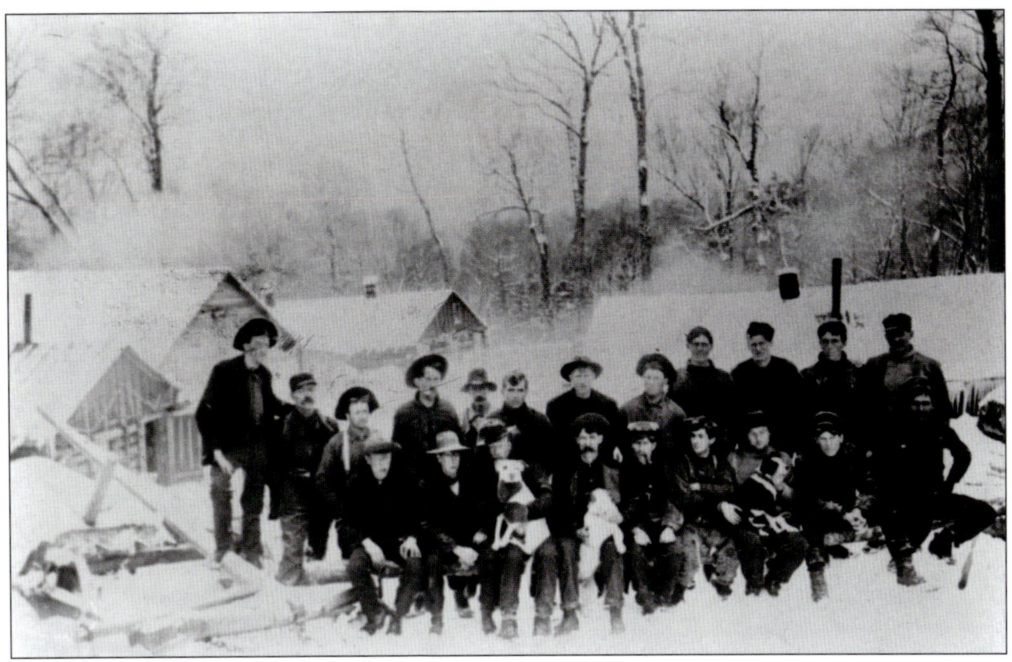

The Johnson Lumber Company owned a stand of spruce on the Pemigewasset Wilderness side of Mount Liberty, but could not reach it from the Gordon Pond Railroad because the terrain was too steep and it was surrounded by land owned by the East Branch & Lincoln Railroad. George Johnson, owner of the Johnson Lumber Company, made a deal with J.E. Henry and Sons to haul the timber out using the East Branch & Lincoln Railroad. The 21 woodsmen and three dogs in the above c. 1910 photograph are believed to be at the old Johnson camp that was located on the side of Mount Liberty in the Pemigewasset Wilderness. A few artifacts (below) remain at the site today. (Above, courtesy of the Upper Pemigewasset Historical Society; below, author's collection.)

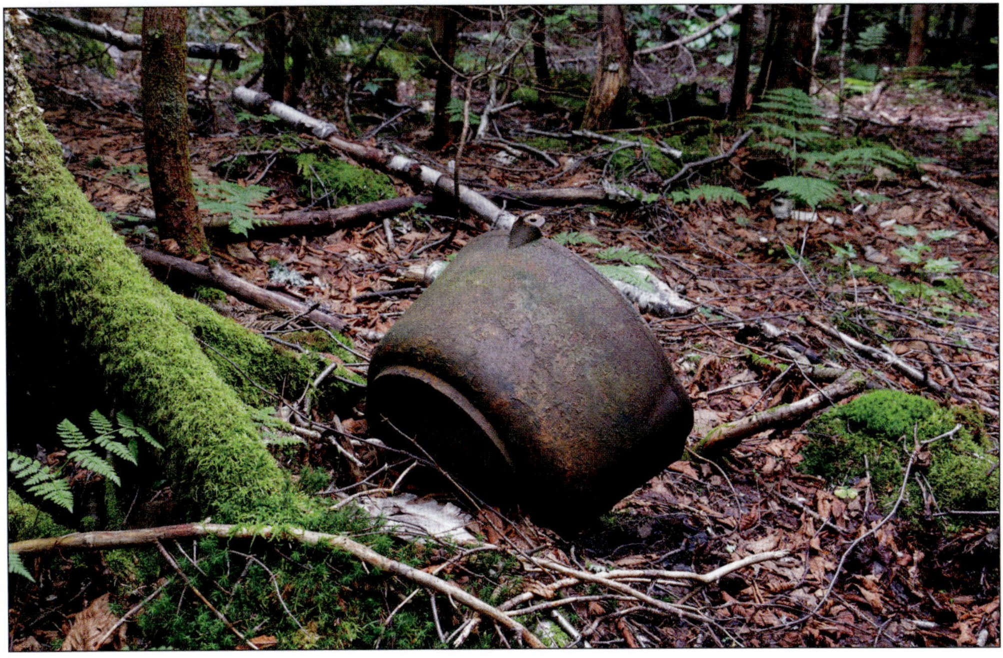

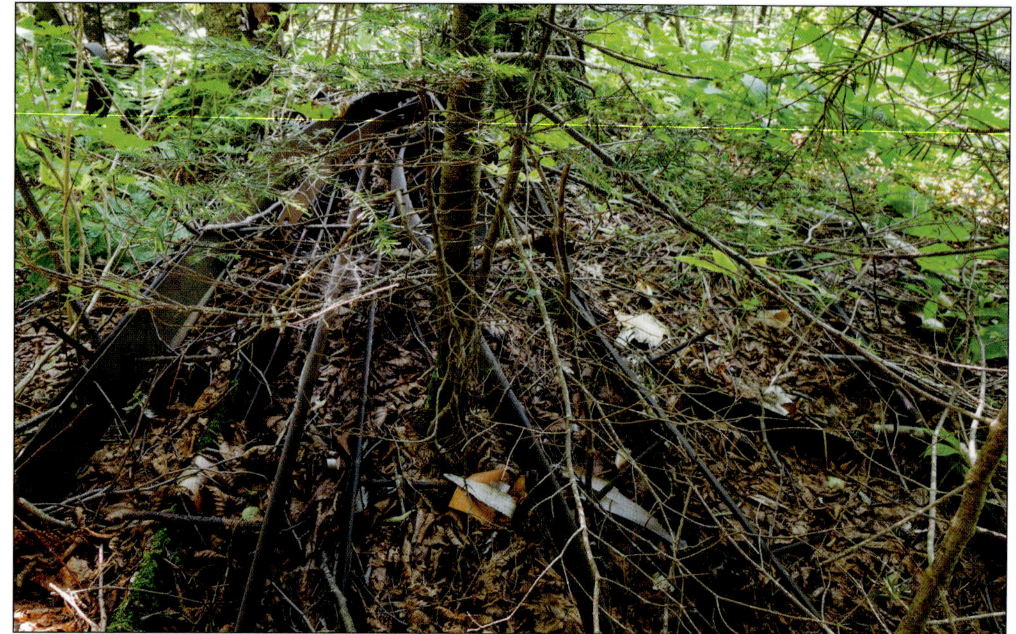

There were two Camp 12s along the railroad. One was located north of Liberty Brook at the end of the Lincoln Brook Branch (above), and the other was south of Twin Brook on the Franconia Brook Branch. The other camp numbers along the railroad that were duplicated were 7, 8, 9, 13, and 14. (Author's collection.)

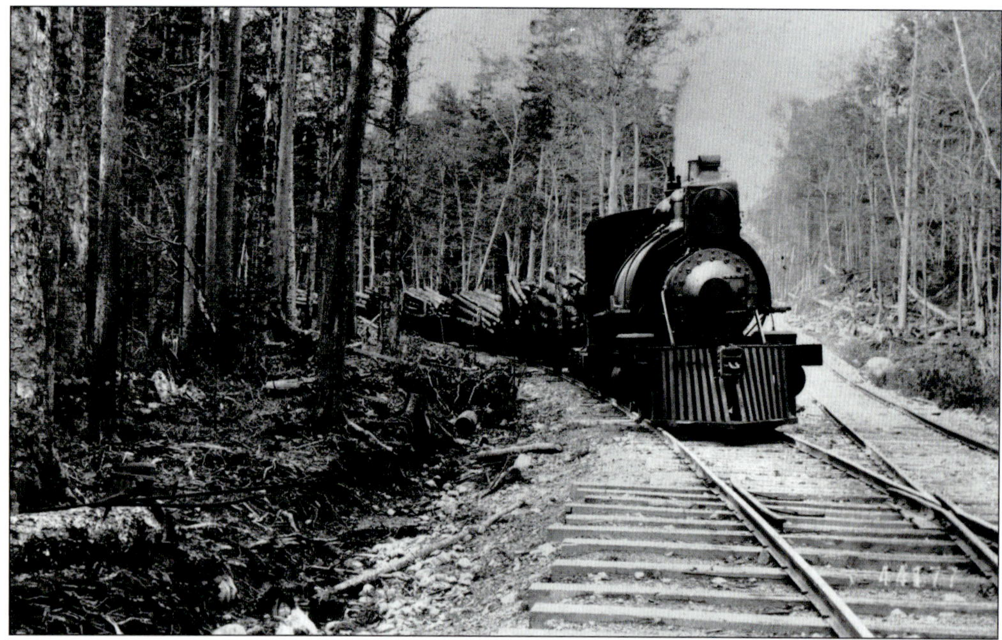

One of the Baldwins is coming off the Lincoln Brook Branch with a load of logs and switching onto the Franconia Brook Branch just above Camp 10 in this 1903 view. With the exception of a short trail reroute near Camp 9, the Franconia Brook Trail follows the entire length of the old railroad bed of the Franconia Brook Branch. (Courtesy of the National Archives & Records Administration.)

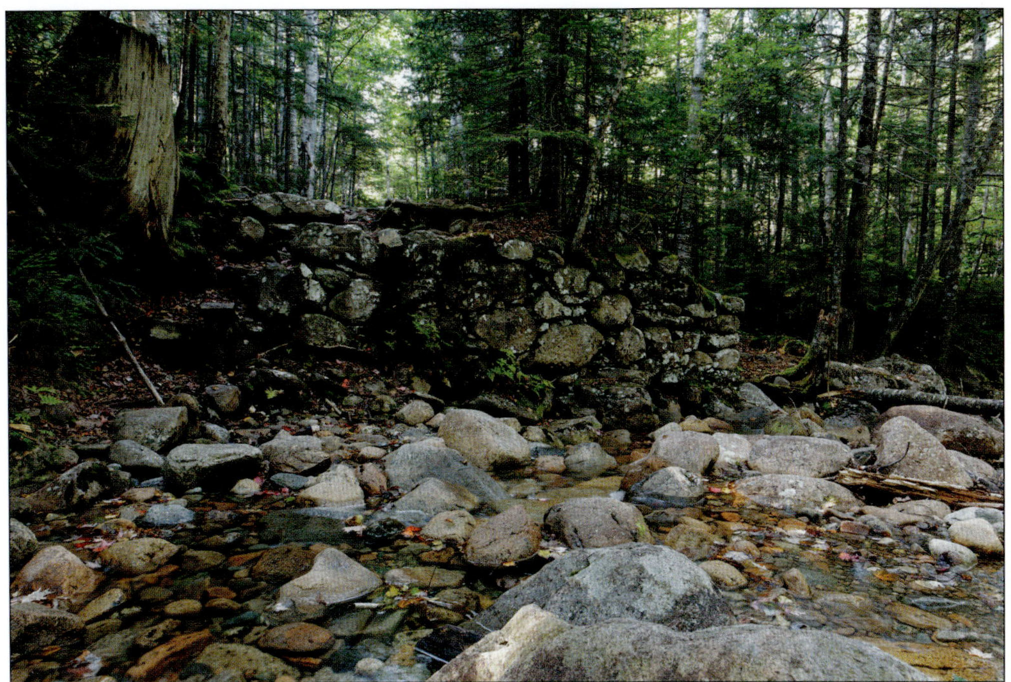

Including trestle No. 7 at the start of the Franconia Brook Branch, there were at least nine bridges and trestles on the Franconia Brook Branch—eight on the mainline to Camp 13, and one on the Camp 9 spur line. Very little remains of the bridges and trestles, and up until 2011, there was a beautiful stone bridge abutment at the Redrock Brook crossing. The abutment almost looked natural, and one could hike by it without realizing what it is. Unfortunately, in August 2011 Tropical Storm Irene washed away most of it (below), and the craftsmanship from a forgotten era can now only be seen in photographs. (Both, author's collection.)

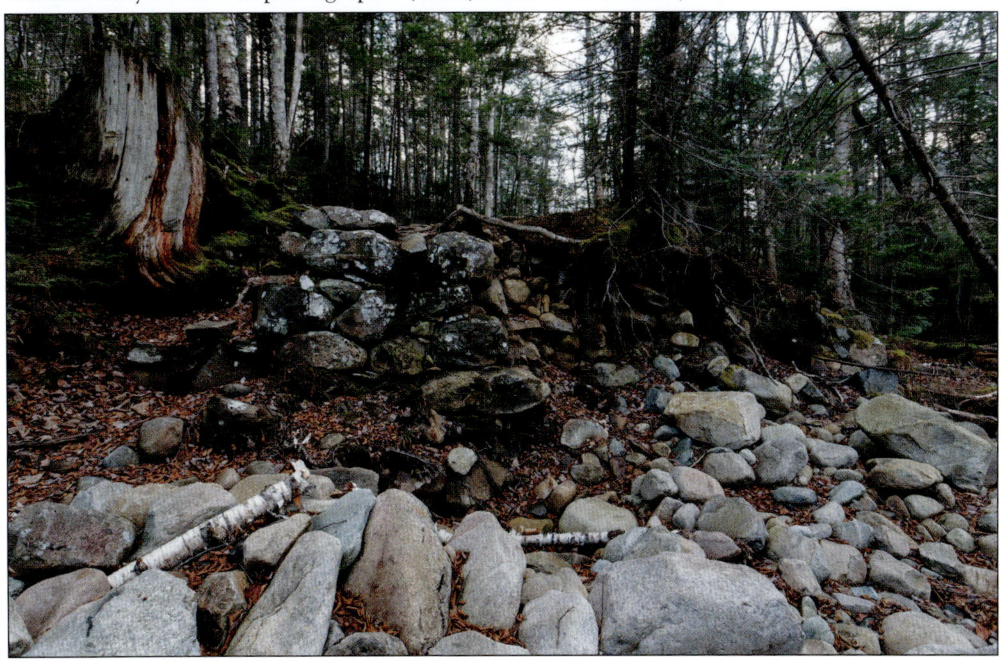

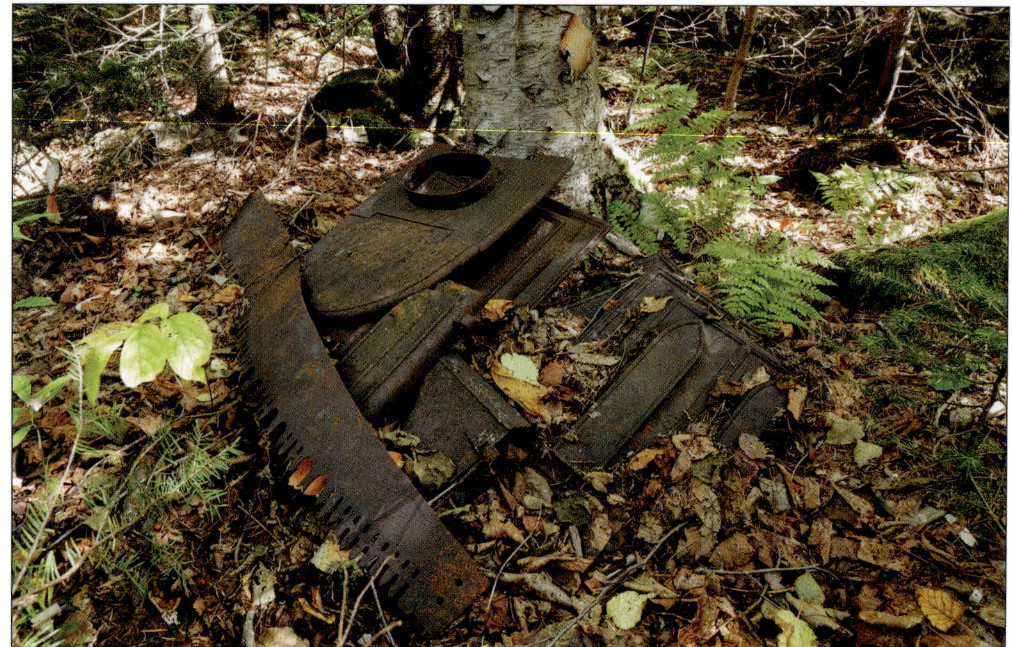

A spur line between Camps 10 and 12 came off the Franconia Brook Branch and traveled into Redrock Ravine, ending at Camp 14. These stove pieces and crosscut saw, both protected artifacts, mark the general location of where the logging camp was. Camp 14 was one of the duplicated camp numbers. The other Camp 14 was located in the Pine Brook valley, off the Hancock Branch. (Author's collection.)

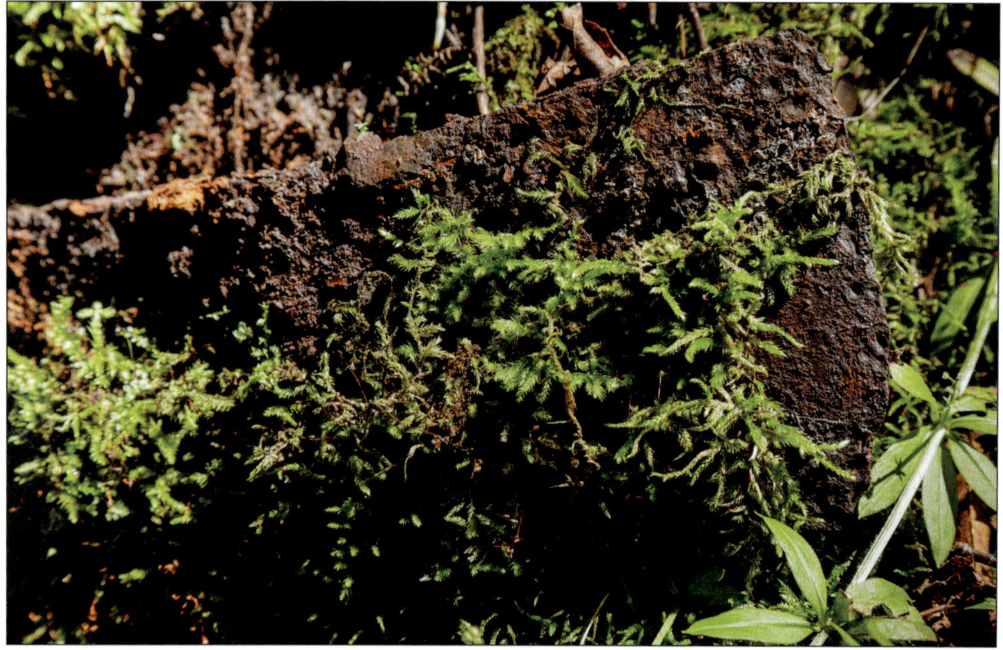

The logging camps on Franconia Brook Branch and the Lincoln Brook Branch date back to over 100 years ago. The artifacts that remain along these branches are slowly being swallowed up by nature. This rusted axe head near Camp 12 is almost unrecognizable. (Author's collection.)

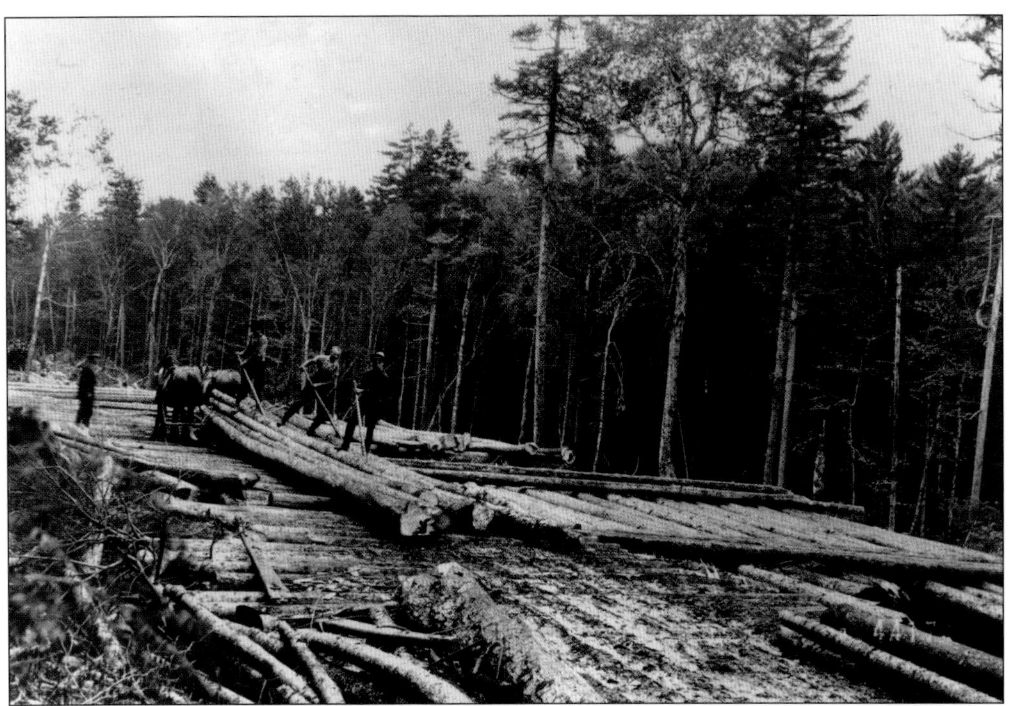

A teamster and his horses have just dragged a load of logs from the woods onto a landing along the Franconia Brook Branch in the 1903 photograph above. Below, the three-man landing crew, each equipped with a peavey (a logging tool used to roll logs) is in the process of rolling the logs onto a wooden frame log car sitting on the rails just below the landing. (Both, US Forest Service photographs, courtesy of the Upper Pemigewasset Historical Society.)

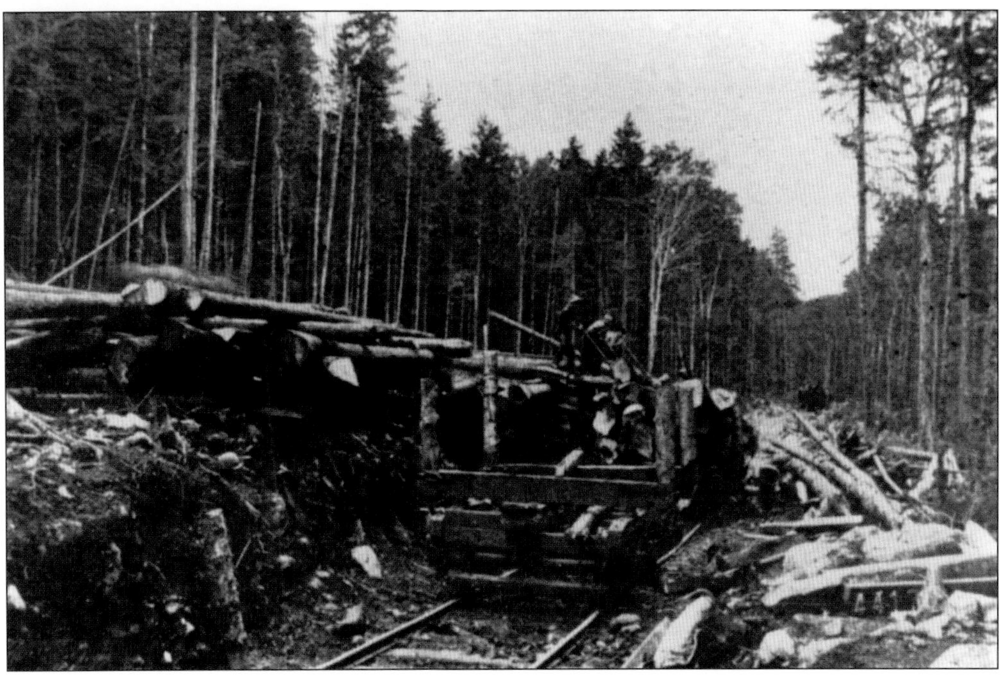

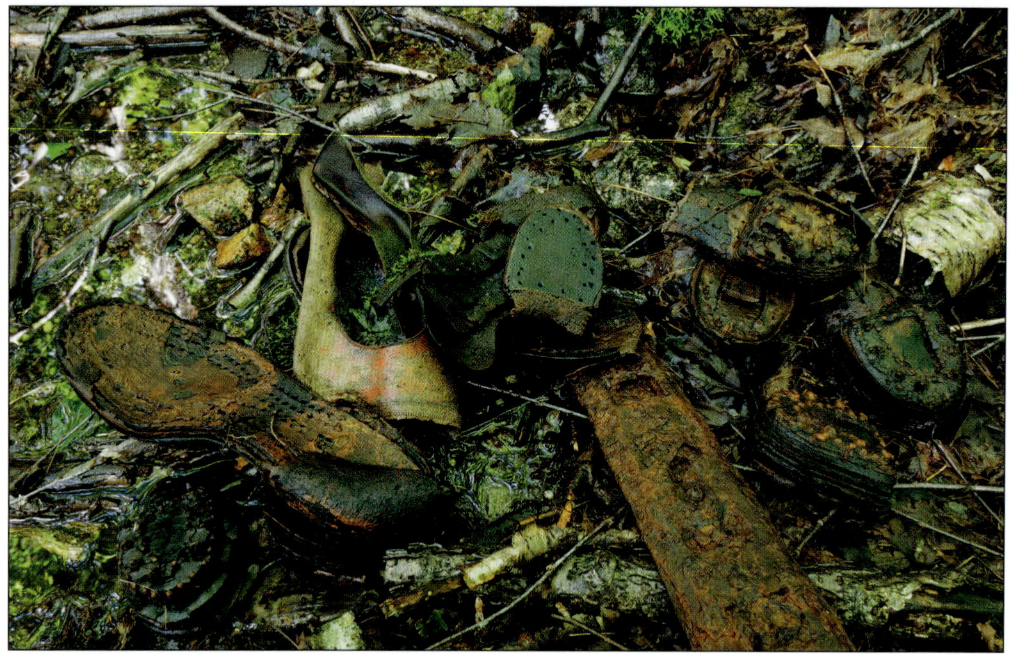

Camp 13 was located at the very end of the Franconia Brook Branch in the area of today's Thirteen Falls. From this camp, it was just under 13 miles by rail back to the mill in Lincoln village. The railroad siding for the log landing was located right at the camp. Artifacts like these decaying boots are scattered throughout the logging camp area. (Author's collection.)

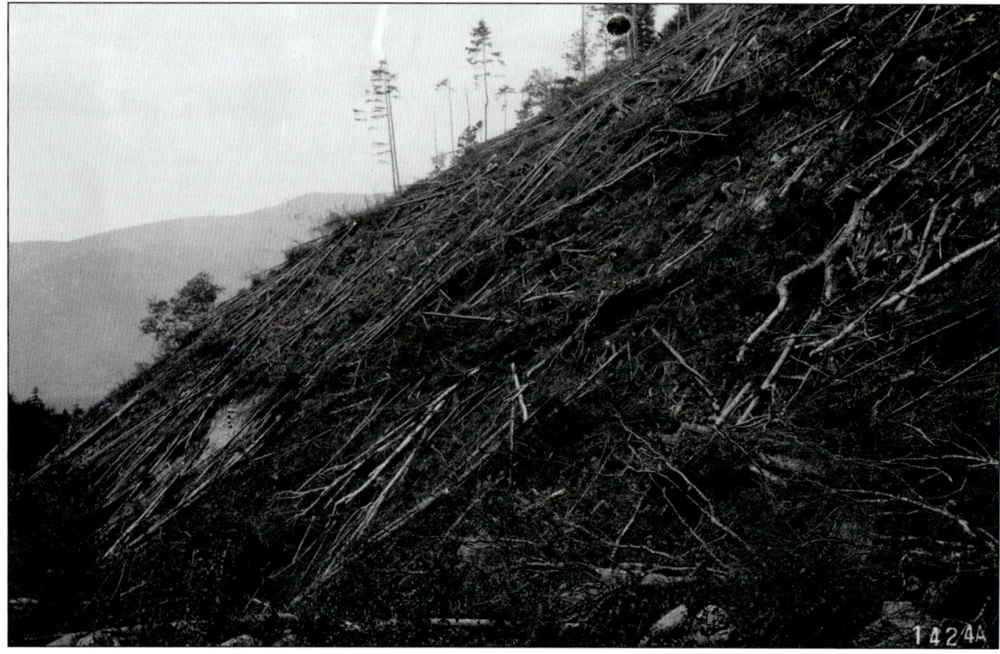

The unsustainable logging practices used during the late 19th and early 20th century logging railroad era left the mountainsides littered with logging slash (wood debris left behind from logging). Logging slash fueled a number of forest fires in the White Mountains during this era. (US Forest Service photograph, courtesy of the Upper Pemigewasset Historical Society.)

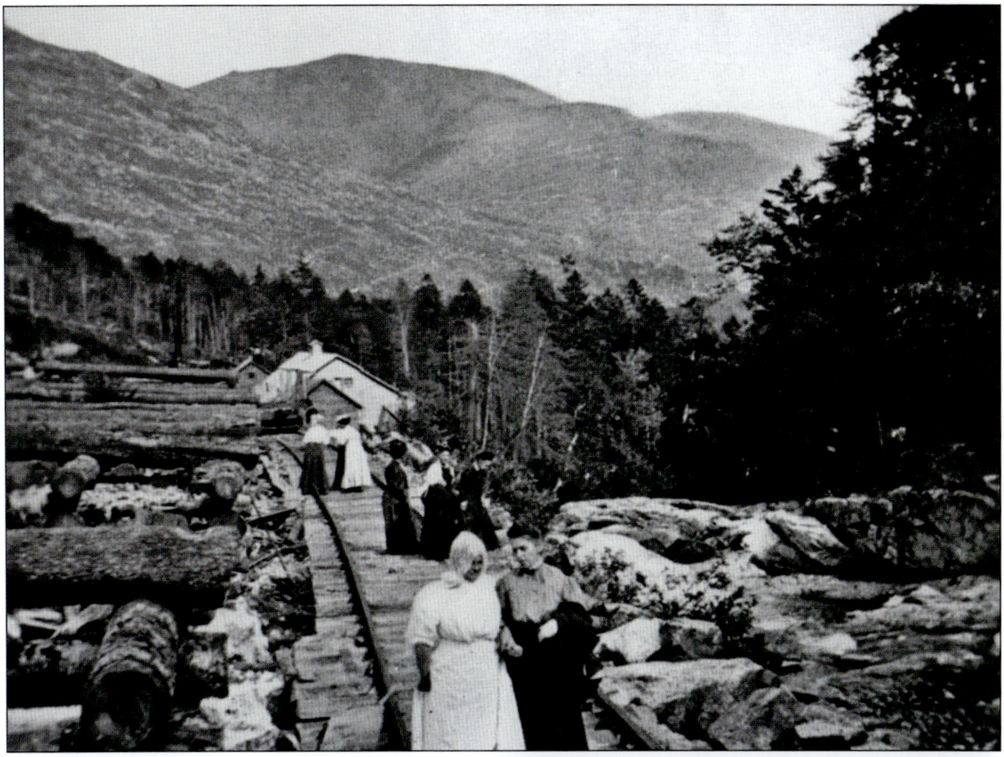

The East Branch & Lincoln Railroad was known for running excursion trains into Lincoln Woods. J.E. Henry and Sons customized some of the flatcars with benches so passengers could sit. For a fee, riders would be taken on a train ride into Lincoln Woods to view the scenery, and were fed a meal at one of the logging camps. During blueberry season, blueberry pickers would be taken to areas along the railroad where blueberries could be found. In the above undated photograph, excursion train riders are visiting Camp 13. An added bonus to visiting Camp 13 was viewing Thirteen Falls (right). Today, a visit to Thirteen Falls requires a 16-mile round trip hike from the Lincoln Woods Trail trailhead. (Above, courtesy of the Upper Pemigewasset Historical Society; right, author's collection.)

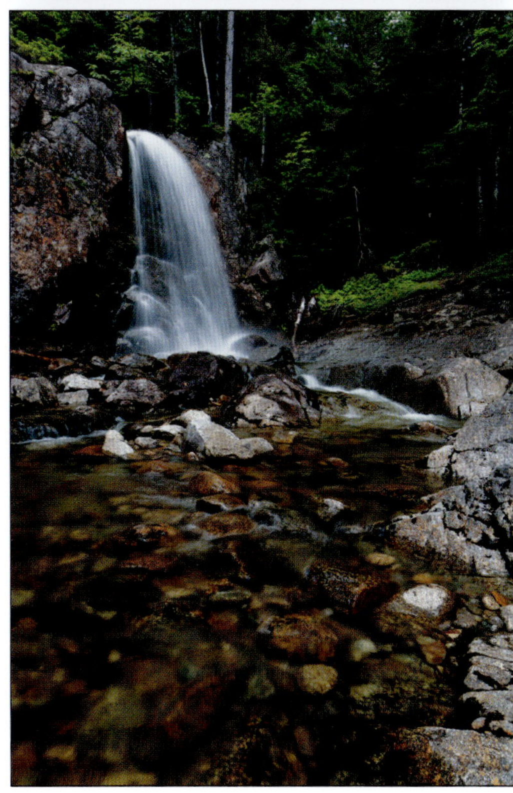

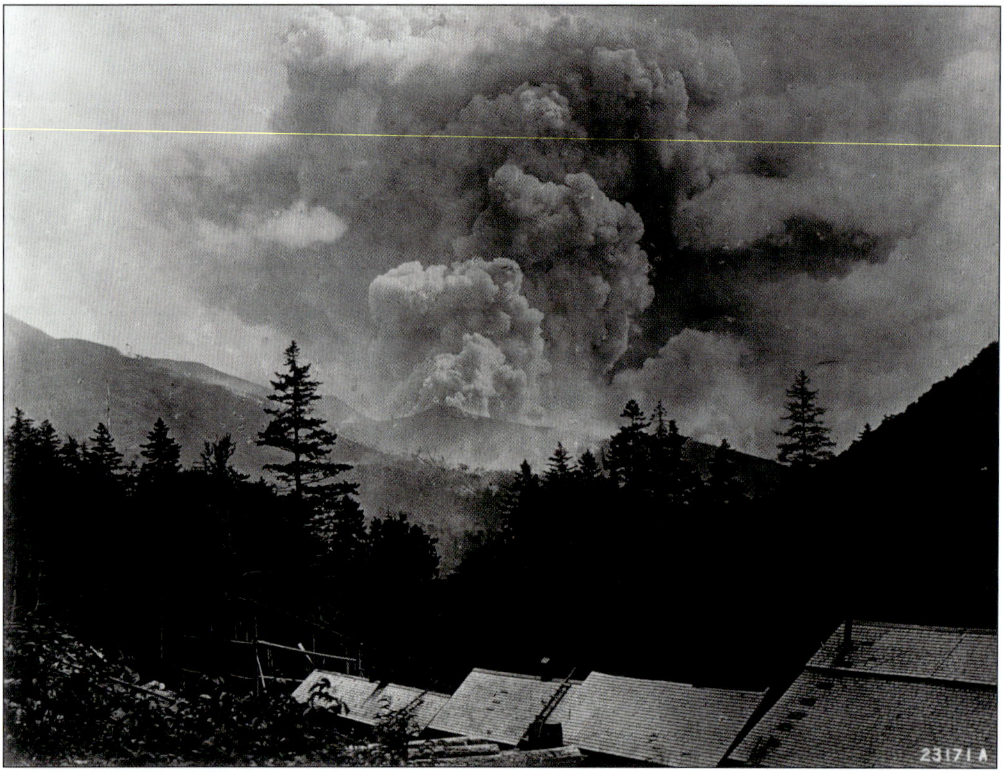

In August 1907, a lightning strike ignited a devastating forest fire on Owls Head Mountain in the Pemigewasset Wilderness that lasted for days. The smoke from the fire could be seen from miles away, and an estimated 10,000 acres were burned. Logging slash fueled the fire. The above 1907 photograph shows the forest fire from Camp 13 at the end of the Franconia Brook Branch, and the photograph below, taken from near Little Haystack Mountain on Franconia Ridge, shows the area where the fire took place. Both ends of Owls Head Mountain suffered damage. (Above, US Forest Service photograph; below, author's collection.)

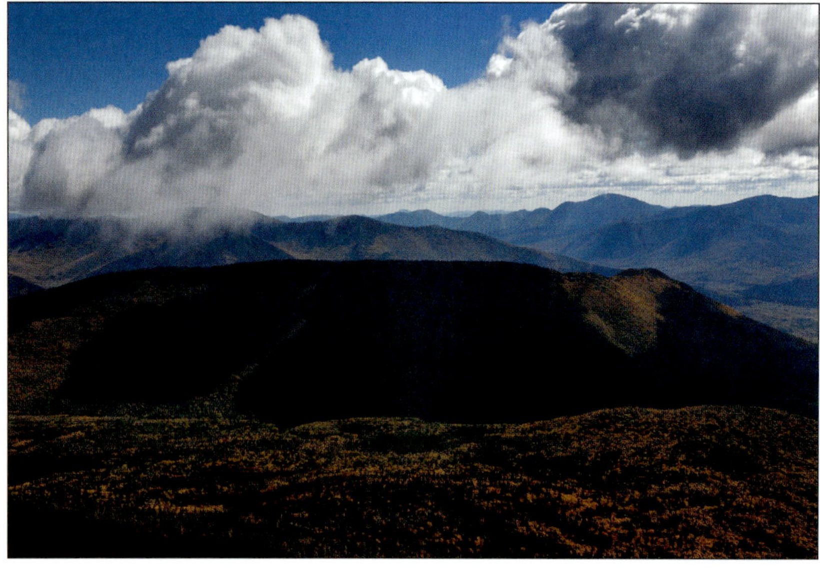

Four

Upper East Branch

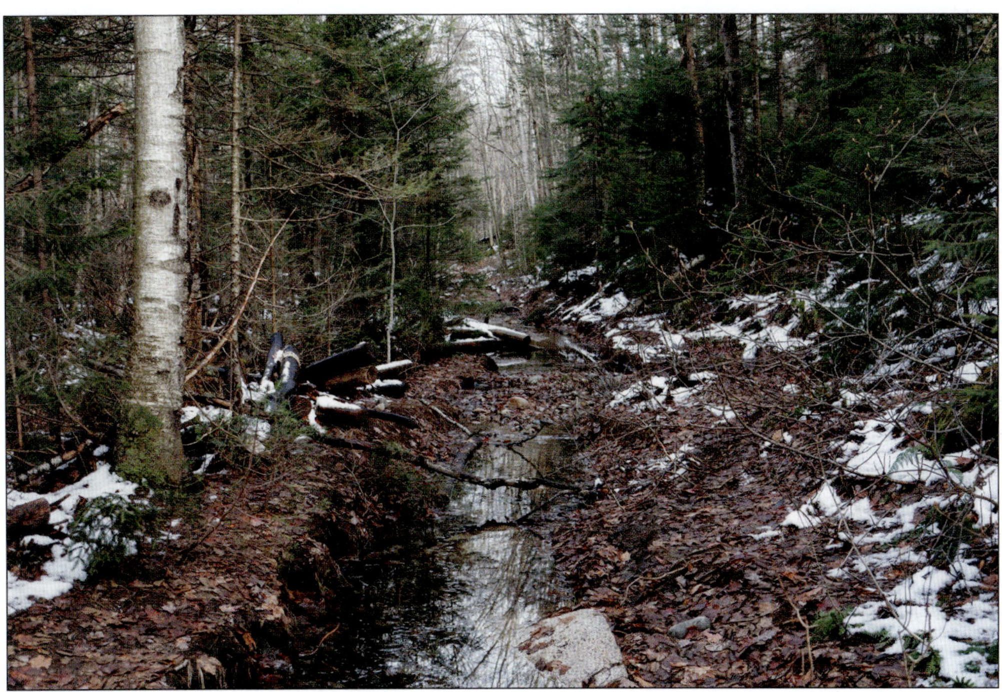

About half a mile above trestle No. 7 (see page 29), a spur line came off the mainline, crossed the East Branch of the Pemigewasset River, and traveled up this section of the closed Pemi East Trail, ending in the general area of Cedar Brook. In 2011, flooding from Tropical Storm Irene uncovered railroad ties that had been buried along the trail. (Author's collection.)

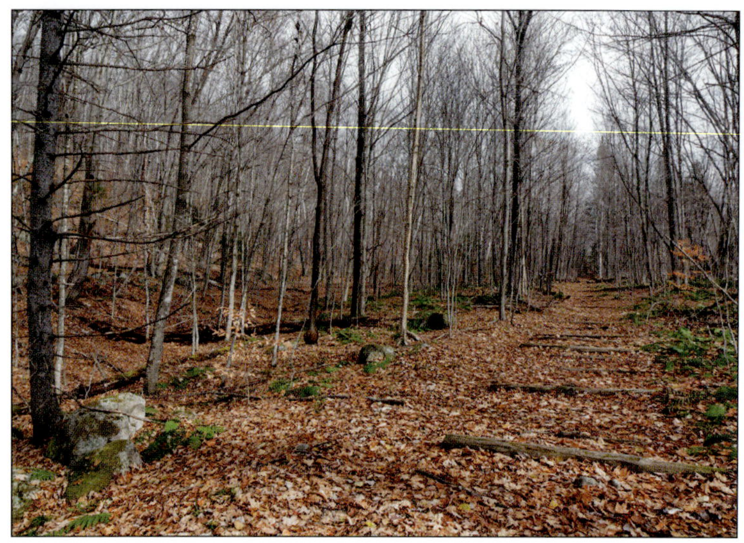

The Upper East Branch ran about six miles to Stillwater Junction, and including trestle No. 7 at the start of the branch, there were at least nine bridges and trestles on this branch. Four rail-side logging camps were located along this branch: Camps 15, 16, 17, and 18. Seen here is the site of Camp 15. The log landing was on the left. (Author's collection)

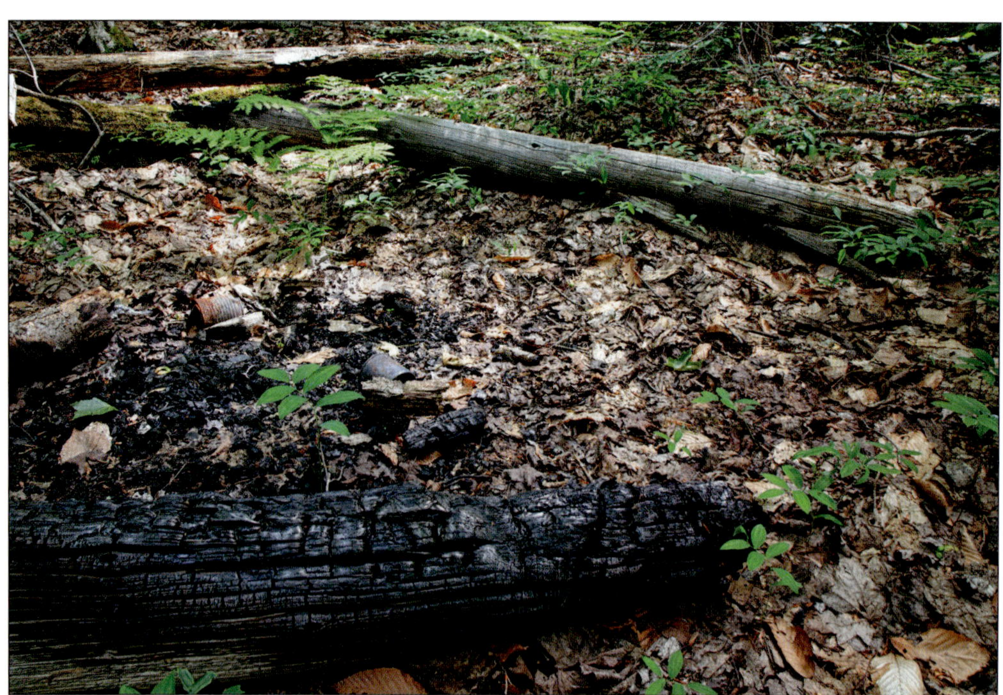

Telephone wires were strung from utility poles along the East Branch & Lincoln Railroad to the numerous logging camps. In some areas along the railroad, side mounted wooden telephone peg holder pins nailed directly to trees were used in place of utility poles. Only a handful of these poles remain standing along the railroad. In 2011, one near Camp 15 was knocked down and burned in a campfire. (Author's collection.)

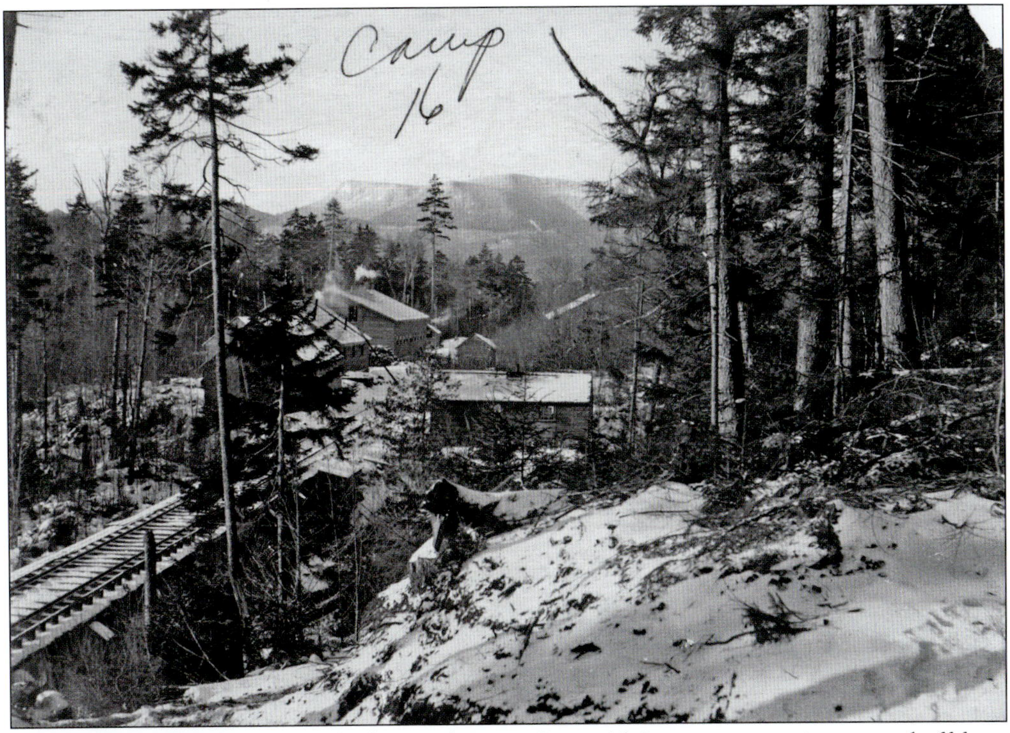

Seen in the undated photograph above is logging Camp 16. It was in operation on and off from 1906 to 1947. In 1946, a truck road was built from Camp 8 on the lower East Branch to Camp 16, and pulpwood was hauled out with trucks. The still standing trestle No. 16, which crosses Black Brook (or Bear Brook on older maps) is on the left. Today, various artifacts (below) remain at the camp. Over the years, the Camp 16 clearing was a favorite spot for backcountry camping, but camping is no longer allowed at this site. (Above, courtesy of the Upper Pemigewasset Historical Society; below, author's collection.)

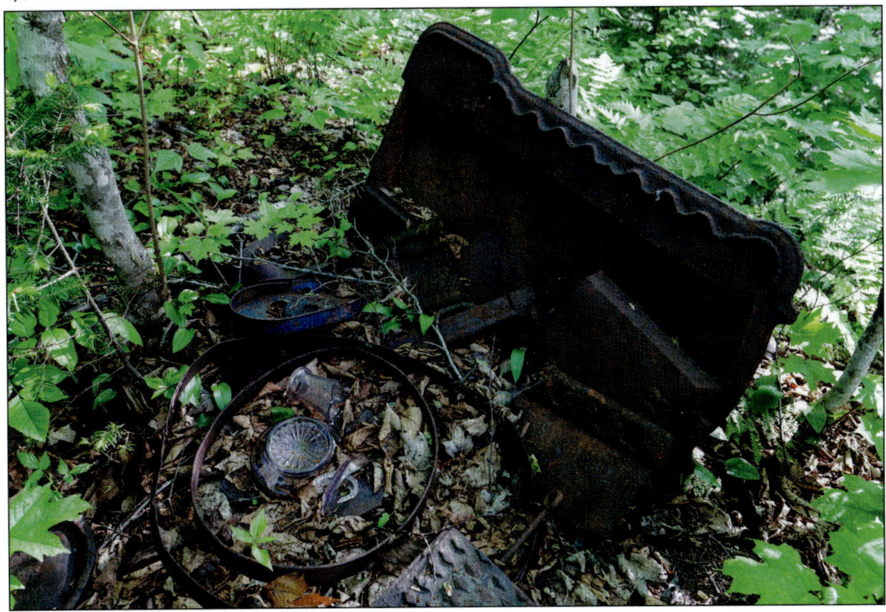

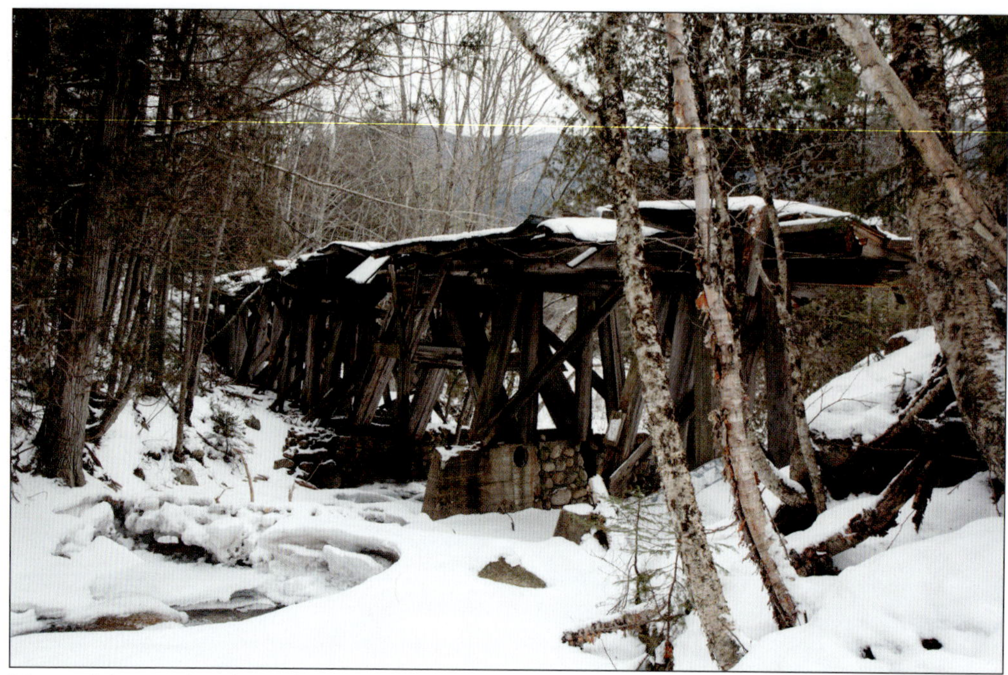

Many of the trestles along the East Branch & Lincoln Railroad were built under the supervision of construction foreman Levi "Pork Barrel" Dumas. Built in the early 1900s, trestle No. 16, which crosses Black Brook near Camp 16, played an important role in transporting logs from remote regions of today's Pemigewasset Wilderness. The last log train rolled over this trestle most likely in the summer or fall of 1946, not long after the Cedar Brook operation was completed. In 2011, flood waters from Tropical Storm Irene washed out one of the stone abutments, causing a section of the trestle to drop about two feet. Most of the rocks on the right below are from the abutment that washed out. (Both, author's collection.)

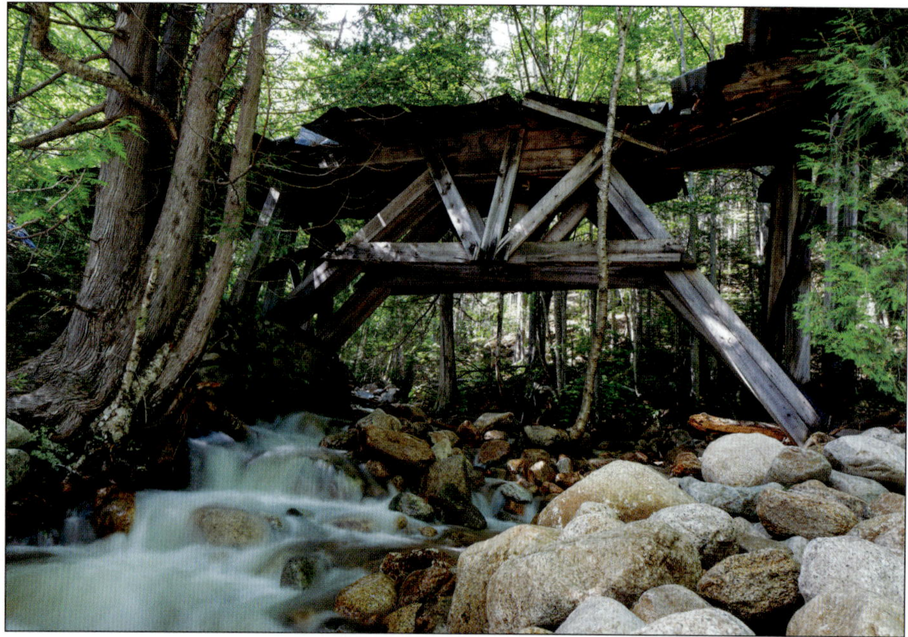

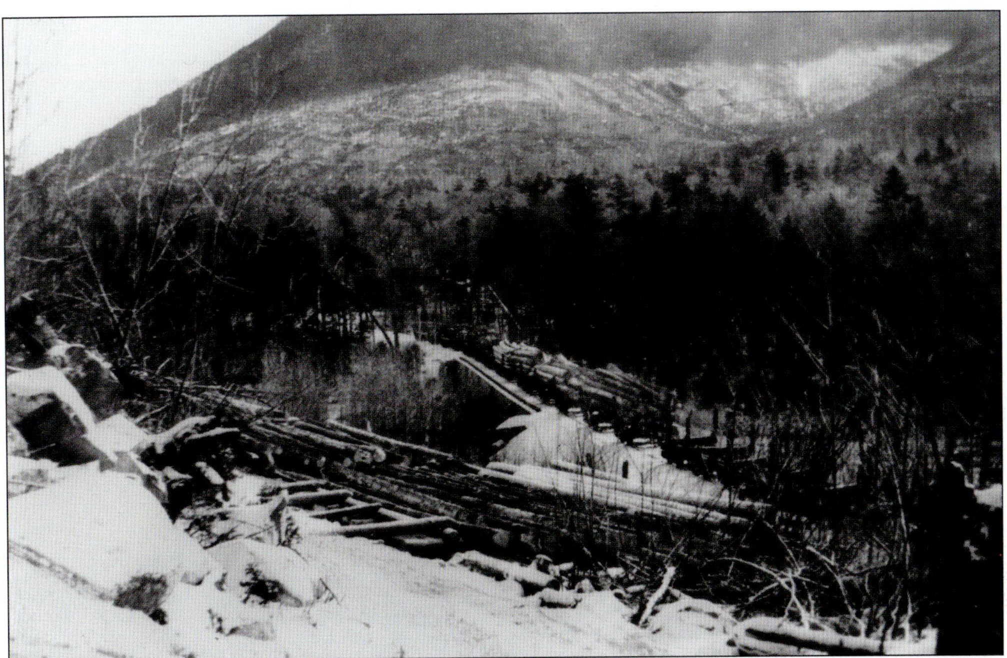

At least seven loaded log cars can be seen on trestle No. 17 in the undated photograph above. This trestle spanned the East Branch of the Pemigewasset River near Camp 17. The cutover slopes of a spur of Mount Hancock can be seen in the background. The log landing in the foreground and a siding for the landing were on the north side of the river in the area where a hiking trail formerly accessed the 180-foot suspension bridge seen on page 60. Remnants of the landing and stone abutments for the trestle are still visible. Below is a north-facing view of the trestle site today. (Above, courtesy of the Upper Pemigewasset Historical Society; below, author's collection.)

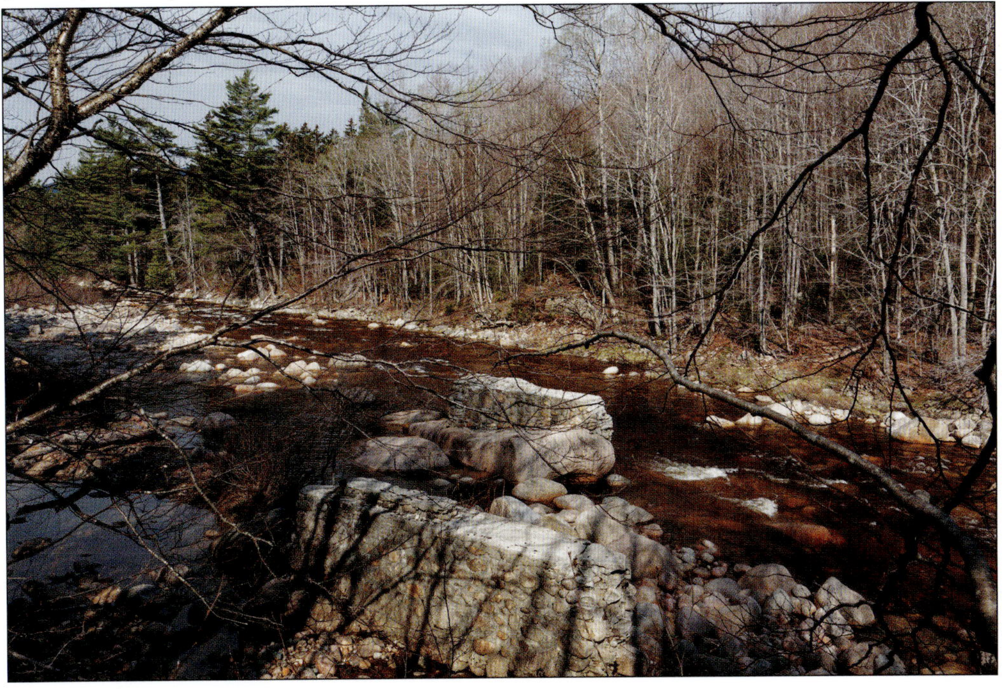

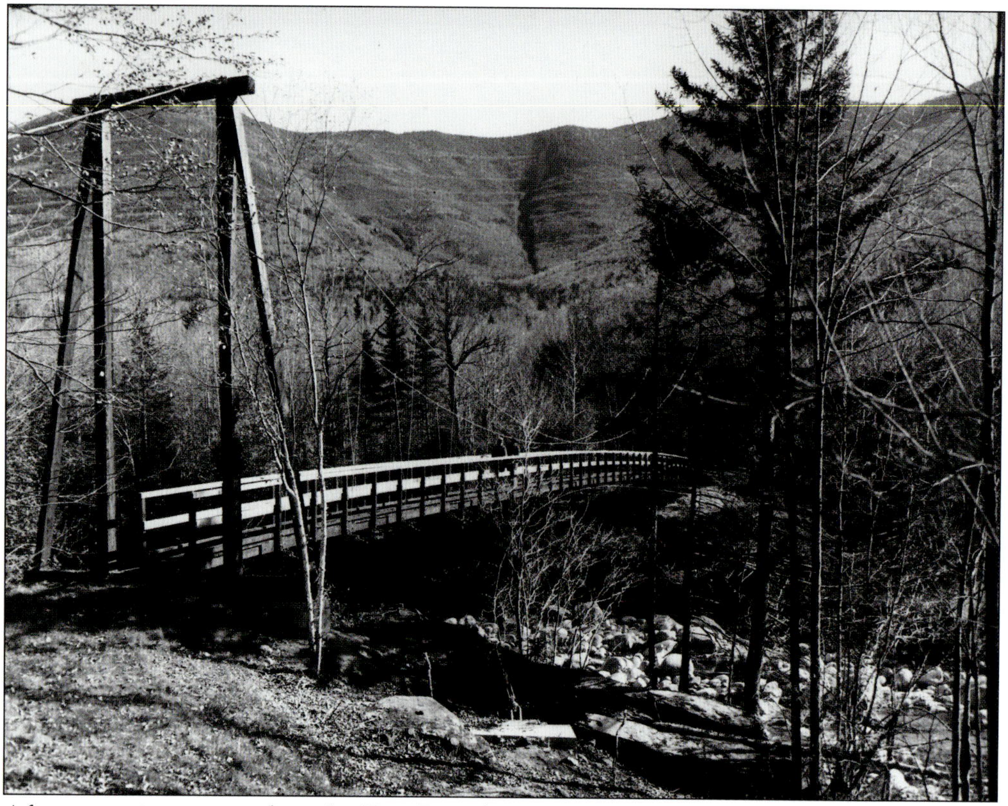

After operations stopped on the East Branch & Lincoln Railroad in 1948, a 180-foot-long suspension bridge for hikers was built across the East Branch of the Pemigewasset River to replace trestle No. 17. The footbridge, built in 1959–1960 and seen here in 1961, was dismantled in 2009 because of safety reasons. The outline of sled roads can be seen on the mountainside. (Courtesy of the Forest History Society.)

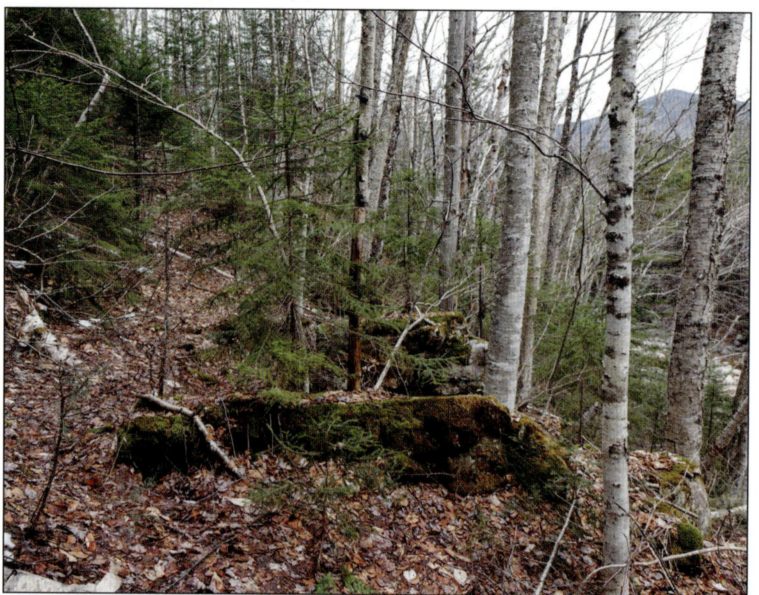

Not all of the trestles along the East Branch & Lincoln Railroad crossed water features. Along the mainline, a short distance east of the junction of the North Fork Branch, a trestle crossed the side of a steep hillside. The stone abutments from the trestle remain in place today. (Author's collection.)

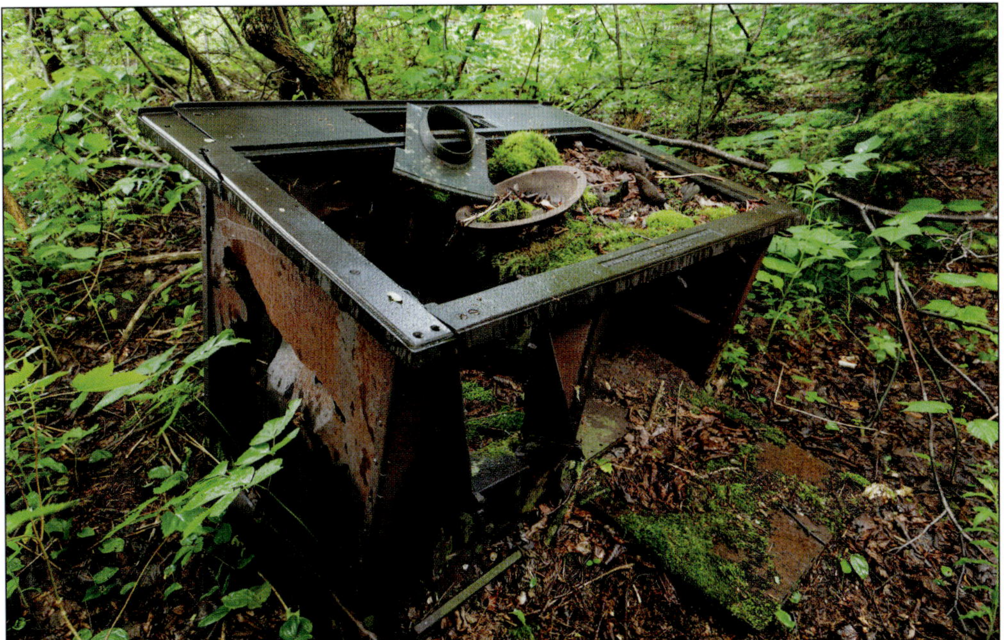

This Home Comfort Stove made by Wrought Iron Range Company in St. Louis, Missouri, marks the site of Camp 18. For many years, this artifact was easily overlooked because it was located in thick brush along the Wilderness Trail, but in 2011 a trail crew rerouted a section of the trail to avoid a wet area, and the trail now travels right next to it. (Author's collection.)

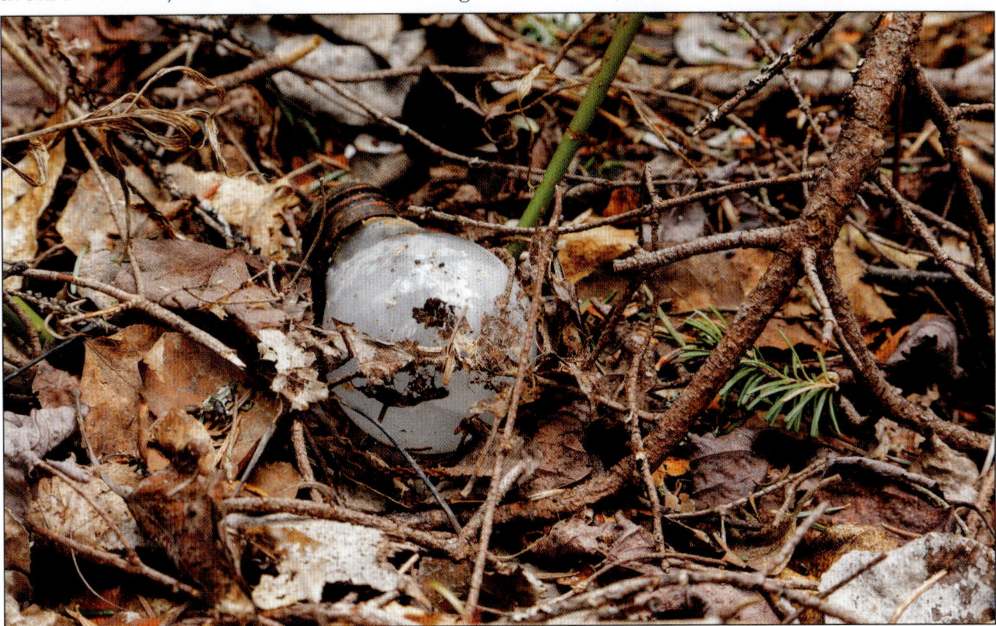

According to *JE Henry's Logging Railroads* by Bill Gove, electric lights first came to the logging camps in 1909. A gasoline motor and generator were set up at Camp 18, producing a 32-volt system with 50-watt bulbs. This GE Mazda light bulb at Camp 18 was manufactured from 1909 to about 1945, and this shape globe was manufactured between about 1920 and 1940. It was not one of the first used. (Author's collection.)

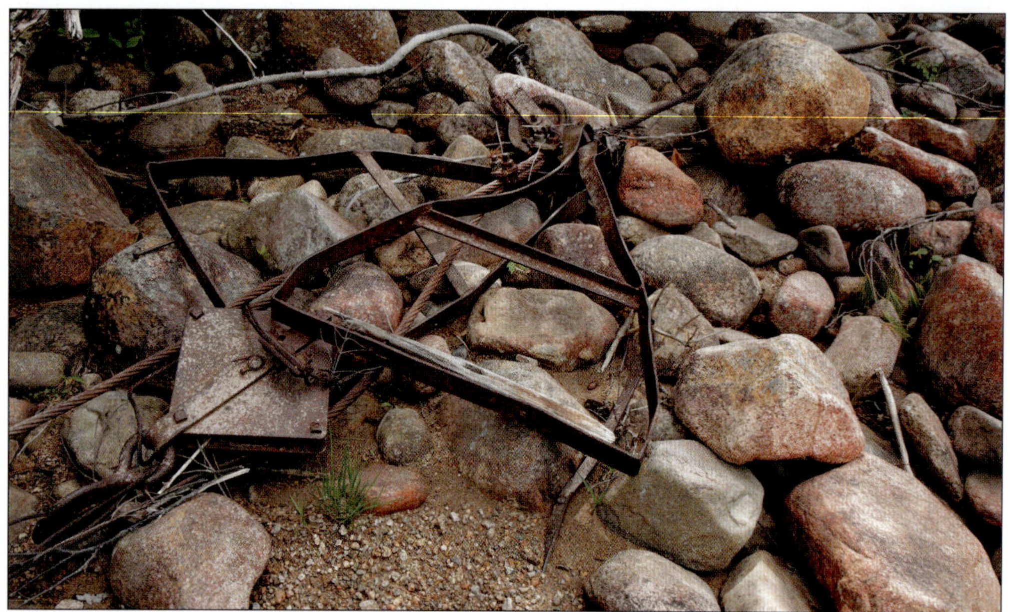

In the early years of the Wilderness Trail, the trail began on the south side of trestle No. 17 and followed much of the old railroad bed to Stillwater Junction. At the first crossing of the East Branch of the Pemigewasset River above Camp 18, a cable car was used during the 1940s to cross the river. These are likely remnants of it. (Author's collection.)

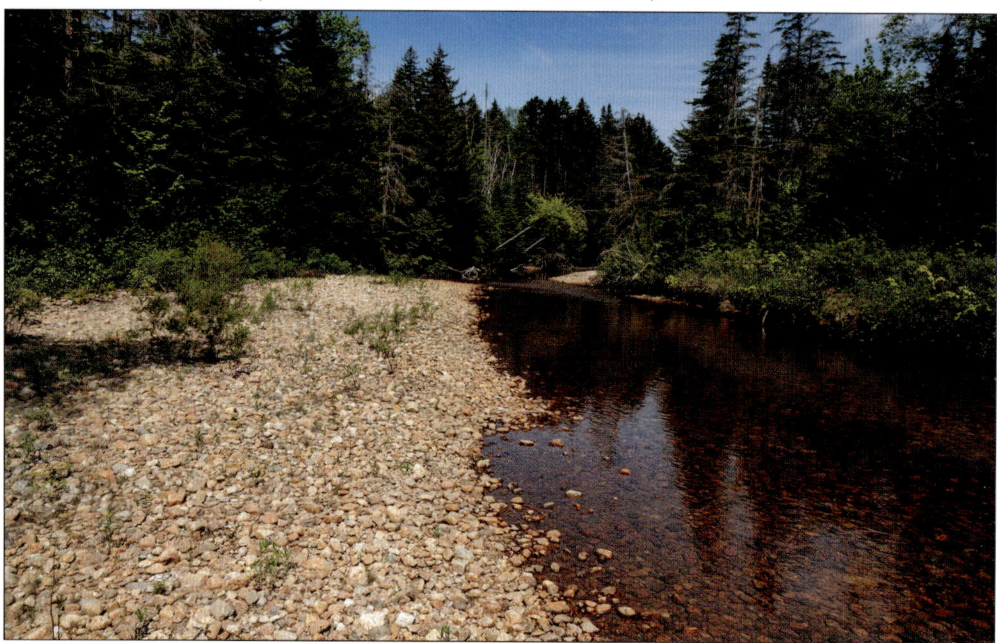

In 1919–1920, the Parker-Young Company planned to build a dam and power station on the East Branch of the Pemigewasset River in the area known as Stillwater. Referred to as the Stillwater Power Project, the dam was to be built near the confluence of the East Branch and Carrigan Branch, and this area where the railroad entered into Stillwater would have been flooded. The Osgood Construction Company began construction on the project, but it was never completed. (Author's collection.)

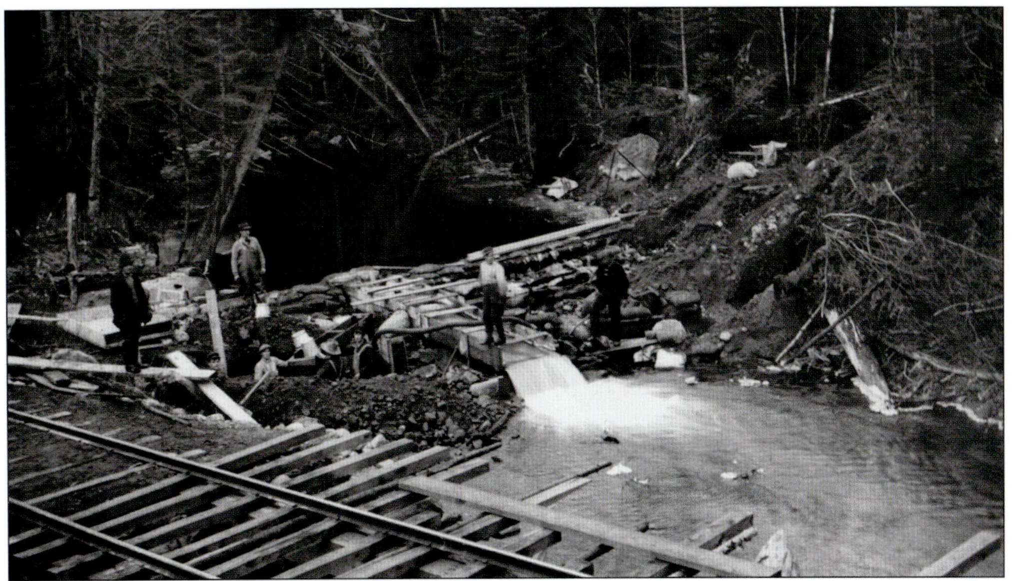

At Stillwater Junction, the railroad split into two branches. The Anderson Brook Branch traveled to Camp 19 in the Anderson Brook and Norcross Brook region, and the Shoal Pond Brook Branch traveled to Camp 21 in the Shoal Pond region. Each branch required a small bridge to cross Anderson Brook. The Anderson Brook Branch, seen in the November 1911 photograph above, crossed the brook at an angle just below the Anderson Brook gauging station. At the time of this photograph, the Anderson Brook gauging station was in the process of being built. The below photograph shows the station as it looked in 2009. This abutment has since fallen over. (Above, courtesy of the National Archives & Records Administration; below, author's collection.)

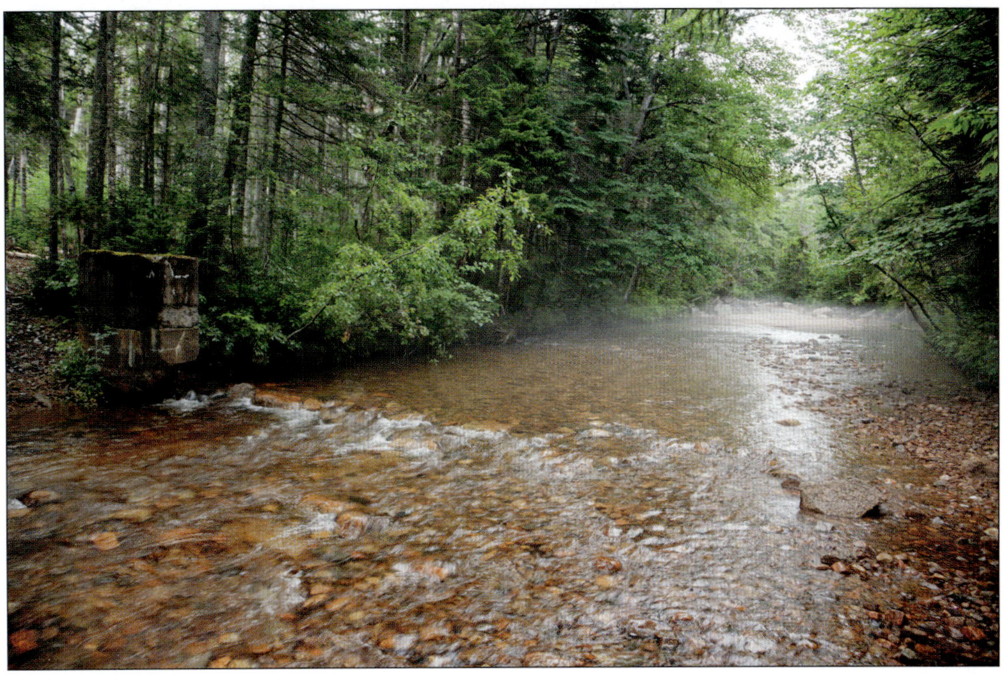

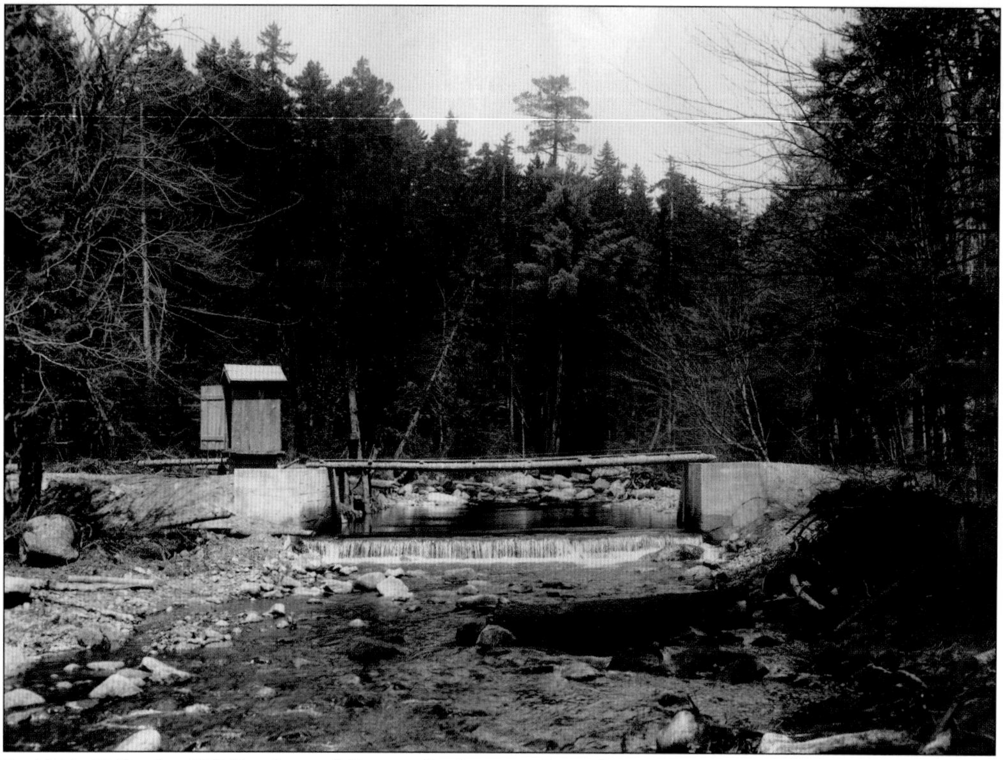

In 1911–1912, the US Geological Survey built a number of stream gauging stations in the White Mountains to determine the effects of deforestation on stream flow. There were at least four in the general area of Stillwater: Anderson Brook, Burnt Brook, Covert Brook, and Shoal Pond Brook. Above is the Shoal Pond gauging station, located near the Shoal Pond Branch of the railroad, in the summer of 1912. Below is the Burnt Brook station in April 1912. The results of these studies showed that cutting trees from the forest affected streamflow. (Both, courtesy of the National Archives & Records Administration.)

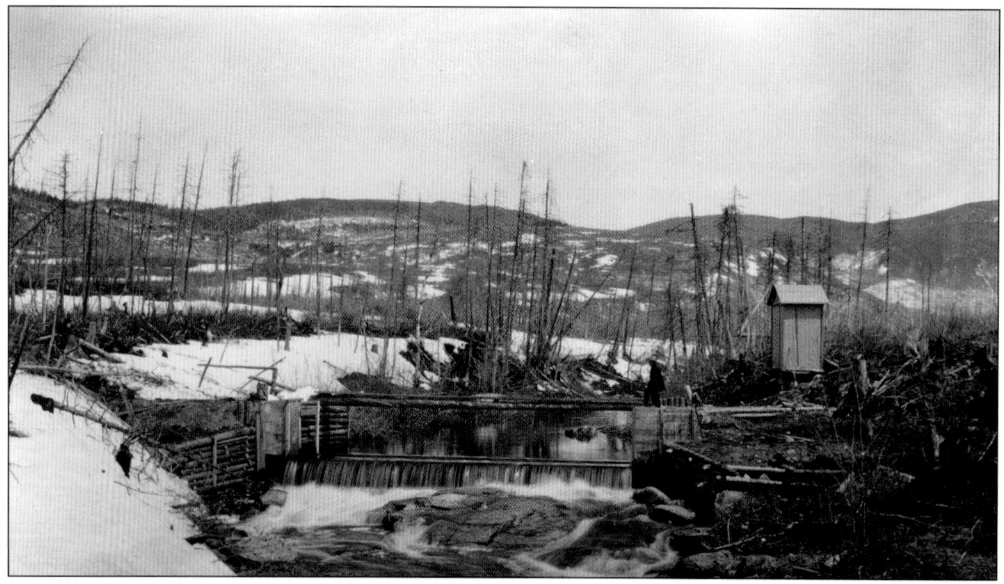

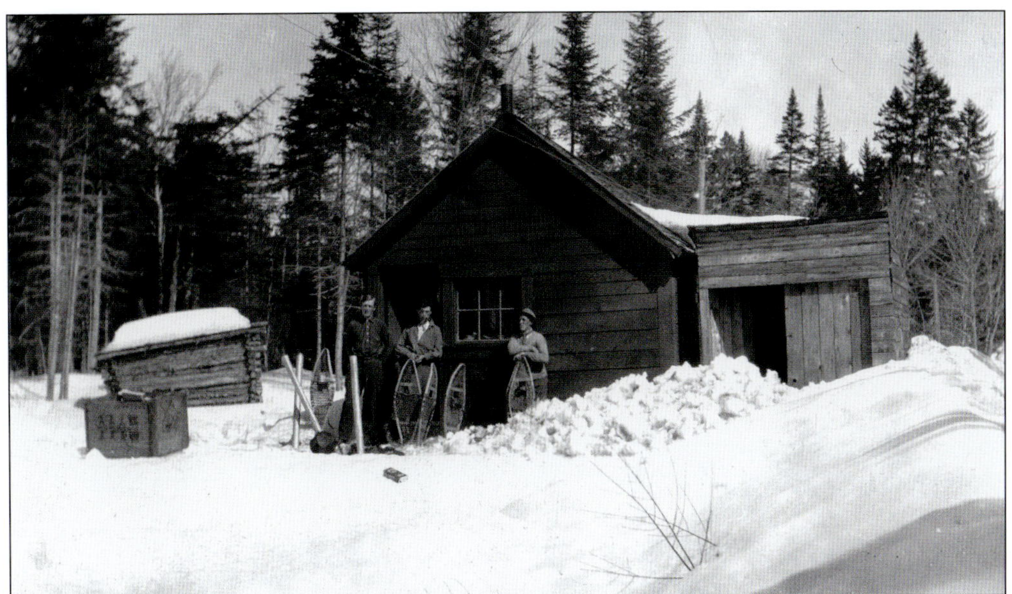

Also located at Stillwater was the Stillwater Camp. Seen here in 1912, this camp housed the men who monitored the stream gauging stations during the 1911–1912 streamflow study. The men had to check the gauges frequently, and during the winter months, they used snowshoes to get around the area. (Courtesy of the National Archives & Records Administration.)

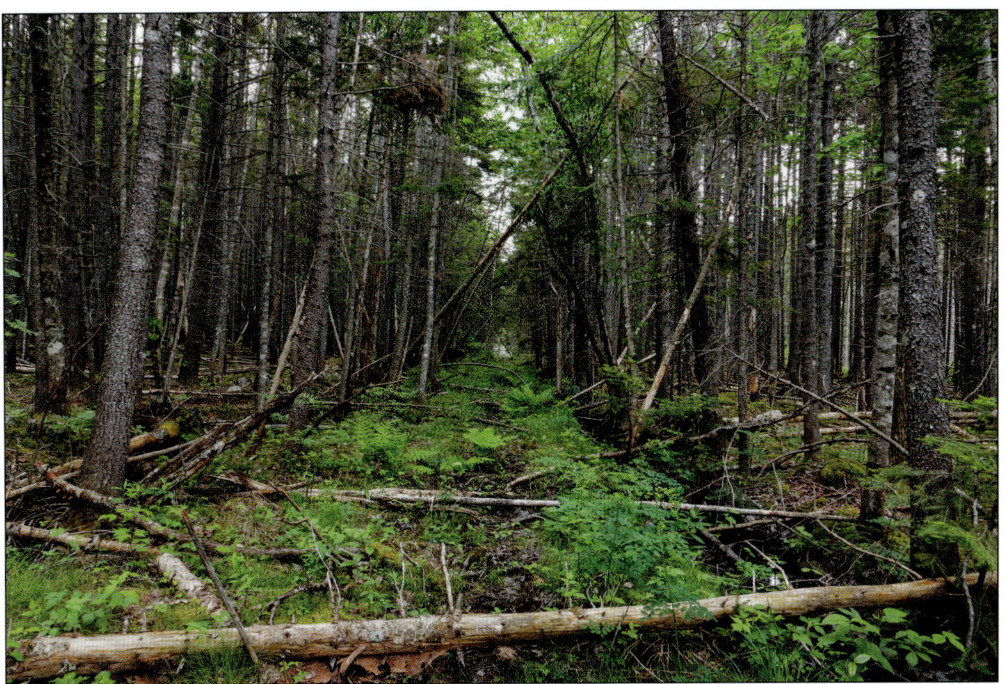

Above Stillwater Junction, the Anderson Brook Branch crossed Anderson Brook three times—twice below Camp 19, and once above the camp. The railroad passed Camp 19, crossed Norcross Brook, and ended at a log landing. For a short time in the 1940s, hikers used this section of the abandoned railroad above Stillwater Junction to hike into Carrigain Notch. (Author's collection.)

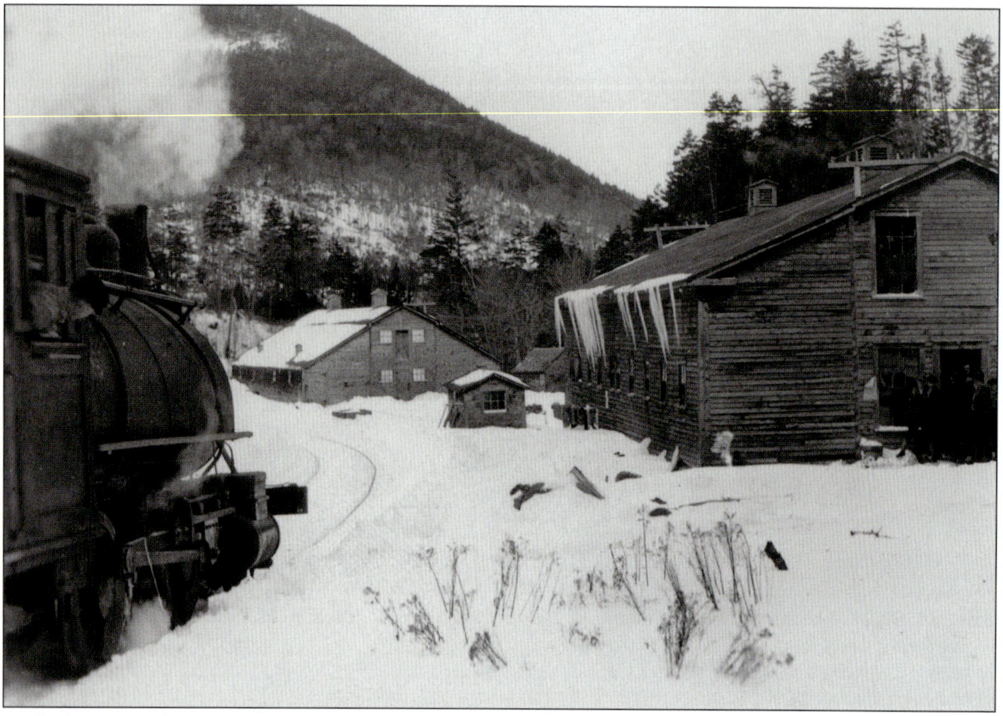

Including spur lines and sidings, the Anderson Brook Branch was about one and a half miles long, and there was only one rail-side logging camp, Camp 19, located on it. Seen in the above undated photograph is the log train at Camp 19. The woodsmen appear to be greeting it as it comes into the camp. The building in the background is the horse barn. Today, the Nancy Pond Trail follows a portion of this branch of the railroad and passes the Camp 19 clearing. Numerous artifacts (below) remain at the camp clearing; of interest is a large pile of bed frames. (Above, courtesy of the Upper Pemigewasset Historical Society; below, author's collection.)

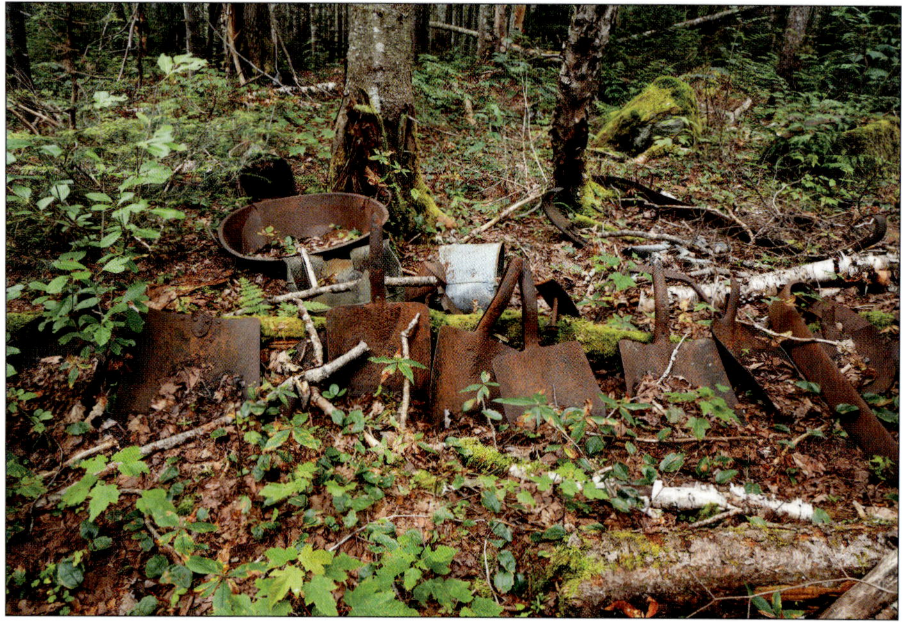

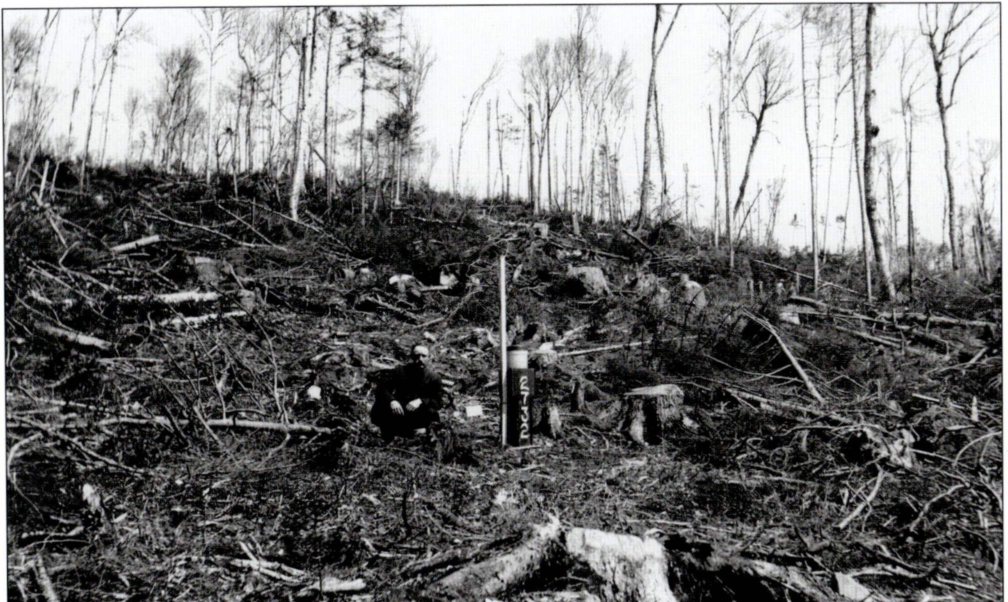

During the 1911–1912 streamflow study by the US Geological Survey, rain and snow gauges were also used during the study. Seen in this c. 1912 photograph is one of the rain gauges in the Anderson Brook watershed. Take note of all the logging slash left behind. (Courtesy of the National Archives & Records Administration.)

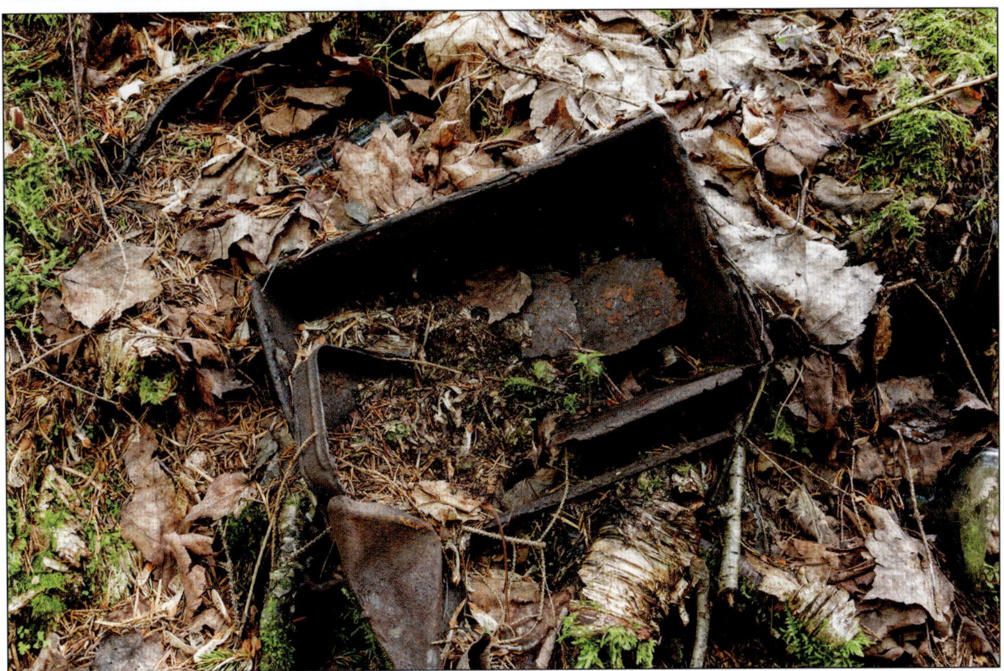

Just west of Camp 19, the Carrigain Branch came off the mainline and traveled in a south to southwest direction, ending just beyond Camp 20. Including spur lines and sidings, this branch was about one and a half miles long. Three bridges were needed to cross Anderson Brook, Notch Brook, and a tributary of Carrigain Branch Brook. Carrigain Notch Trail follows the old railroad, and artifacts mark the camp location. (Author's collection.)

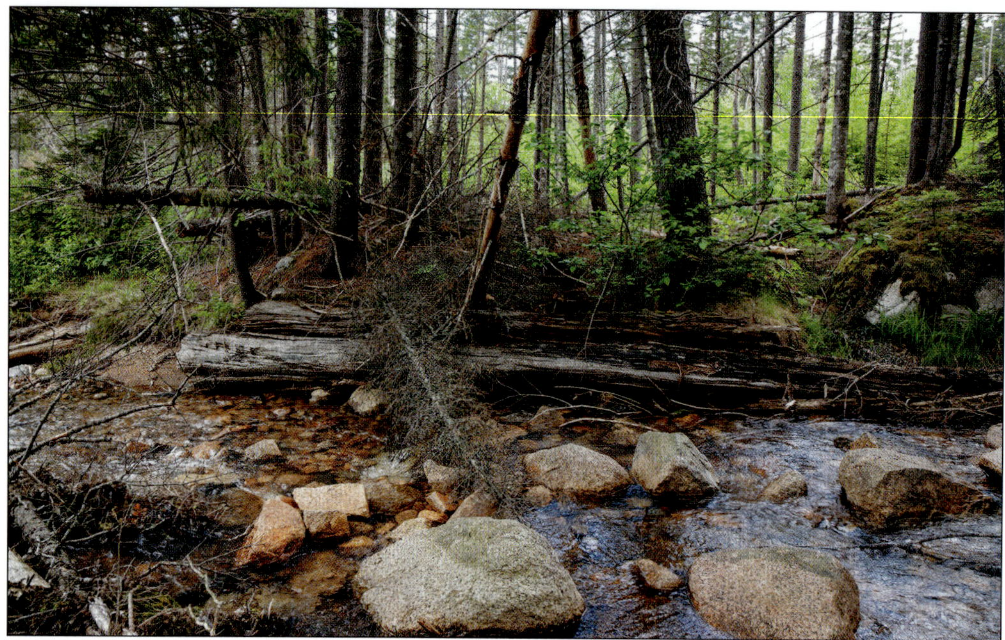

The Carrigain Branch also had a short spur line that traveled into the Notch Brook drainage. It crossed Notch Brook twice and ended in a log landing/work area. This 2009 photograph shows the remnants of one of the two small wooden bridges that crossed Notch Brook. (Author's collection.)

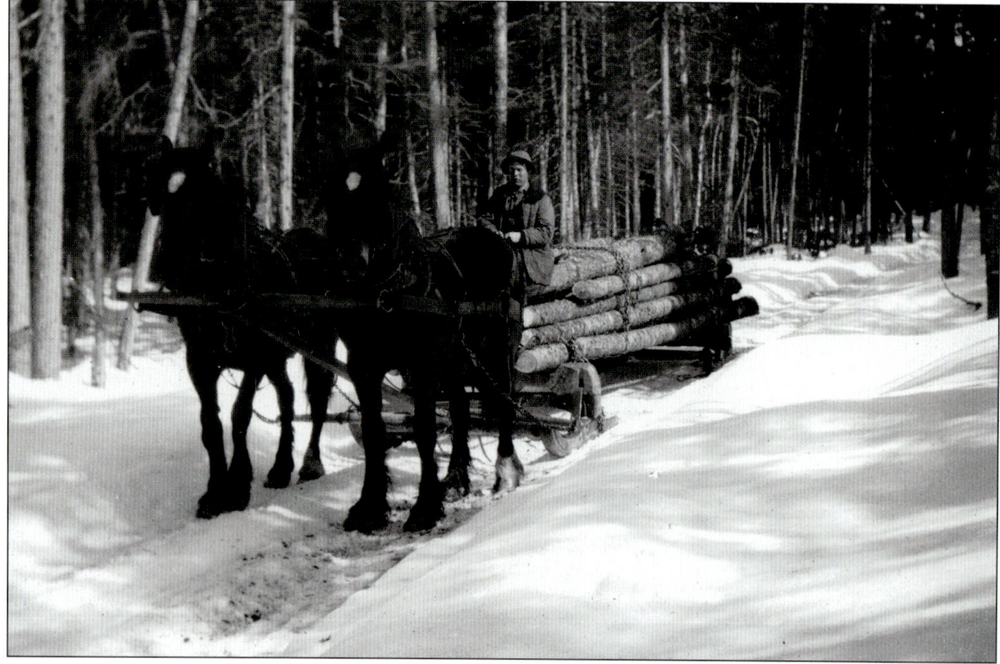

J.E. Henry and Sons were in the timber business to make a profit. Rules and regulations were posted at every logging camp in Lincoln Woods, and over half of the 47 rules applied to the well-being of horses. Seen in this 1912 photograph is a typical horse team with a load of logs in the Shoal Pond Brook drainage. (Courtesy of the National Archives & Records Administration.)

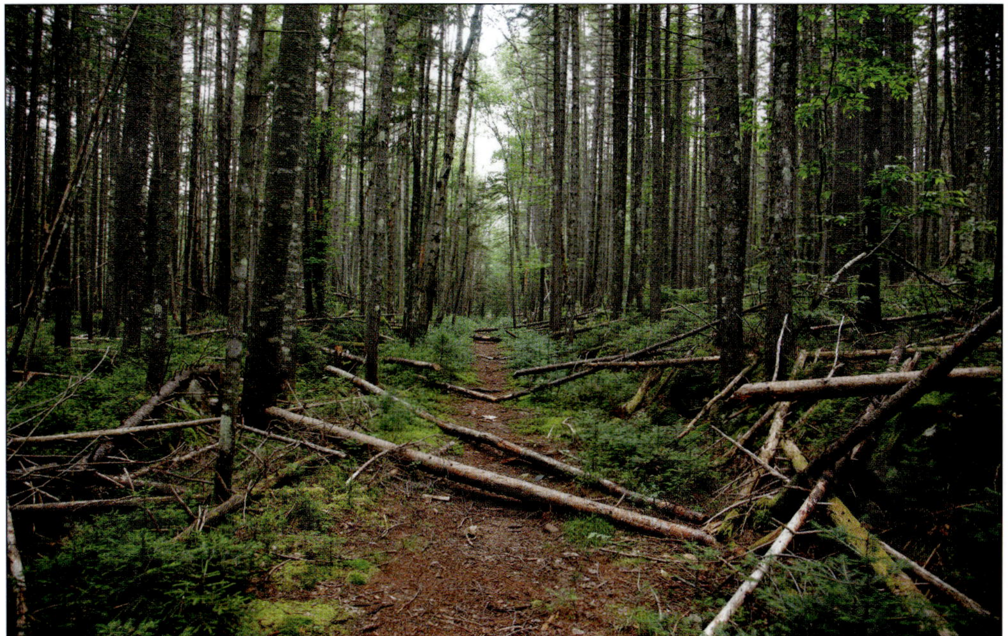

The Shoal Pond Branch of the East Branch & Lincoln Railroad was a little over one mile long, and only two bridges were needed on this branch. It began at Stillwater Junction, crossed Anderson Brook and Shoal Pond Brook, and ended at a log landing just beyond Camp 21. The Shoal Pond Trail follows the entire length of this branch of the railroad. (Author's collection.)

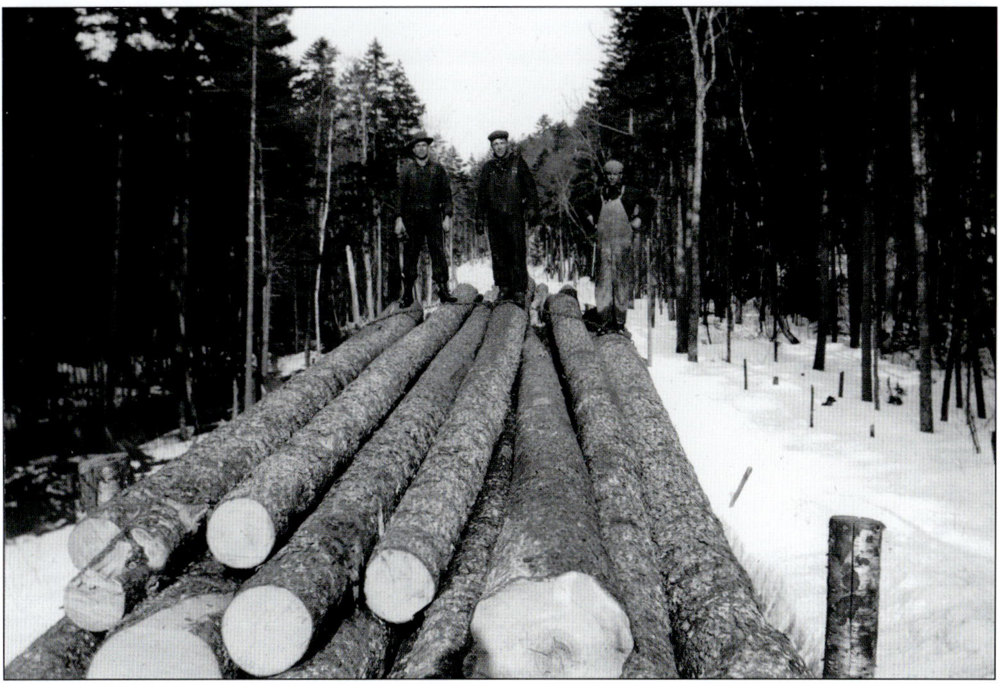

Seen here in April 1912 is the work crew posing on a loaded log train bound for the mill. From the Camp 21 log landing, it was roughly a 15-mile trip by railroad back to the mill in Lincoln village. (Courtesy of the National Archives & Records Administration.)

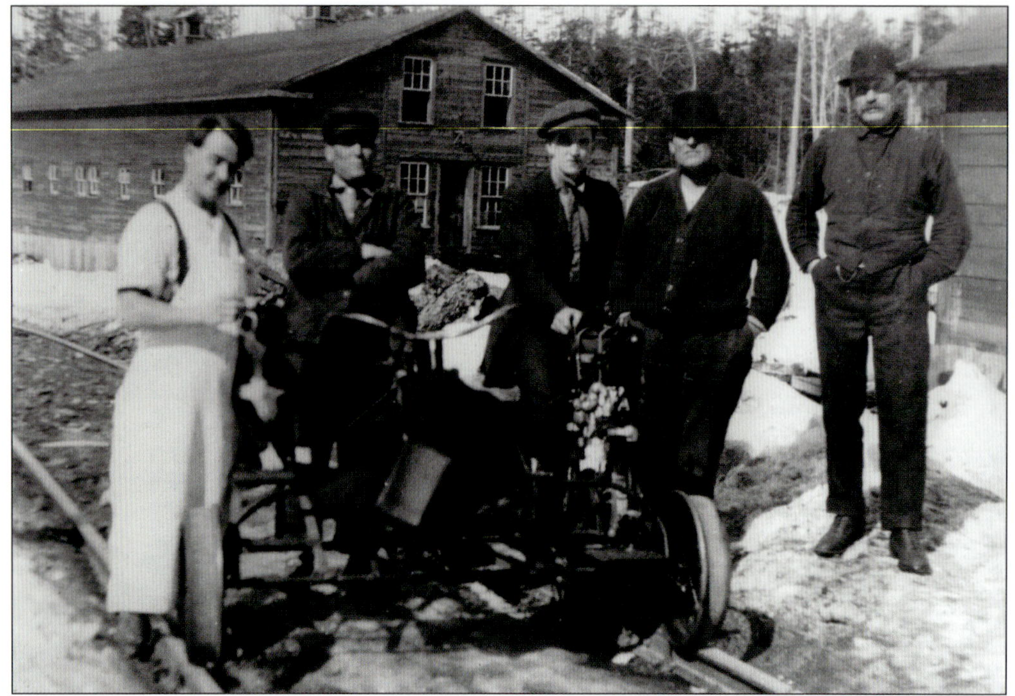

Camp 21 was the only rail-side camp on the Shoal Pond Branch. However, Camp 21A, a mountain camp northeast of Shoal Pond, was associated with this camp. Posing with a track bike in this undated photograph are, from left to right, Jimmy Palmer, Joe Boyle, unidentified, Abe Boyle, and Joe Morrison. (Courtesy of the Upper Pemigewasset Historical Society.)

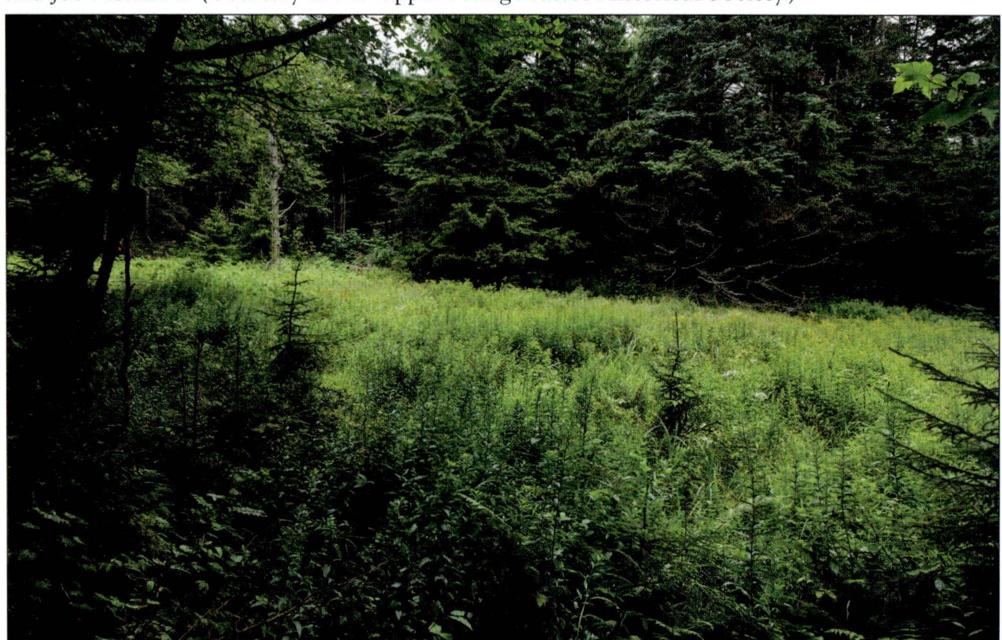

Today, the dwellings of Camp 21 are long gone, but the camp clearing is easy to identify along the Shoal Pond Trail. Many of the camp clearings along the East Branch & Lincoln Railroad are large and attract all types of wildlife. Moose are known to bed down in them. (Author's collection.)

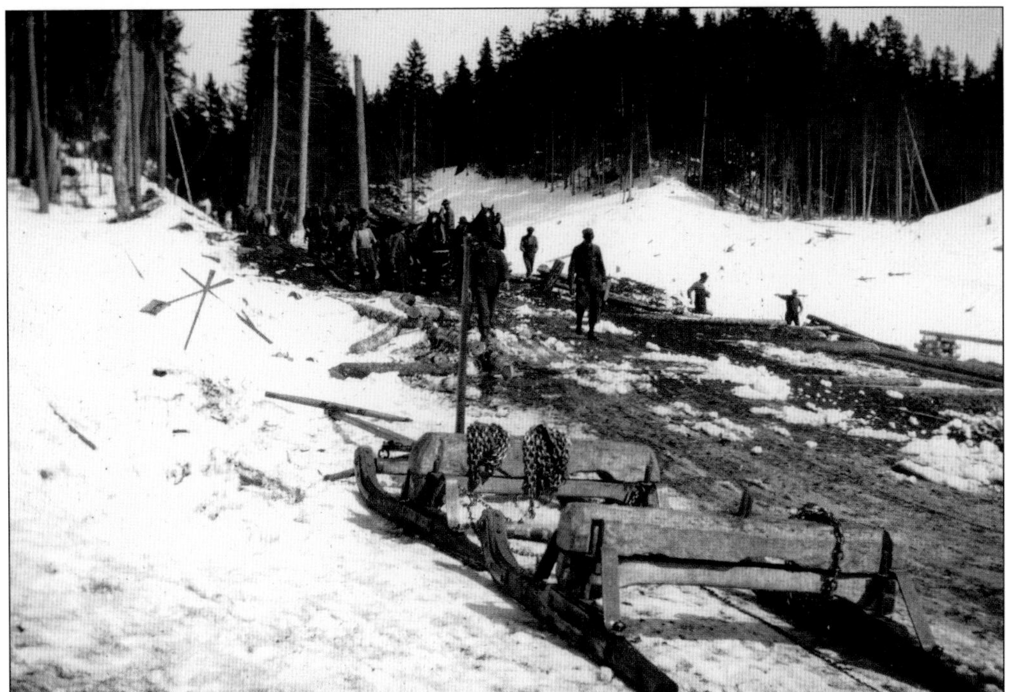

Located at the end of the Shoal Pond Branch just beyond Camp 21 was a log landing. In this 1912 photograph, a group of woodsmen has congregated at the Camp 21 landing. It may have been quitting time, and the woodsmen were coming out of the woods for the day. The railroad is out of view on the right below the landing. (Courtesy of the National Archives & Records Administration.)

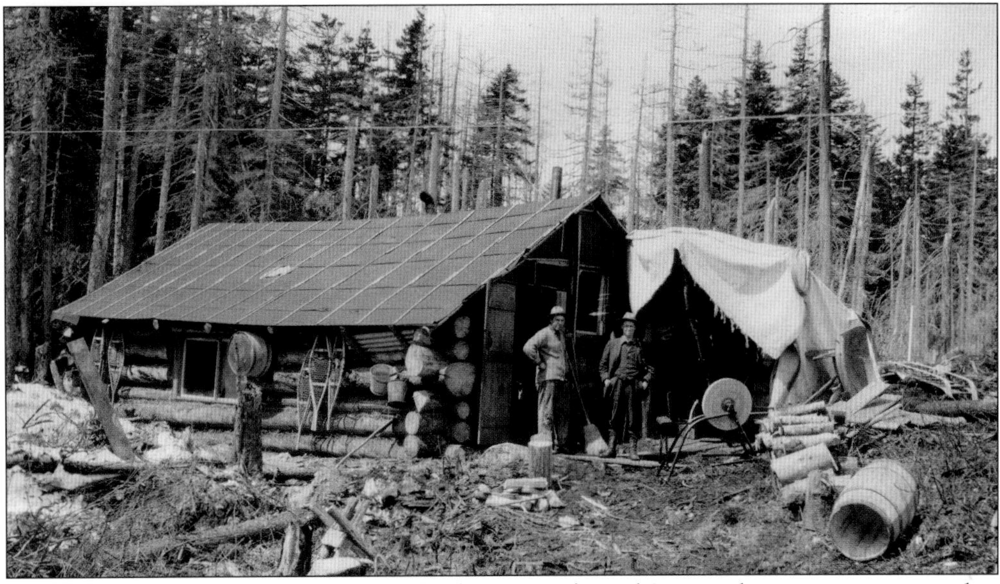

During the 1911–1912 streamflow study by the US Geological Survey, there were two camps that housed the men who monitored the stream gauging stations. One was at Stillwater, and the other was north of Camp 21 at Shoal Pond. Seen here in 1912, the Shoal Pond Camp was a typical 1900s backcountry cabin. Take note of the grinding wheel. (Courtesy of the National Archives & Records Administration.)

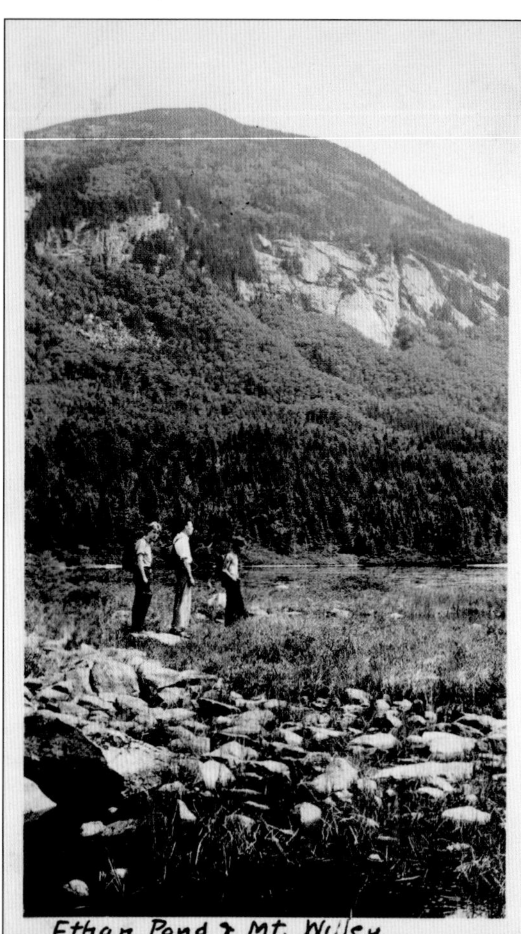

Camp 21A was on the outer edge of East Branch & Lincoln Railroad territory in the Shoal Pond region. With this camp, Henry's woodsmen were able to cut the mountainsides of Mount Field and Mount Willey. Seen here is Mount Willey and Ethan Pond in 1936, some 20 years after the area was logged. (Courtesy of the Appalachian Mountain Club Library & Archives.)

This April 1912 photograph showing duff burnt from under stumps in the Burnt Brook (North Fork of the East Branch of the Pemigewasset River) drainage shows the devastation from forest fire. In addition to the flow-measurement gauging station on Burnt Brook, the US Geological Survey placed nine rain gauges and 18 snow gauges in the Burnt Brook drainage during the 1911–1912 study. (Courtesy of the National Archives & Records Administration.)

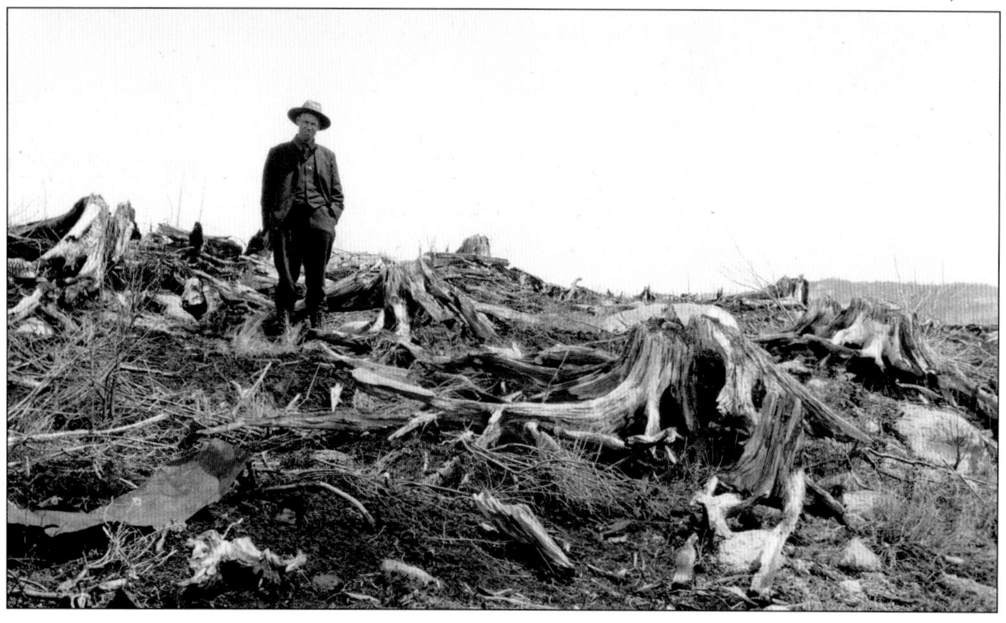

Five

North Fork Branch

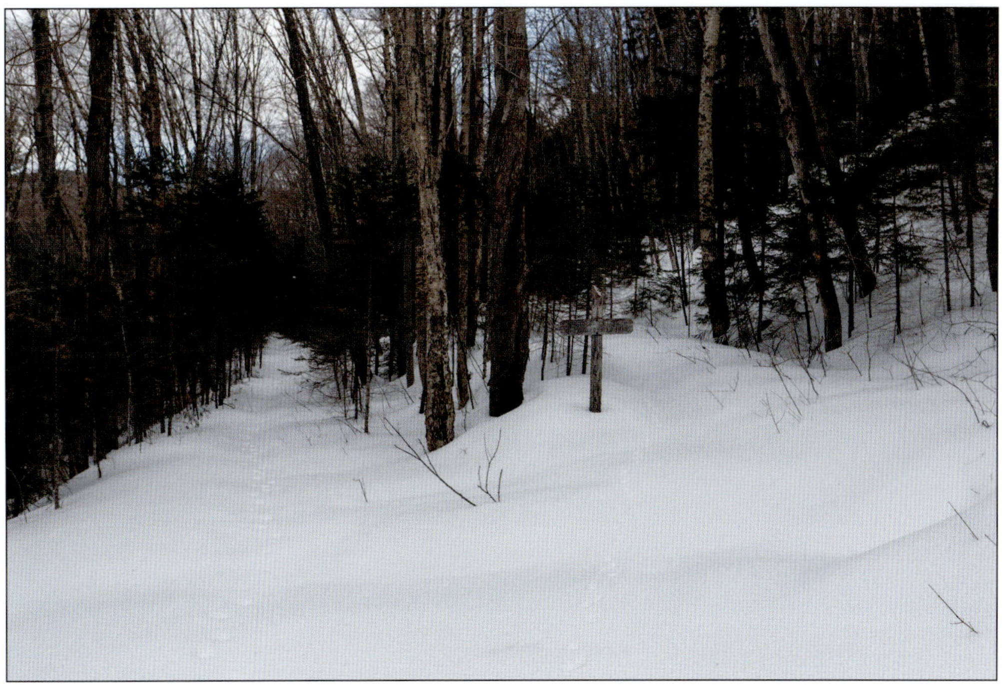

The North Fork Branch of the East Branch & Lincoln Railroad began off the mainline at today's junction of the Thoreau Falls Trail (left) and Wilderness Trail (right, to Stillwater) at North Fork Junction. Including spur lines and sidings, this branch was roughly four and a half miles long. With the exception of a short section of trail, the Thoreau Falls Trail follows 2.1 miles of the old railroad bed. (Author's collection.)

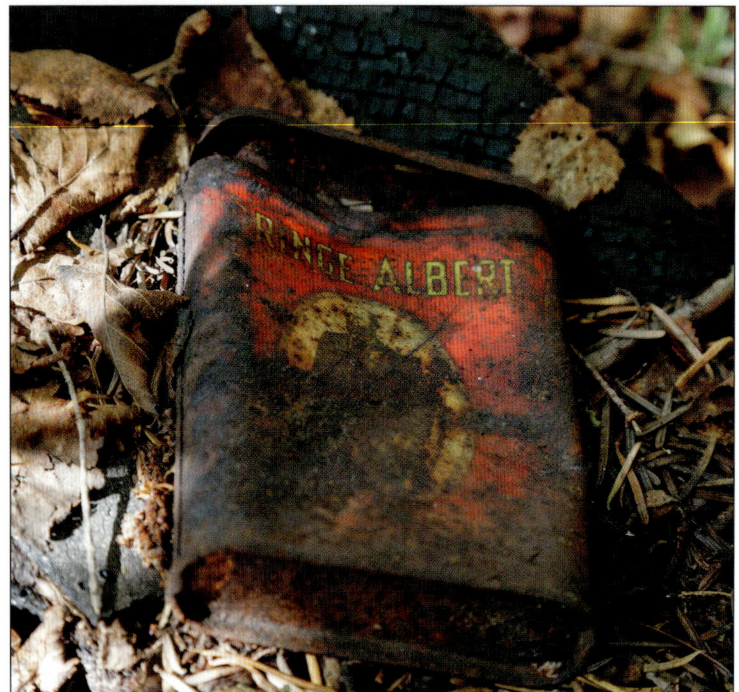

Tobacco was widely used among the logging railroads in the White Mountains. Prince Albert tobacco, an American brand made public in 1907 by R.J. Reynolds Tobacco Company, seemed to be the most popular brand among the pipe smoking woodsmen who worked in the East Branch & Lincoln Railroad country. (Author's collection.)

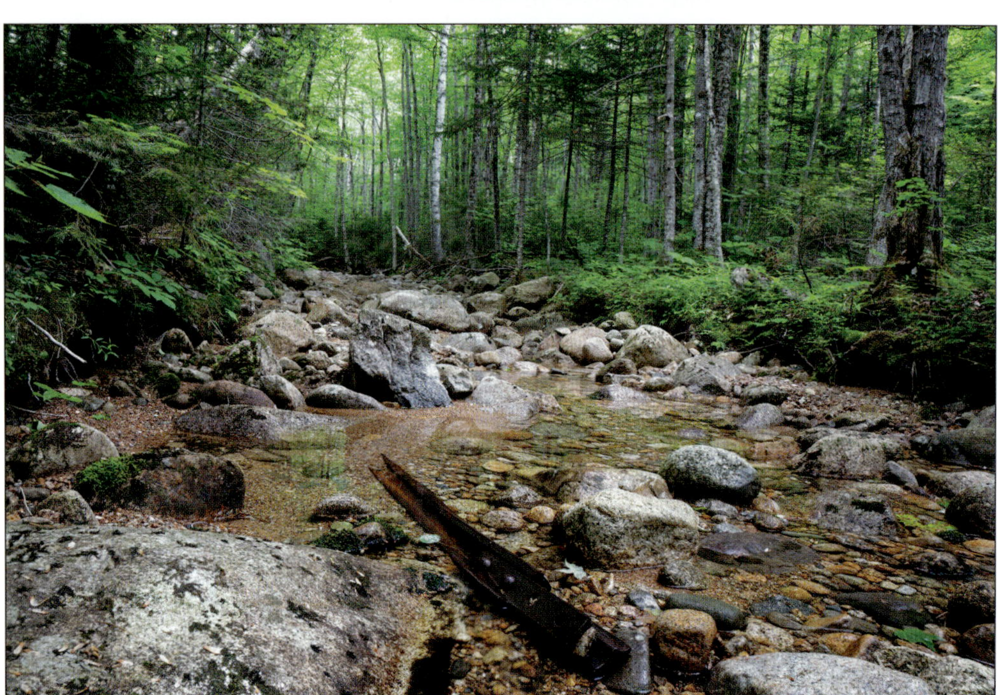

Just south of the North Fork Junction trestle, two spur lines branched off the North Fork Branch. The first one was a short line that traveled up this rocky brook bed. It may or may not have crossed the East Branch of the Pemigewasset River above the North Fork trestle. Flooding from Tropical Storm Irene covered up this piece of railroad track and other artifacts along this spur. (Author's collection.)

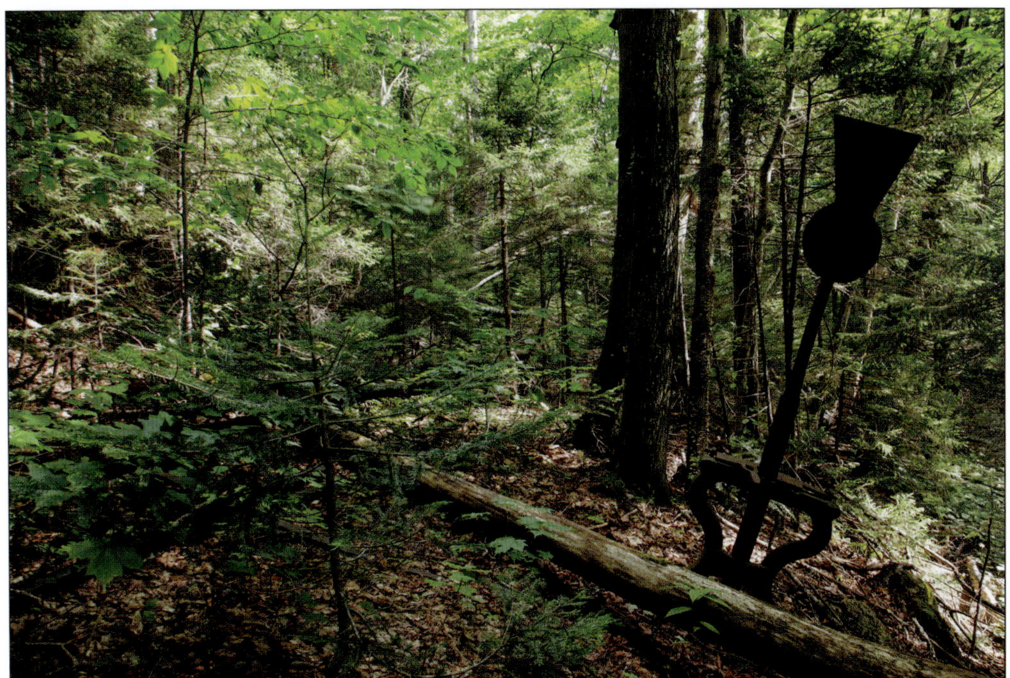

The second spur line branched off the North Fork Branch just north of the first one. It traveled northwest off the mainline, crossing the East Branch of the Pemigewasset River just below the confluence of the North Fork and East Branches of the Pemigewasset River. It then traveled north alongside the North Fork of the East Branch of the Pemigewasset River for about three quarters of a mile, eventually ending in a landing/work area. The railroad track and two harp switch stands, protected artifacts, remain in place along this spur line. The landing/work area is now flooded. (Both, author's collection.)

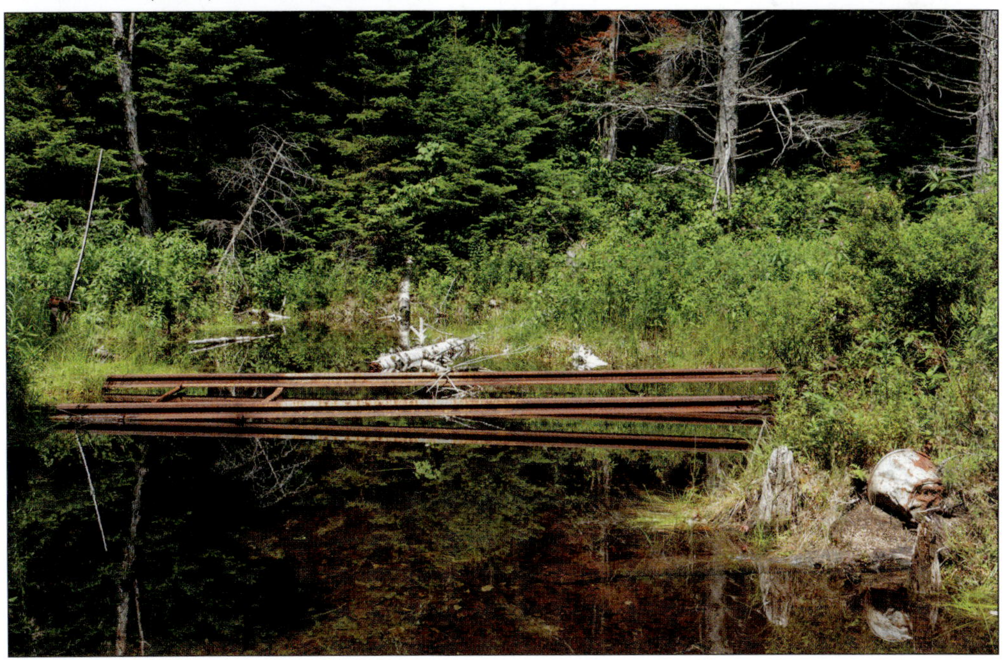

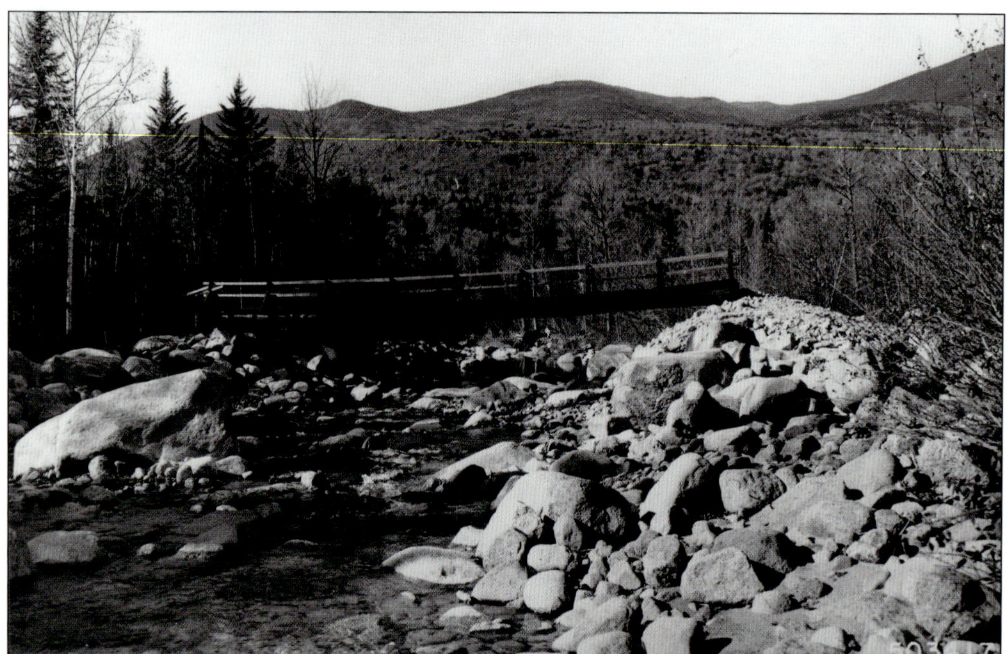

Including the trestles on the spur lines, there were at least six bridges and trestles on the North Fork Branch, four of them on the mainline. The first trestle on the mainline and the longest on this branch was just below where today's Thoreau Falls Trail footbridge crosses the East Branch of the Pemigewasset River at North Fork Junction. These two photographs face downstream at the footbridge in October 1961 (above), around the time when it was built, and in 2011 (below), showing natural forest regeneration on the riverbank over a 50-year period. This bridge was damaged during Tropical Storm Irene in 2011. (Above, courtesy of the Forest History Society; below, author's collection.)

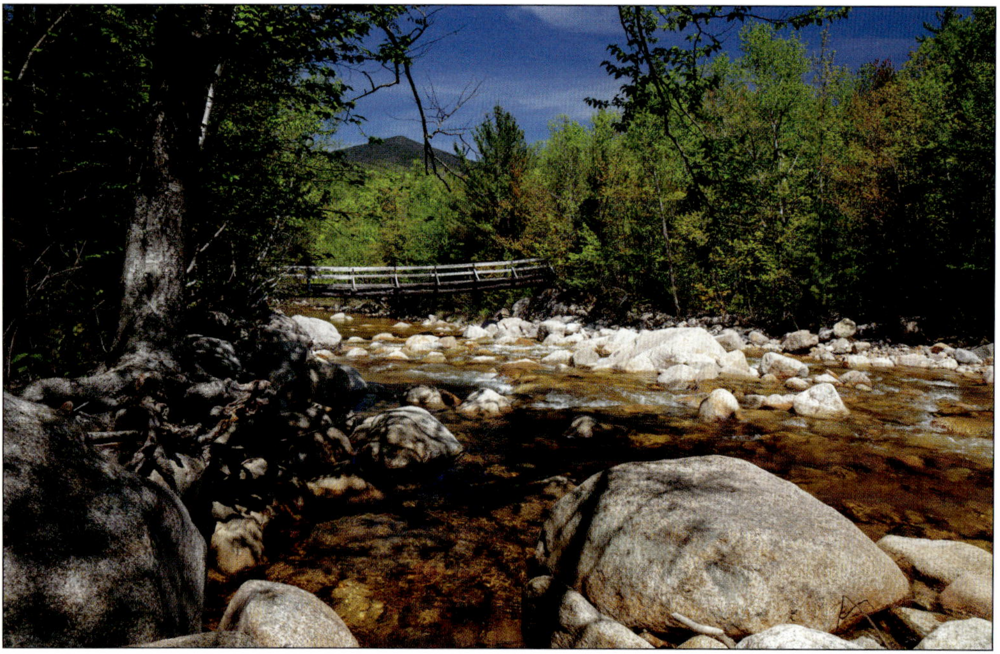

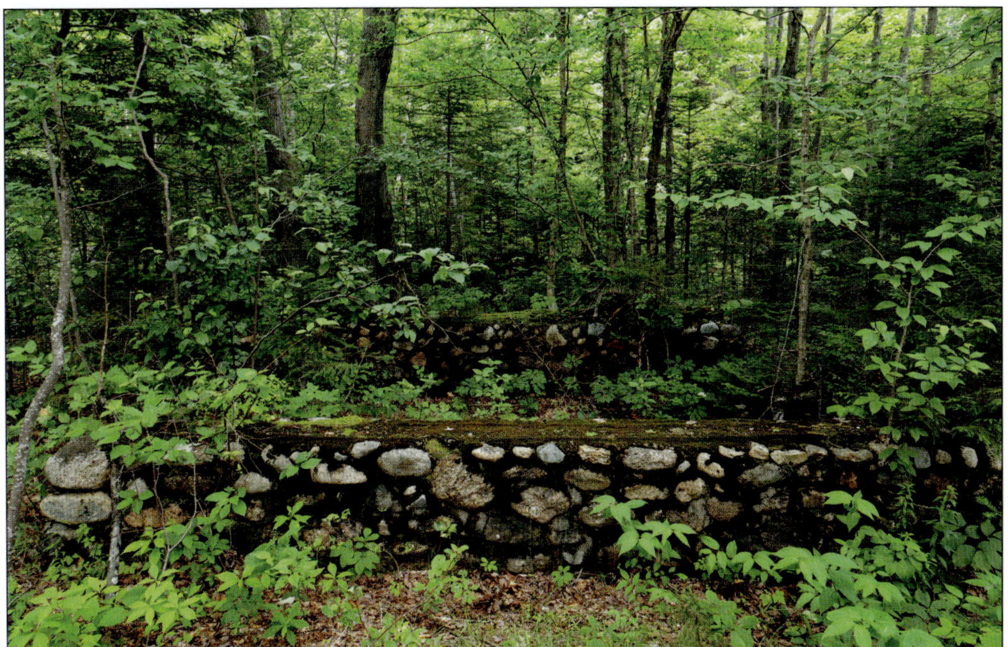

Remnants of the trestle that crossed the East Branch of the Pemigewasset River at today's Thoreau Falls Trail footbridge site can still be found on both sides of the river. These stone abutments are just downstream from the footbridge on the north side of the river. (Author's collection.)

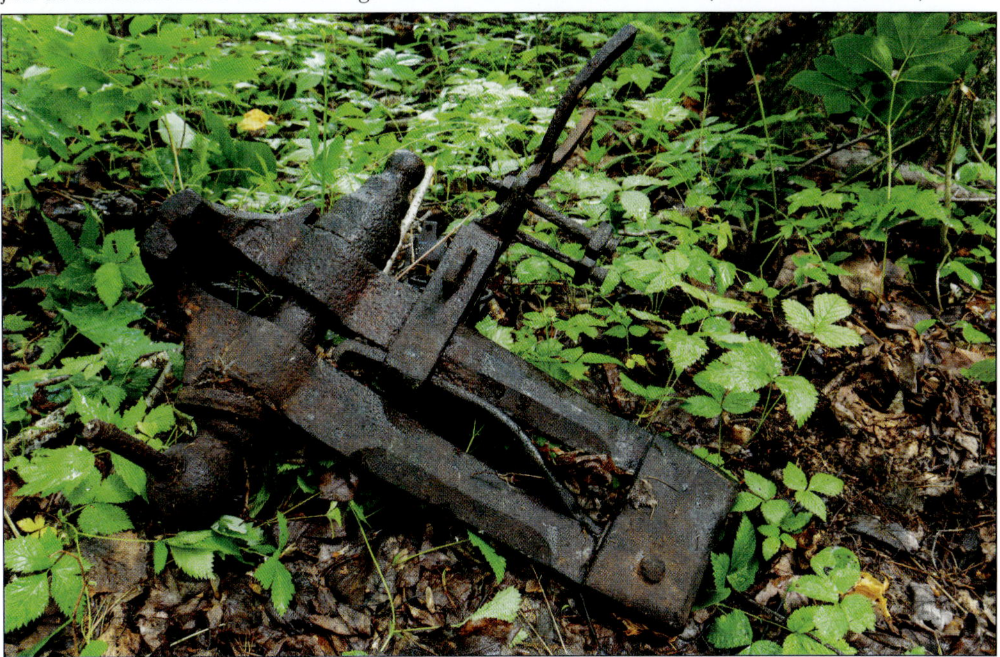

There were three rail-side logging camps located along the North Fork Branch: Camp 22, "New" Camp 22, and Camp 23. There were also two mountain camps: Camps 22A and 23A, off this branch that housed choppers high on the mountainside of Mount Bond. The rail-side camps had blacksmith shops; this old vise at Camp 22 was one of the tools used by the blacksmiths. (Author's collection.)

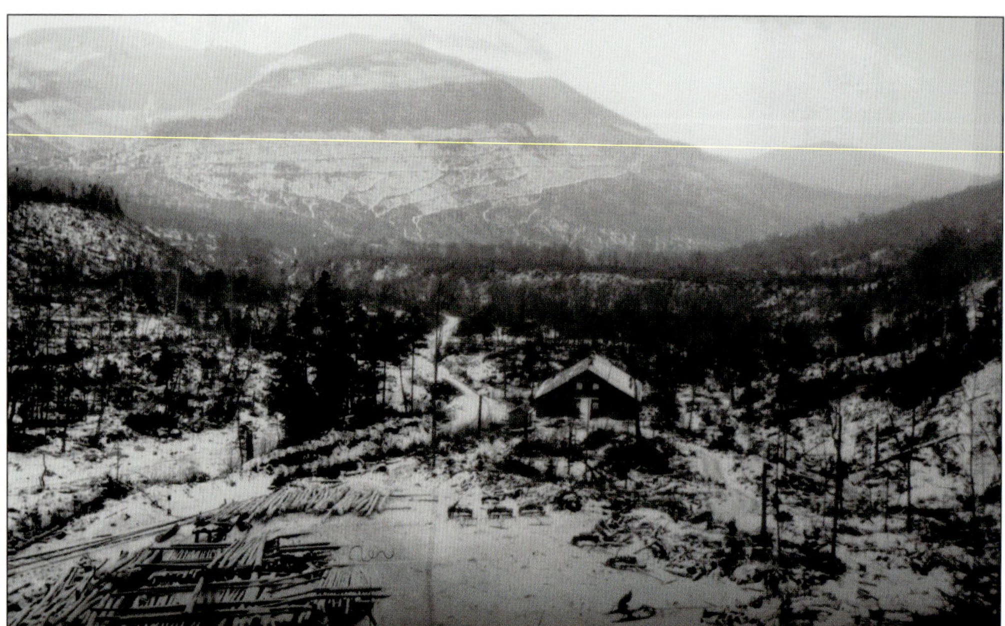

This 1928 photograph looking south from New Camp 22 shows the maze of sled roads on the side of Mount Hancock. Teamsters and their horse teams used these sled roads, mostly during the winter months, to drag logs off the mountainsides down to the log landings along the railroad. The men responsible for cutting these roads were referred to as "swampers." The log landing for this logging camp is in the foreground, and the short bridge that crossed the North Fork of the East Branch of the Pemigewasset River can be seen behind what looks to be the horse barn. Today, the artifact below marks the location of this forgotten camp. (Above, courtesy of the Upper Pemigewasset Historical Society; below, author's collection.)

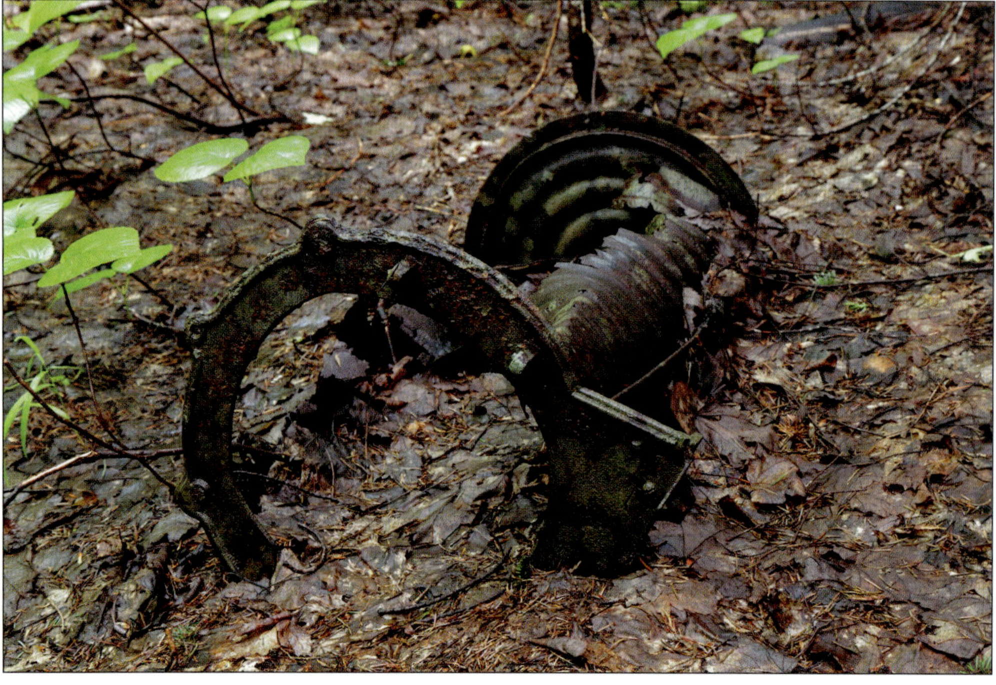

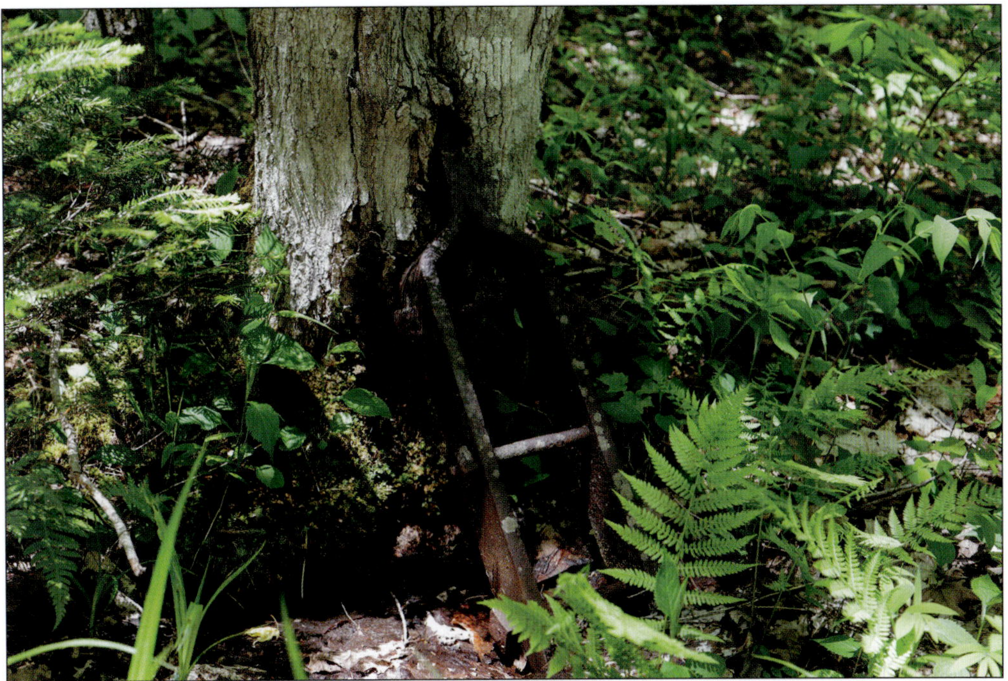

Log cars on the East Branch & Lincoln Railroad used a link-and-pin coupler system to connect the cars to one another. Once loaded, a "reach" (a spruce beam) would be used to connect the loaded log cars. This metal bracket was bolted to each end of the reach and was anchored into the link-and-pin coupler pocket with an iron pin. (Author's collection.)

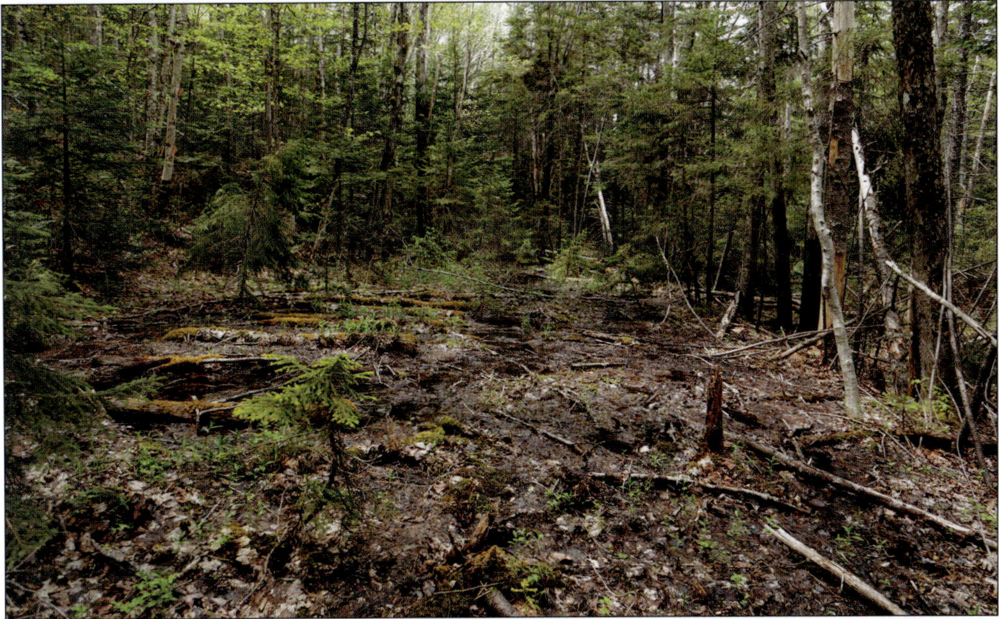

A spur line began off the mainline just north of Jumping Brook. It crossed the North Fork of the East Branch of the Pemigewasset River and traveled a short distance on the east side of the river, eventually ending at a landing/work area. Two sections of track were on this spur, and near the end of it, railroad ties are still visible in this wet area. (Author's collection.)

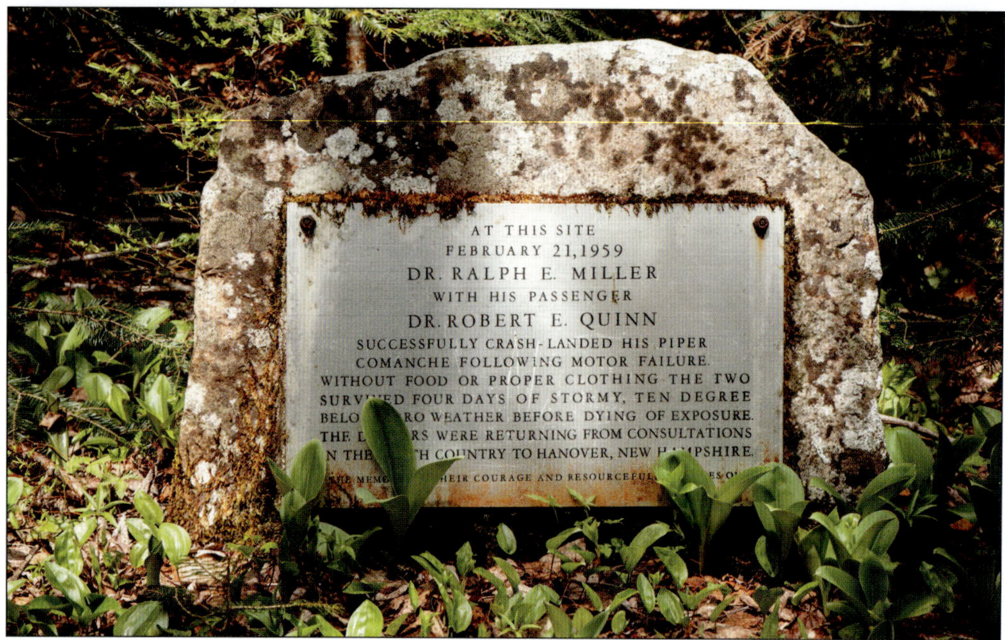

On February 21, 1959, a Piper Comanche airplane took off from the Berlin, New Hampshire, airport destined for Lebanon, New Hampshire. Dr. Ralph E. Miller and his passenger, Dr. Robert E. Quinn, successfully crash-landed in a remote area of the Pemigewasset Wilderness near New Camp 22 on the abandoned North Fork Branch of the East Branch & Lincoln Railroad. With medical supplies, they were able to build snowshoes out of tree branches. They attempted to follow the railroad bed until it appeared to abruptly end, so they turned around and went back to the plane. Unknown to them, the spot where they turned back was only a short distance from the US Forest Service's fully supplied North Fork Cabin. The doctors survived for four days before dying of exposure. (Both, author's collection.)

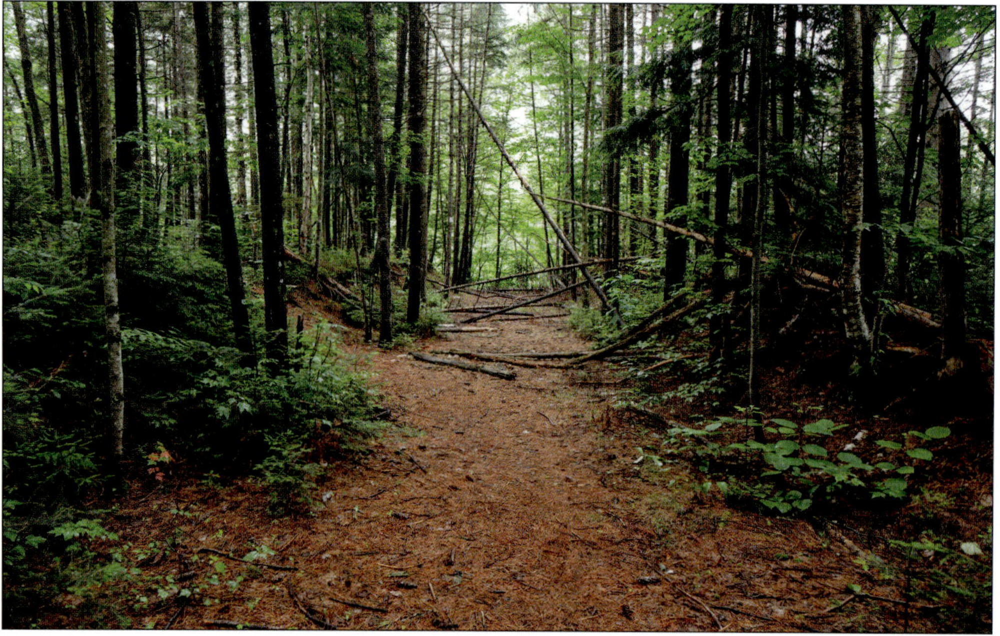

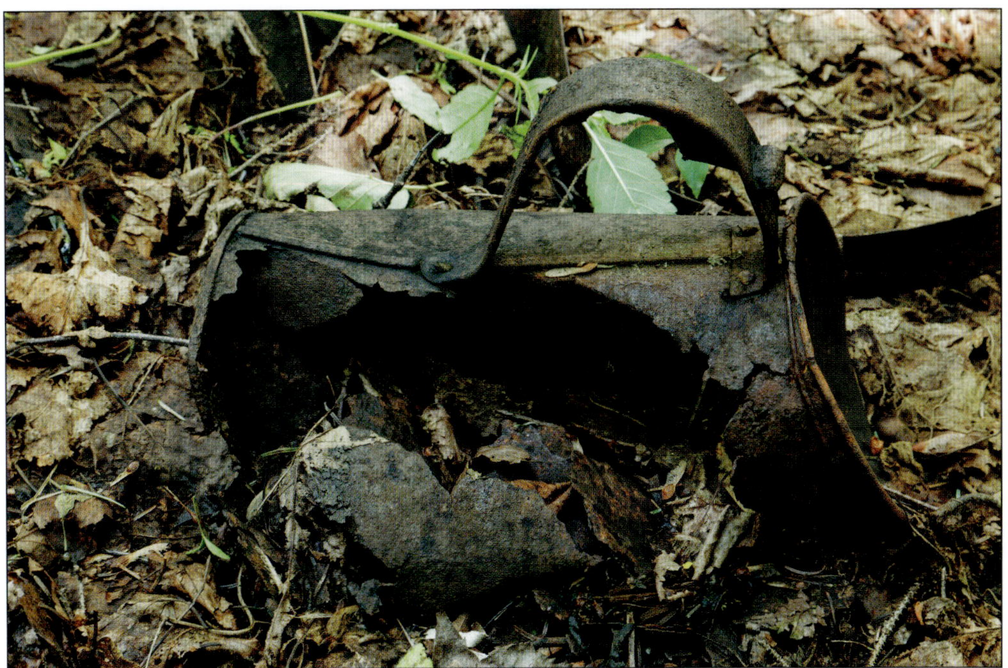

Camp 23 was located near the end of the North Fork Branch of the East Branch & Lincoln Railroad. It was one of the larger logging camps along the railroad. In February 1923, the Lynn, Massachusetts, chamber of commerce held its first annual winter outing at the Lincoln Hotel. During their stay in Lincoln, an excursion train took them into Lincoln Woods to Camp 23 where they were served hot coffee, doughnuts, and desserts. Today, typical items of a logging camp are scattered around the old camp site. Tools of the woodsmen can still be found along the sled roads that traveled from this camp to the mountainsides of Mount Bond and Mount Guyot. (Both, author's collection.)

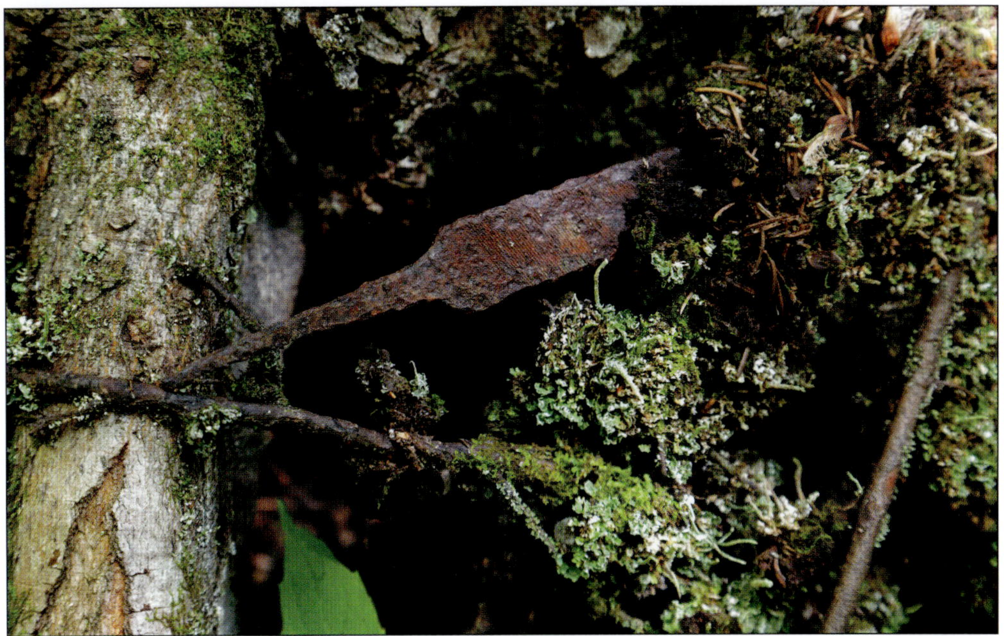

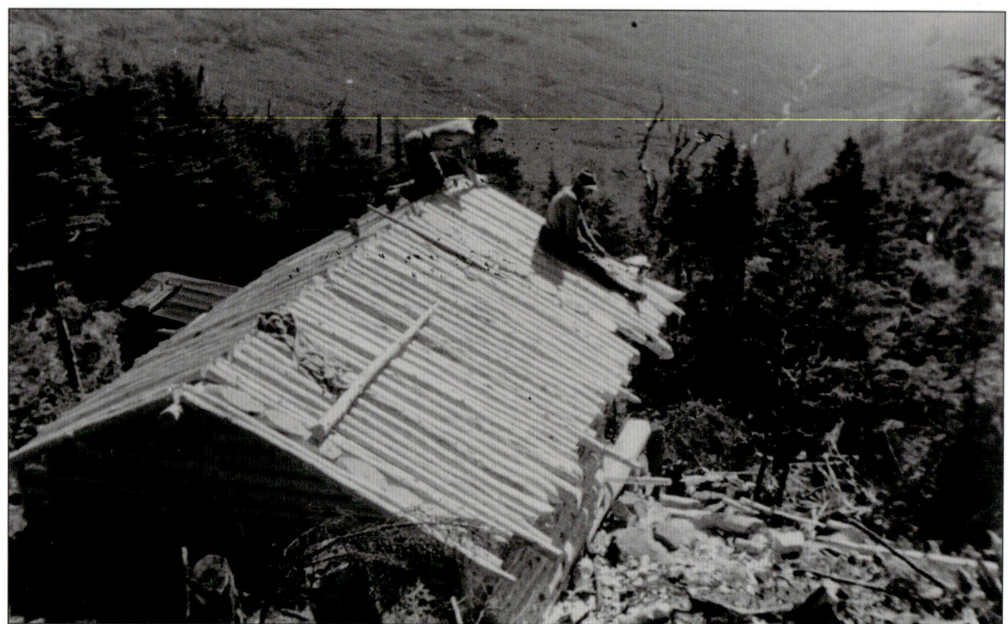

In this 1939 photograph of the building of Guyot Shelter, the Jumping Brook drainage on the eastern slopes of Mount Guyot can be seen in the background. The eastern slopes of Mount Guyot and Mount Bond were logged from the three rail-side camps on the North Fork Branch: Camp 22, New Camp 22, and Camp 23. (Courtesy of the Appalachian Mountain Club Library & Archives.)

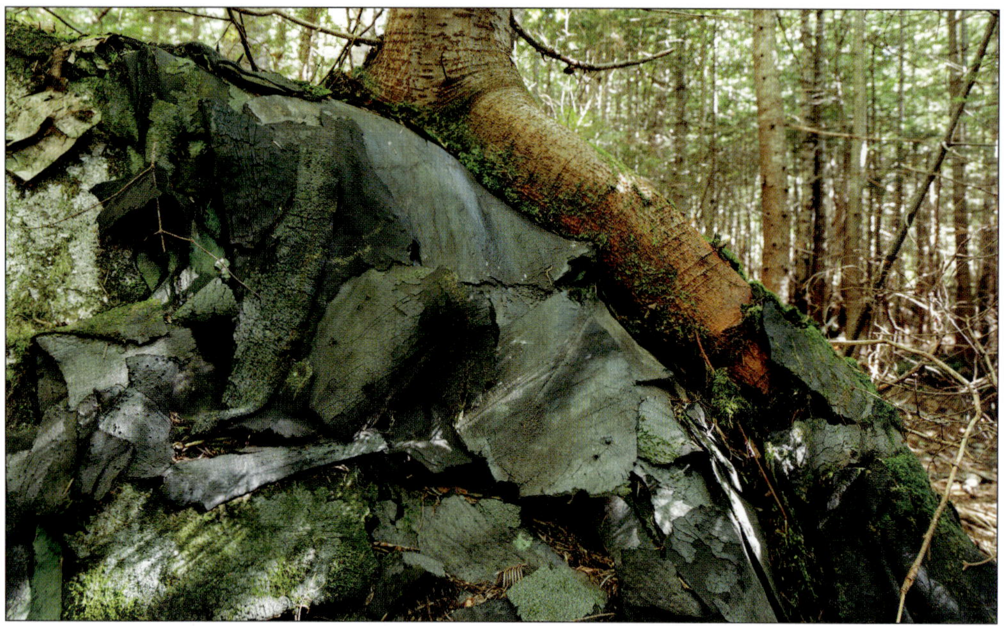

There were two mountain camps associated with the rail-side camps on the North Fork Branch: Camp 22A and Camp 23A. Built in the fall of 1925, Camp 23A, seen here, housed choppers from logging Camps 22 and 23. The mountain camps were small dwellings, usually made of logs, and when the woodsmen were done with them, they would burn them down to discourage further usage of them. (Author's collection.)

Six

Cedar Brook Branch

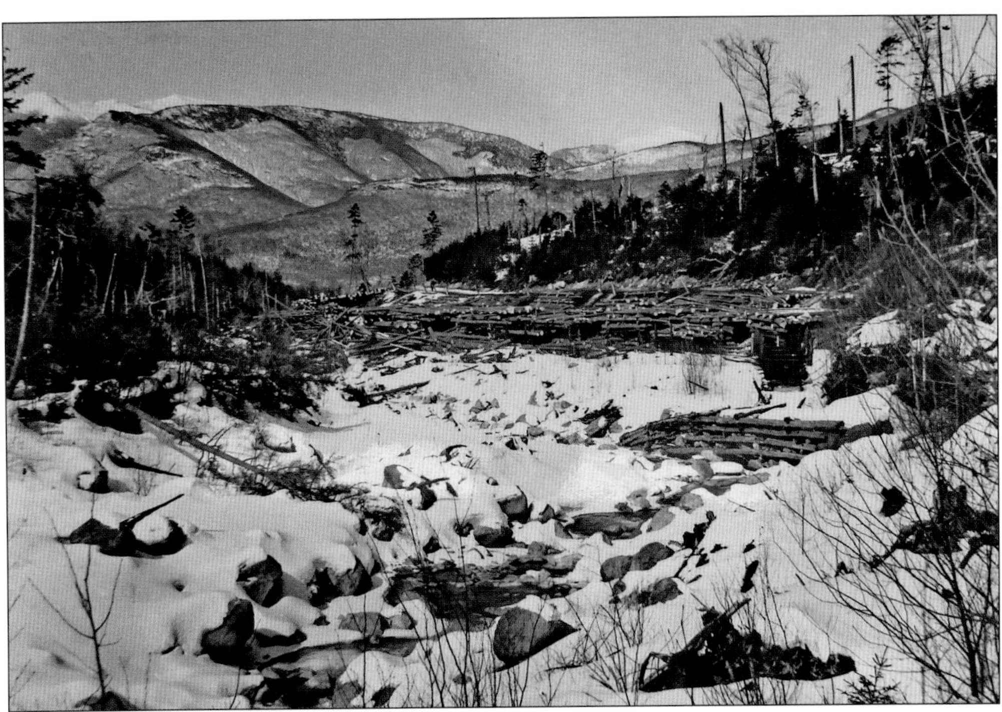

During the Parker-Young Company years in 1928, a two-mile branch of the railroad was built into the Cedar Brook valley. Three logging camps were established in the valley during the 1930s. Camp 24 was a rail-side camp, and Camps 24A and 24B were mountain camps located off the railroad. This undated photograph shows the log landing at the end of the Cedar Brook Branch. (Courtesy of the Upper Pemigewasset Historical Society.)

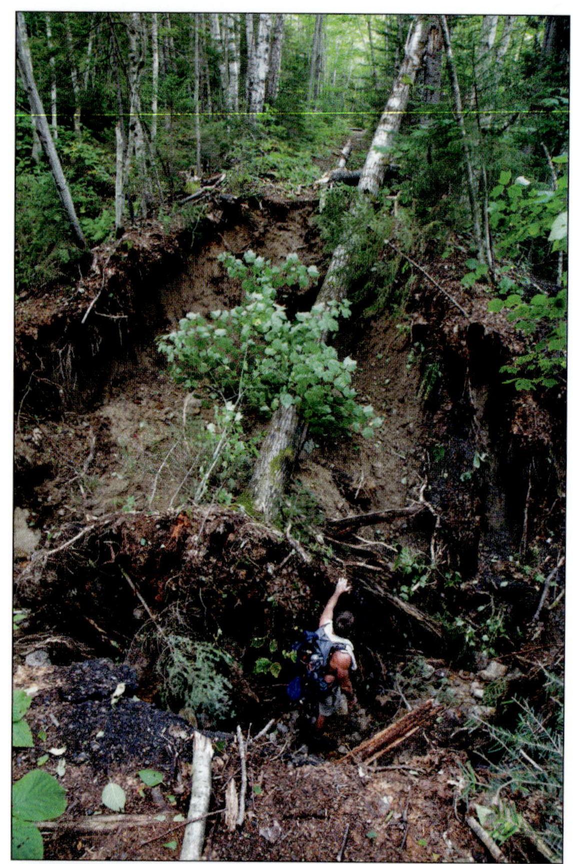

The Cedar Brook Branch began off the mainline at the southern end of trestle No. 17 (see page 59), near Camp 17, and traveled southwest into the Cedar Brook valley. Today's Wilderness Trail follows the lower section of the old railroad bed (from the trestle No. 17 site to its junction with the Pemi East Side), and the Cedar Brook Trail from its junction with the Pemi East Trail follows the top section. In 2011, heavy rain from Tropical Storm Irene washed out a section of the railroad bed above Camp 17 and uncovered artifacts (below) from a previously unknown historical site along the railroad. (Both, author's collection.)

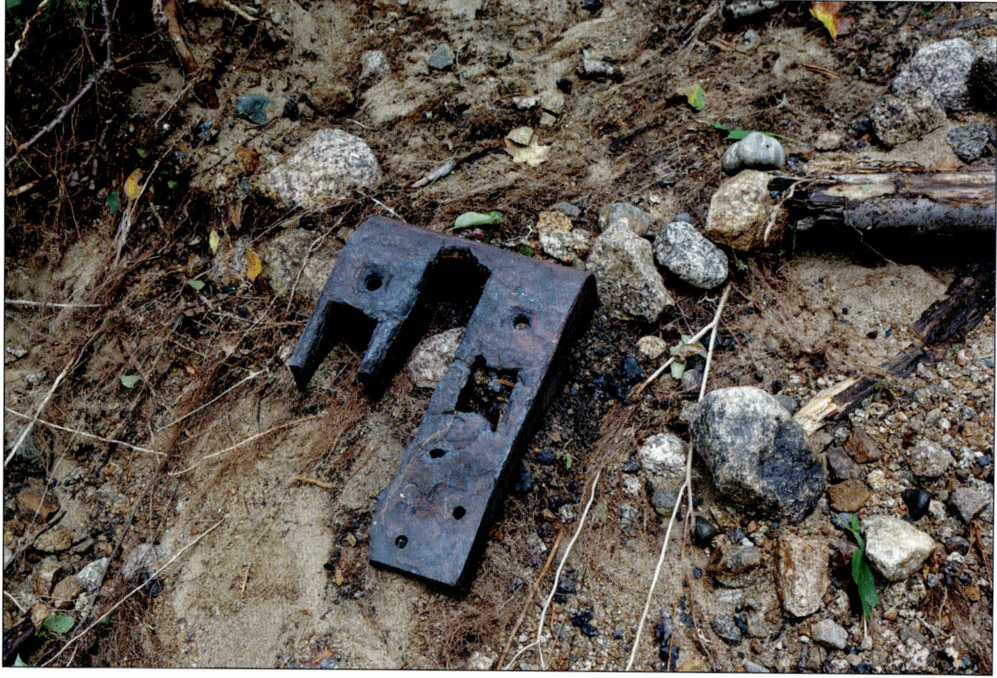

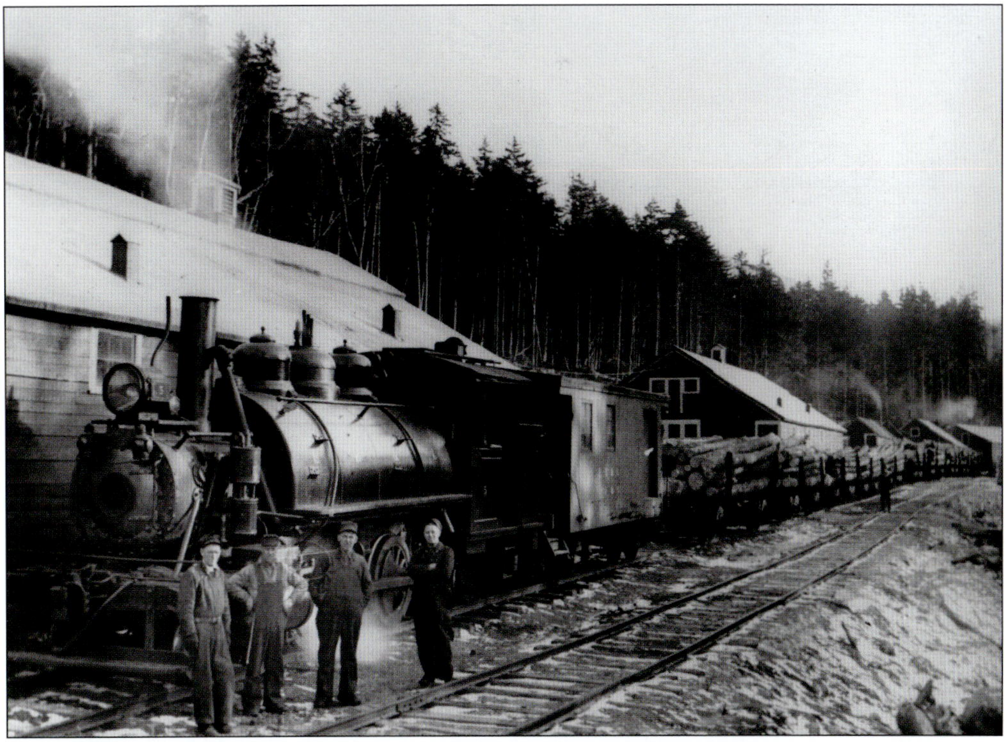

Operated during the Parker-Young era, Camp 24 was the largest logging camp along the East Branch & Lincoln Railroad, and at a seven percent grade, the Cedar Brook Branch had the steepest grade on the railroad. Seen here is the Baldwin No. 5 at Camp 24 with a full load of logs. The train crew are, from left to right, Ed Perry, Blaise Duguay, Louis Boyle, and Billy McGee. The blacksmith forge table below is one of the many remnants of Camp 24. (Above, courtesy of the Upper Pemigewasset Historical Society; below, author's collection.)

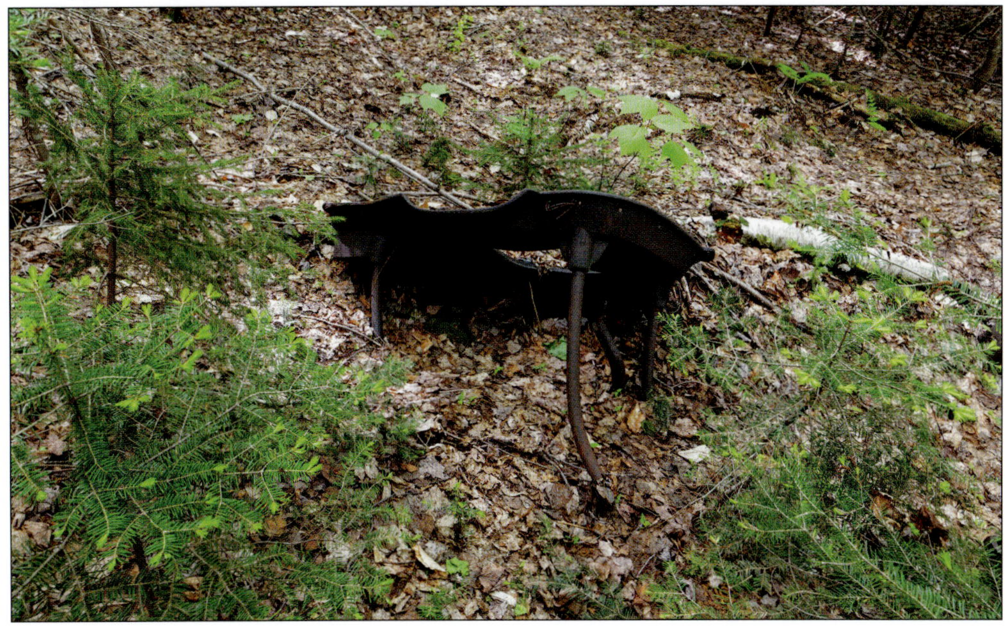

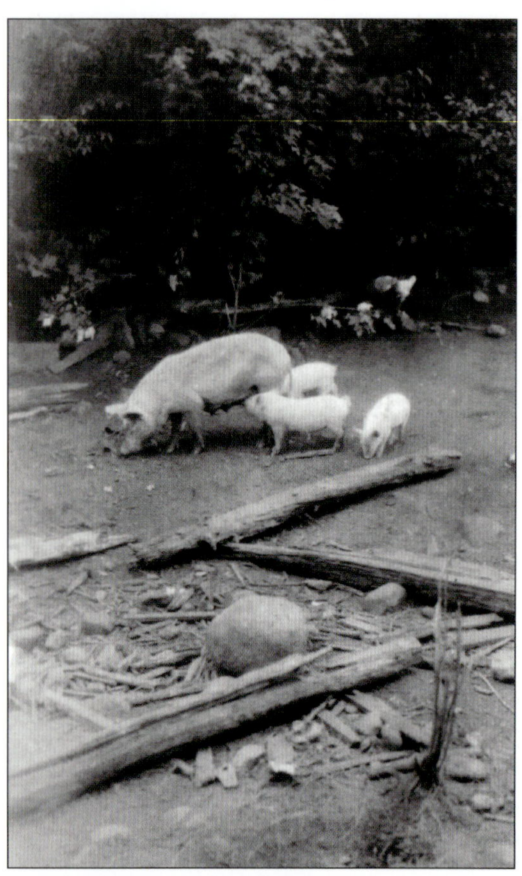

Many of the logging camps along the East Branch & Lincoln Railroad raised pigs to supply fresh pork for meals for the woodsmen. Rule 46 on J.E. Henry and Sons' rules and regulations applied to the throwing of food and unnecessary loud talk while eating meals at the table. Any woodsmen caught doing either would be fined. (Courtesy of the Appalachian Mountain Club Library & Archives.)

Wet areas along the sled roads were corduroyed with small logs laid crossways. The corduroyed sections acted like a bridge and made it possible for the teamsters and their horse teams to drag loaded bobsleds across the wet area down to the log landings that lined the railroad bed. (Author's collection.)

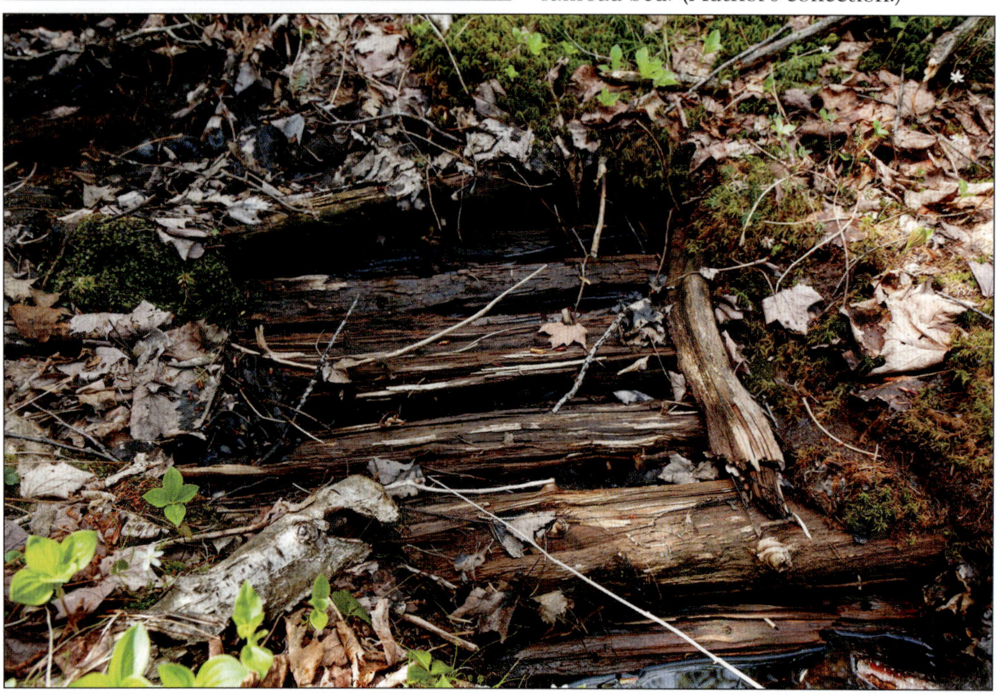

Built in 1930, little remains of Camp 24A. This rusted can once contained Flit, an insecticide product mainly used for killing flies and mosquitoes. It also killed ants, bed bugs, fleas, lice, moths, and other insects, all of which were common in the logging camps. In the 1930s, Flit powder was promoted as being the best ever developed for crawling insects and fleas on dogs. (Author's collection.)

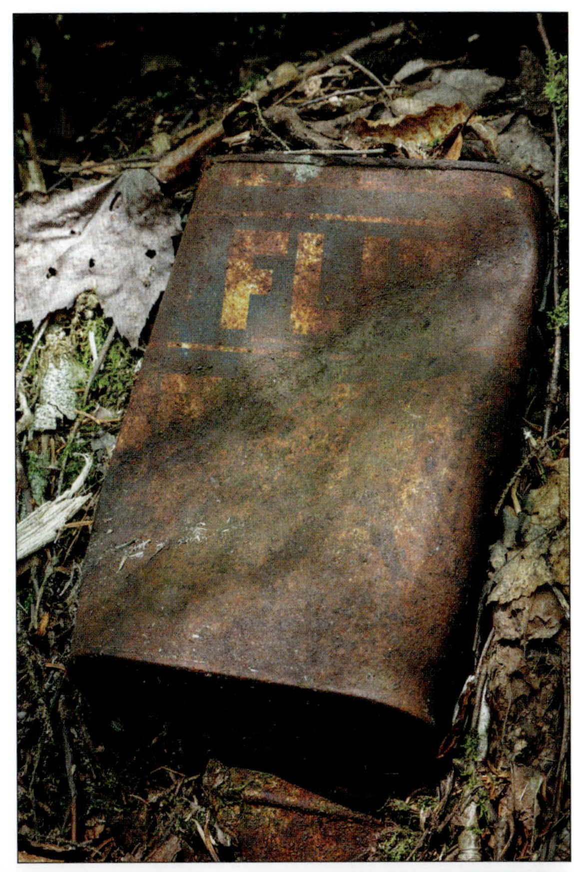

Built in 1934, Camp 24B, located on the eastern slopes of the Hitchcock Mountain Range, was the second mountain camp associated with Camp 24 in the Cedar Brook valley. Living in logging camps for months at a time in Lincoln Woods meant the woodsmen had to sometimes invent things. It is unknown what this tub with holes was used for. (Author's collection.)

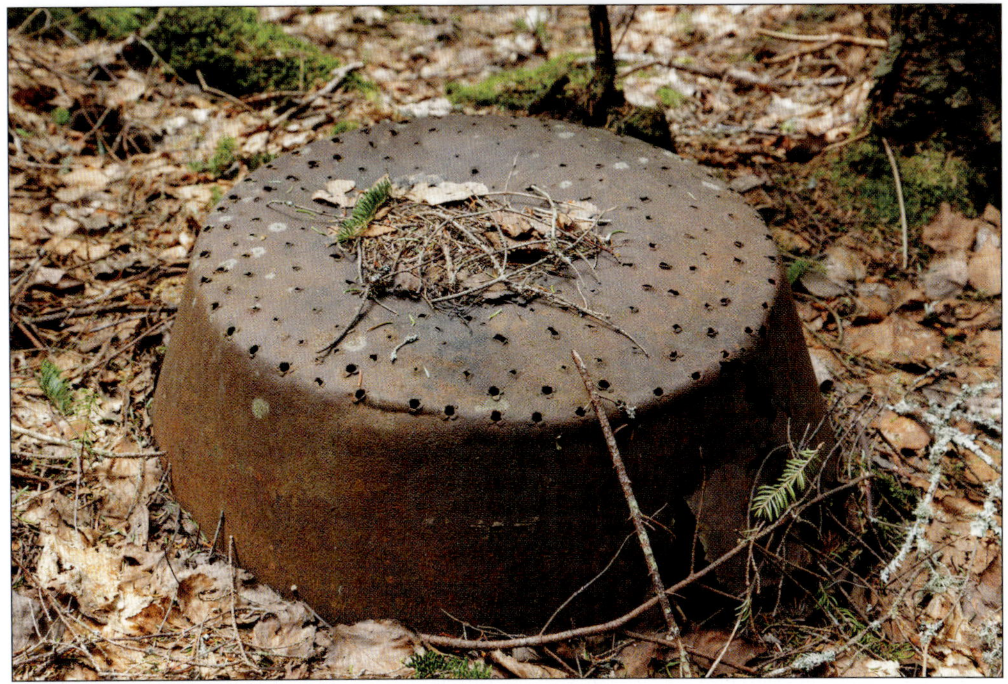

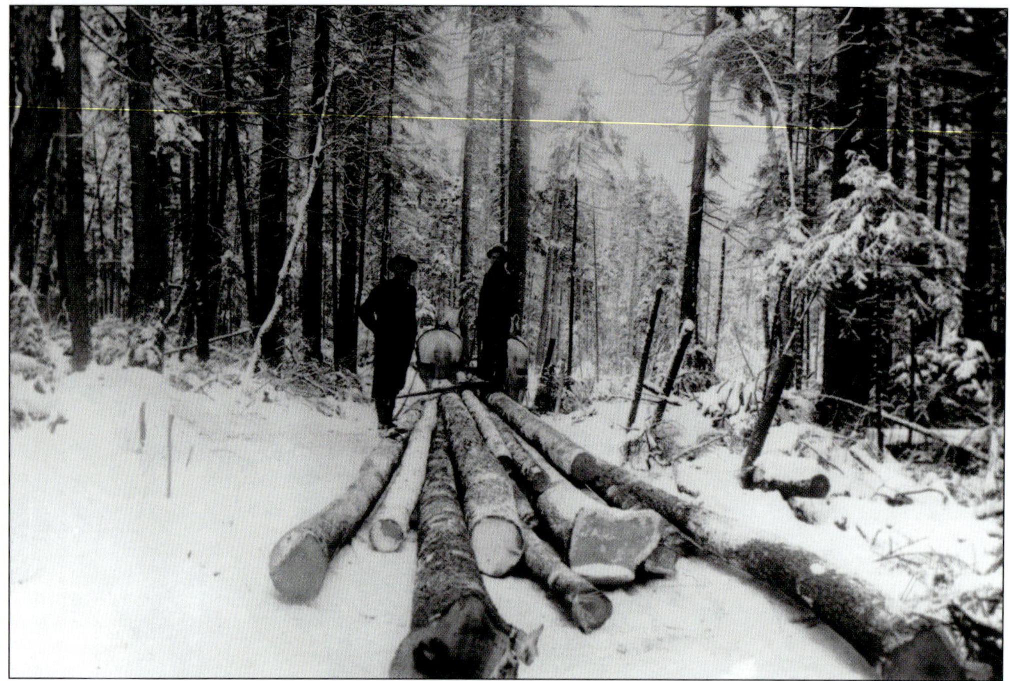

Seen here in an undated photograph is Billy Boyle and a teamster on one of the many sled roads in the Cedar Brook valley. This load of spruce is on its way to the log landing at Camp 24. Once at the landing, the logs were rolled onto the railroad log cars and brought to the mill in Lincoln village. (Courtesy of the Upper Pemigewasset Historical Society.)

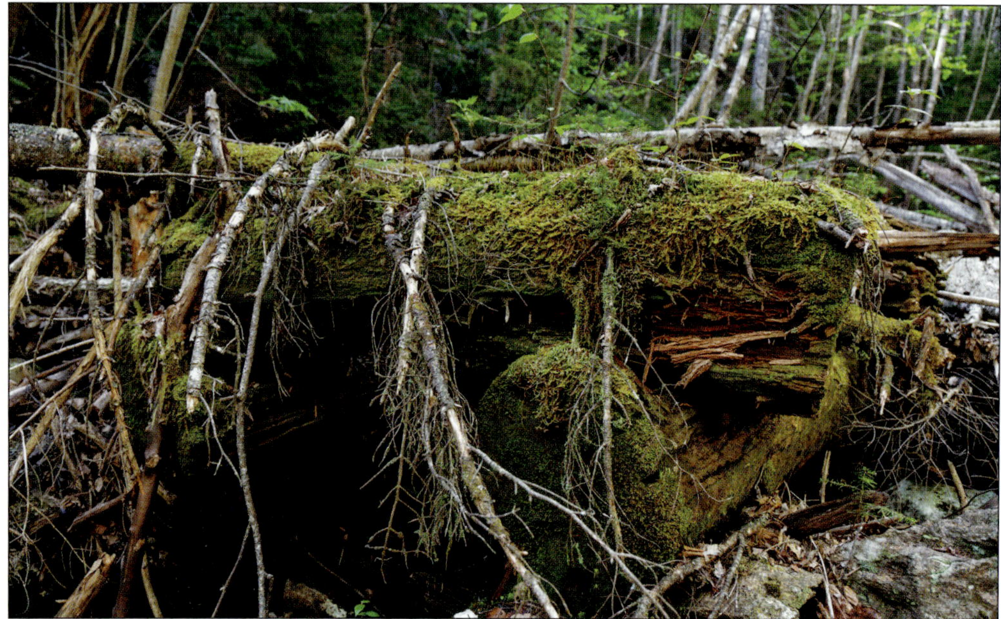

Logging operations went on in the Cedar Brook valley for almost 20 years before coming to an end in 1946. The track was torn up down to Camp 16 in 1946, and work began on the building of a truck road from Camp 8 to Camp 16. The Cedar Brook valley has since recovered from the logging, but evidence of the woodsmen still remains in the forest. (Author's collection.)

Seven

Henry's Woods

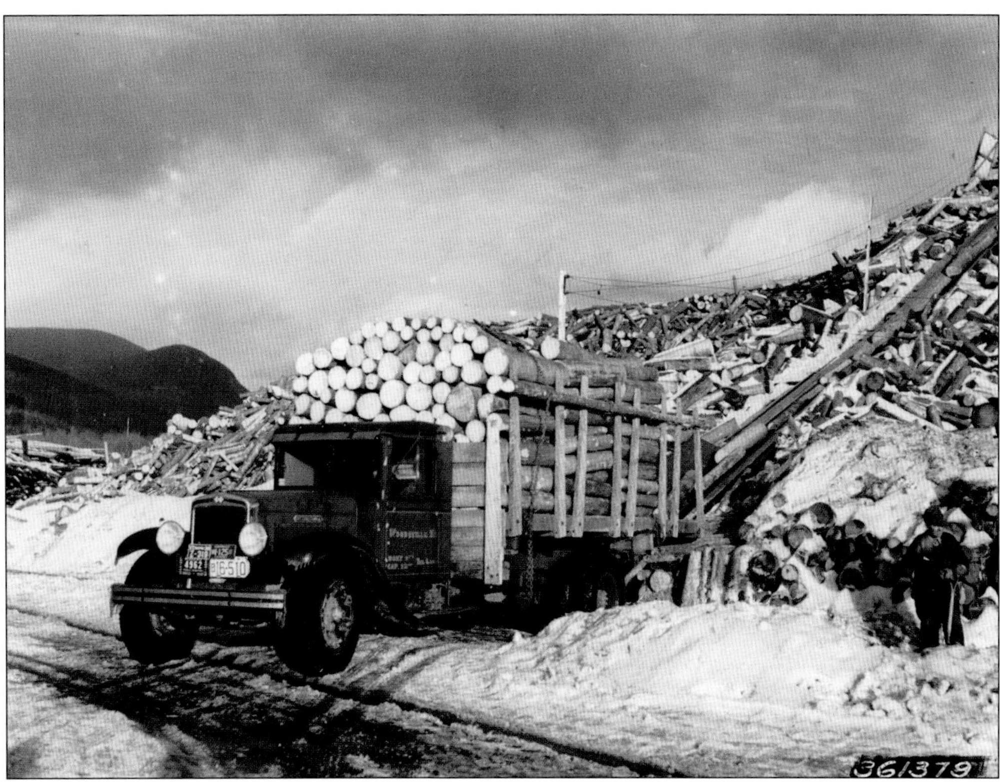

In 1936, under the Weeks Act of 1911, the US Forest Service purchased almost 70,000 acres of land in the East Branch watershed from the Parker-Young Company. In the agreement, Parker-Young retained cutting rights to some of the land for 20 years. By 1942, Parker-Young was starting to use trucks to haul pulpwood out of Lincoln Woods down to the mill in Lincoln village. (Courtesy of the National Archives & Records Administration.)

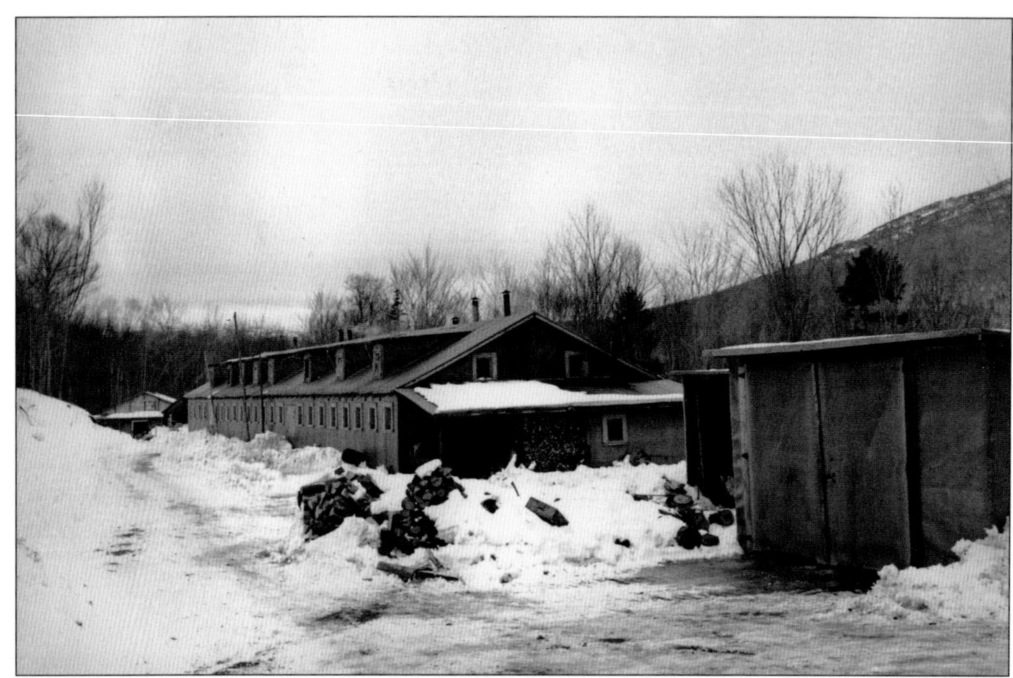

In 1946, the Parker-Young Company sold the mill and what was left of the East Branch & Lincoln Railroad to the Marcalus Manufacturing Company, which reorganized as the Franconia Paper Corporation in 1950. It established a logging camp on Black Mountain in the early 1950s, built a bridge across the Hancock Branch Brook, and trucked the spruce down to Lincoln mill. This camp operated for a few years, and ended up being the last logging operation in Lincoln Woods. Pictured here in 1952 are the bunkhouse (above) and the barn and blacksmith shop (below) at the Black Mountain Camp. (Both, courtesy of the Upper Pemigewasset Historical Society.)

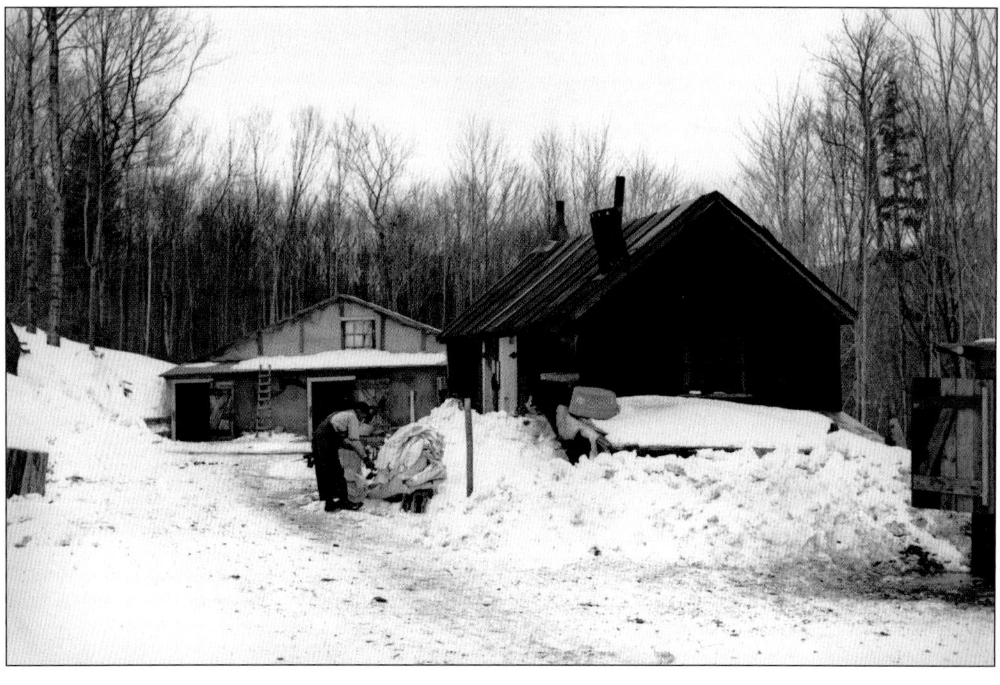

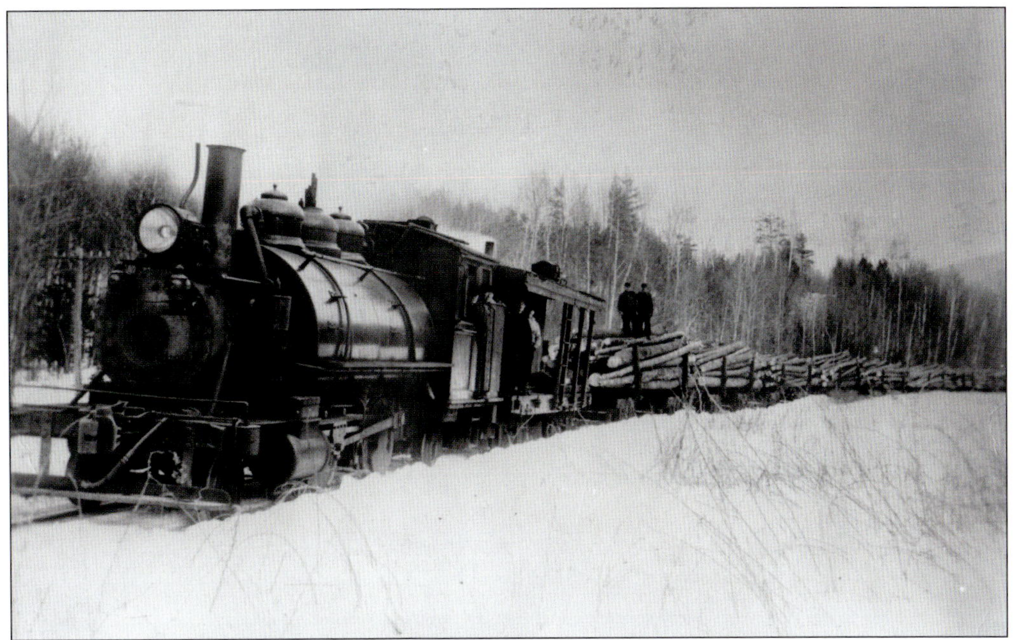

By 1947, trucks were the preferred transportation for hauling pulpwood out of Lincoln Woods, and by January 1948, only the yard track and the mainline to just above Camp 3 were still in place. The largest New England logging railroad ever in operation had come to an end. The Baldwin No. 5, seen here near Dam No. 1, now resides at Clark's Trading Post. (Courtesy of the Upper Pemigewasset Historical Society.)

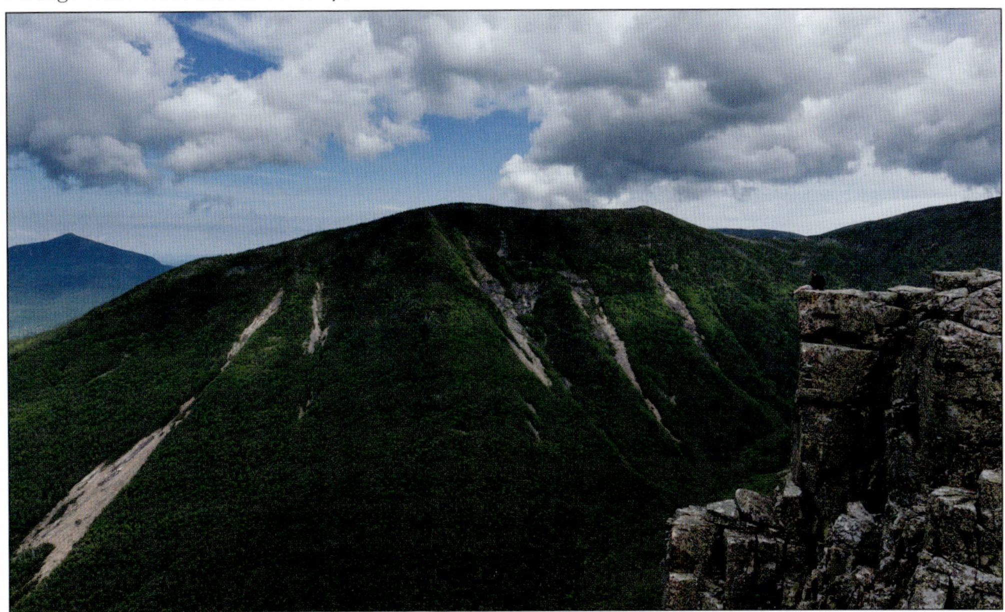

Before James E. Henry's logging railroad took over Lincoln Woods, farmers in the area referred to the land as "wilderness," but it did not have any official wilderness designation at the time. Today, 45,000 acres of this wilderness, the Pemigewasset Wilderness, is governed under the National Wilderness Preservation System and the Wilderness Act of 1964. It has the highest level of protection for federal lands. The serenity of Bondcliff is forever preserved. (Author's collection.)

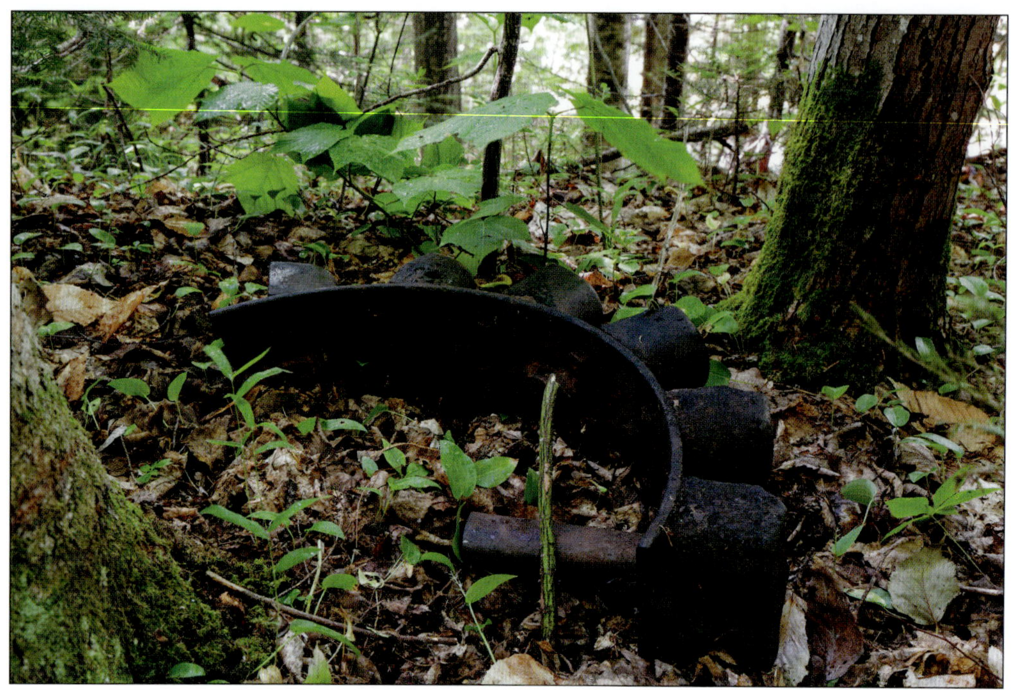

Most of the bottles, metal objects, and other railroad-related items that remain in East Branch & Lincoln Railroad territory today are protected artifacts. Help preserve our heritage and take only pictures. (Author's collection.)

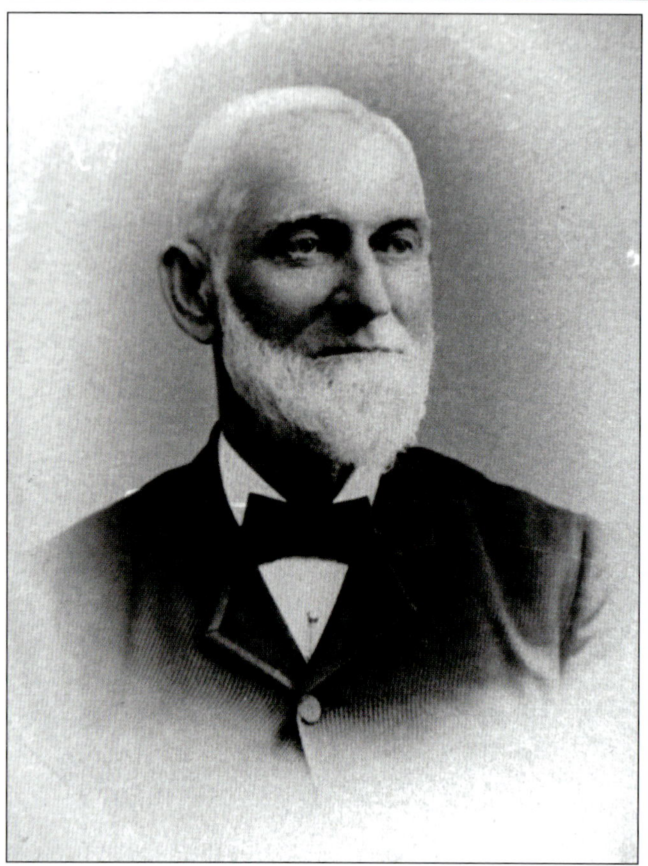

Today, Lincoln is the second-largest town by area in New Hampshire. The town celebrates its rich railroad and mill history in many ways, and James E. Henry's logging practices are used to educate the young and old about land conservation. However, Henry should not be seen only as a timber baron. He was an entrepreneur, and a good one at that. (Courtesy of Mike Dickerman.)

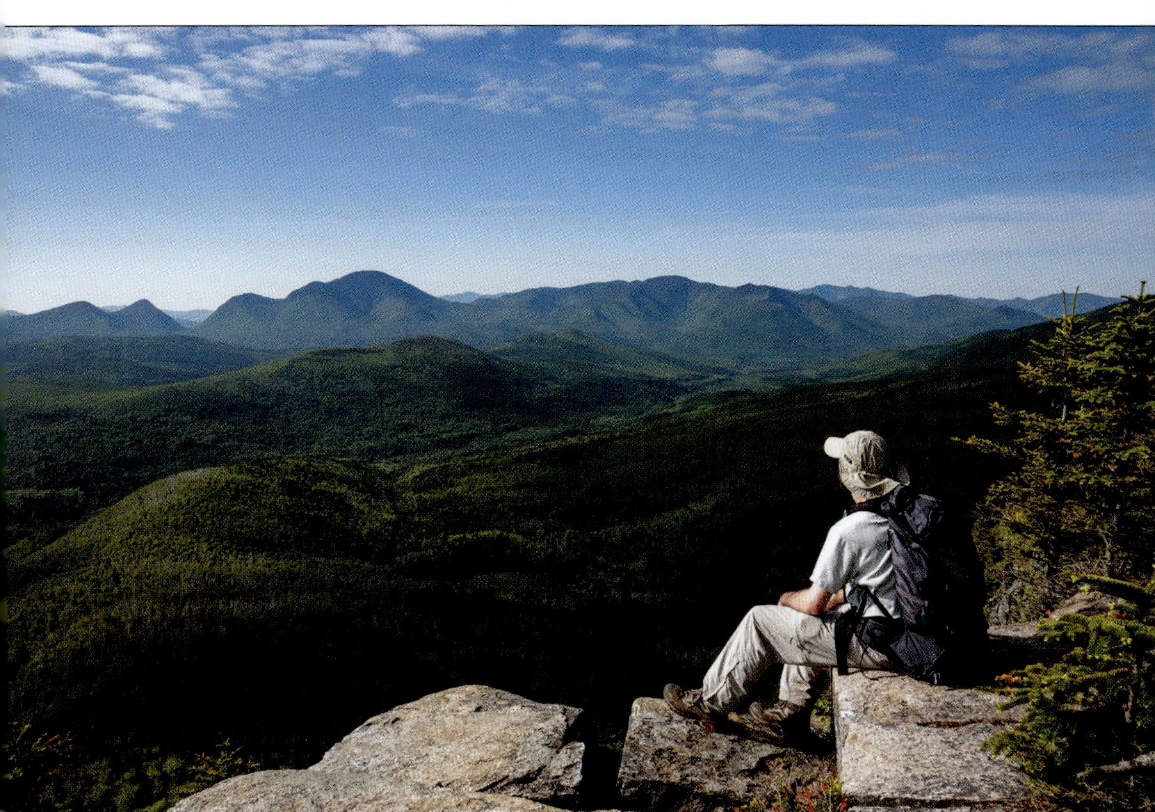

James Everell Henry will always be remembered as a timber baron. But because of his logging practices, one of the most successful pieces of conservation legislation in US history was signed into law in 1911 when Pres. William Taft signed the Weeks Act. Under the Weeks Act, the federal government was able to purchase private land in the eastern United States and maintain it as national forests. To date, the Weeks Act has protected over 20 million acres. Henry also, unknowingly, created one of the greatest trail systems in New England—the Pemigewasset Wilderness trail system. Almost every trail in this designated wilderness follows or utilizes sections of the East Branch & Lincoln Railroad. Today, these flat and wide trails provide easy hiking for all age groups. Would trails exist in the Pemigewasset Wilderness today if the East Branch & Lincoln Railroad did not travel deep into its regions looking for timber? It seems likely that without the railroad there would be far less trails in this wilderness. It will always be Henry's Woods. (Author's collection.)

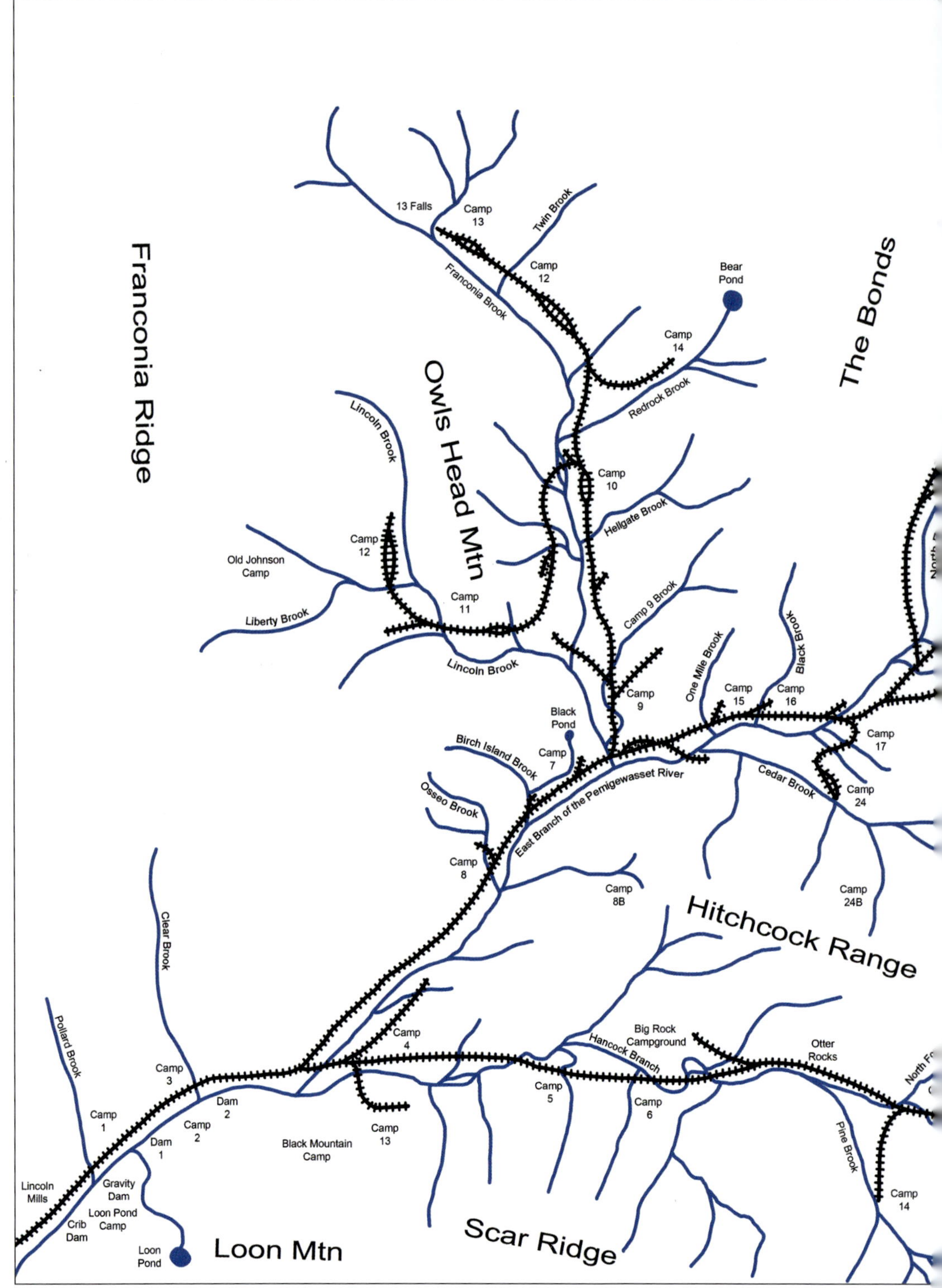

This map shows the numerous logging camps, branch lines, railroad sidings, and the general layout of the East Branch & Lincoln Railroad. Including the many railroad sidings and branch

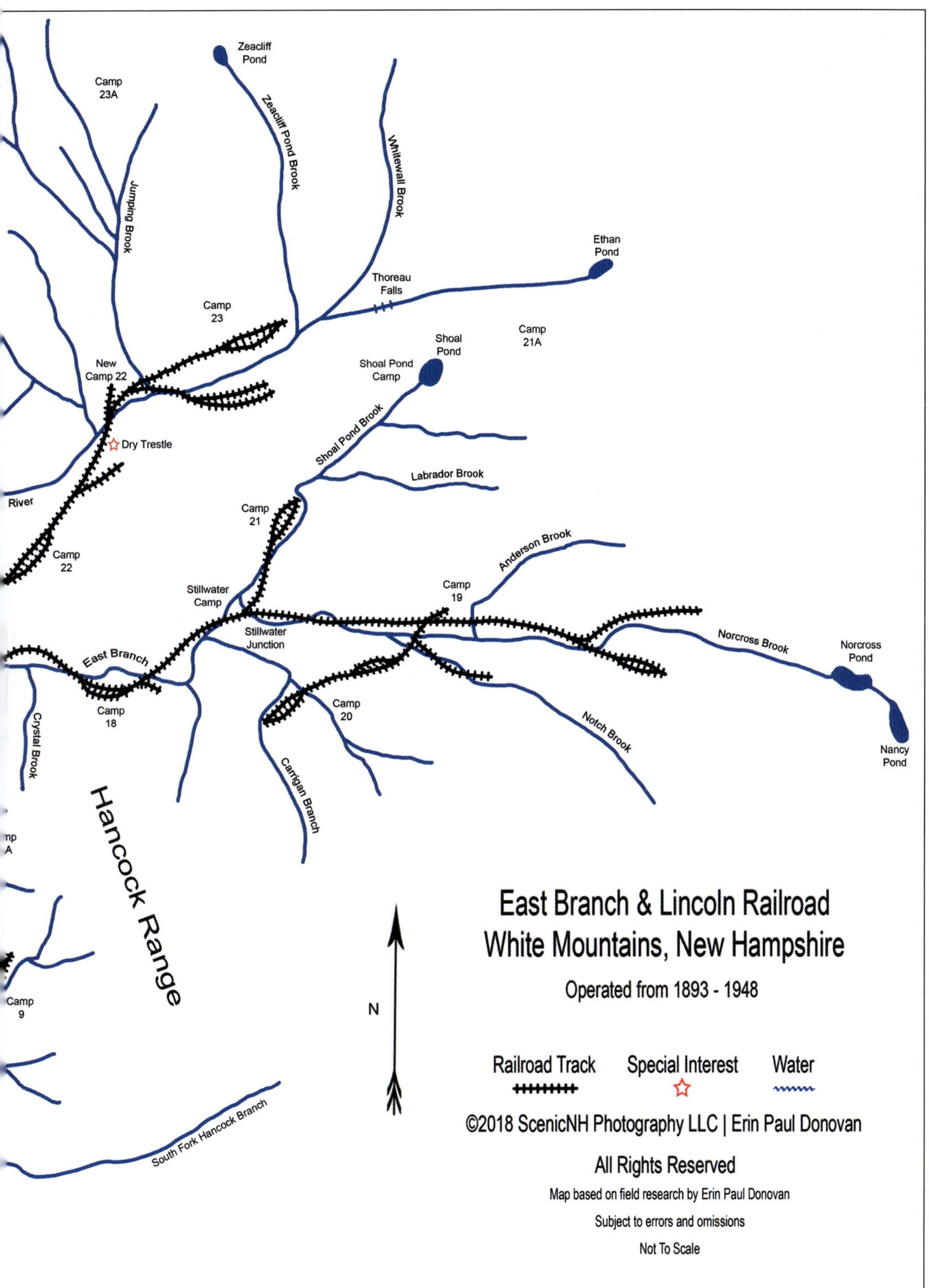

lines, the railroad was estimated to be 50 to 60 miles long. (Author's collection.)

Consistent with our mission to preserve history on a local level, this book was printed in South Carolina on American-made paper and manufactured entirely in the United States. Products carrying the accredited Forest Stewardship Council (FSC) label are printed on 100 percent FSC-certified paper.

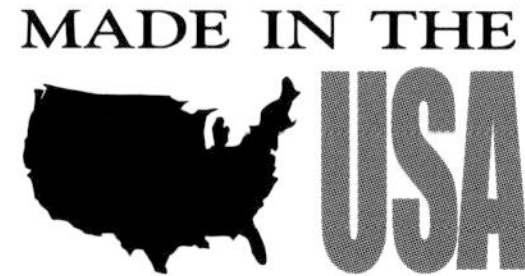